ANCIENT
TRADE
AND
SOCIETY

ANCIENT TRADE AND SOCIETY

LIONEL CASSON

WAYNE STATE UNIVERSITY PRESS
DETROIT 1984

Library of Congress Cataloging in Publication Data

Casson, Lionel, 1914–
  Ancient trade and society.

  Includes bibliographical references and index.
  1. Commerce—History—To 500.   2. Civilization,
Ancient.   I. Title.
HF357.C37   1984   382'.093   83-19880
ISBN 0-8143-1740-5

The publication of this volume to honor Lionel Casson was in good
part made possible by contributions from Virginia L. and Martin
Bernstein; Phyllis Pray Bober; Larissa Bonfante; Blanche and
Milton Brown; Andrea Casson; Bette Cohen; Charles W. Dunmore;
Elsbeth and John Dusenbery; Cleo and James Fitch; Theresa Goell;
Norma and Bernard Goldman; Lillian Herlands and George D.
Hornstein; Dora and Peter Janson; Barry R. Katz; Hope and
Benjamin F. Levene; Annalina Levi; Helen and Naphtali Lewis;
Joy and Philip Mayerson; Elizabeth W. and Henry H. Moulton;
Joan and Richard Scheuer; Nanette and Milton Scofield; Theresa
Shirer; Elaine Brody and David Silverberg; Norman Simon; Morton
Smith; Dita and Robert Stieglitz; Bluma and Max Trell; and Hope
G. Weil.

Contents

Maps and Illustrations

Foreword

C olleagues and friends of Lionel Casson offer this volume of
his essays to mark his retirement from New York University
in 1979, to applaud his past achievements, and to ask for more.
Applause, of course, has not been lacking. His achievements are
well known and much praised. But this seems an appropriate
moment to summarize what he has done, and to offer a material
token of appreciation for both the works and the author of the
works.

There is much to summarize, since Lionel Casson is a man of
parts. Doing one thing in one way apparently has not been
enough for him. He is singular only in the success with which he
has done a number of things in a number of ways.

As a classicist, he began with language. His Ph.D. dissertation
was in papyrology, and later he published, with Ernest L. Hettich,
Excavations at Nessana, vol. 2 *Literary Papyri* (1950). He cares
about literature. He is interested in nonliterary papyri as well,
because of the revelations they contain about people in history.
And papyrology itself appeals to him because he enjoys its particular intricacies—making jigsaw connections of the pieces, puzzling
out the lacunae, grappling with the sentences, and niggling over
jots and tittles, until the answers come.

In reading not only papyri but also ancient literature more
generally, he enjoys the exacting involvement with problems of

9

word meaning and sentence structure. But he cares enough about the larger problems of basic content and esthetic structure to turn his hand to literary translation. Ancient comedy is his specialty. He has published *Masters of Ancient Comedy* (1960), *Selected Satires of Lucian* (1962), *Six Plays of Plautus* (1963; 1971), and *The Plays of Menander* (1971).

Lionel Casson uses language attractively, lucidly, and trippingly. In dealing with ancient comedy, he has developed a particular kind of easy, colloquial style that suits both the original play and the contemporary reader. Also, the content of ancient literature to him is not so much antiquarian as human. People are not scholarly abstractions or classroom stereotypes. The man next door in Menander or Plautus is kin to the man who lives next door to us. All of this together works so well that enthusiastic reviewers have acclaimed his success as a translator of ancient comedy.

Lionel Casson has published many translations of ancient literature, but he has published even more studies in the scholarship of ancient civilization. It is characteristic of him that he has covered a remarkably wide spectrum of subjects, including history, economics, technology, geography, and even travel. Most centrally his name is associated with ancient ships and shipping, a subject on which he is generally considered the generation's best authority. His *Ships and Seamanship in the Ancient World* (1971) is a standard reference book. He is at work even now translating and annotating the first-century *Periplus Maris Erythraei,* a sea captain's guide to ports of call.

The books cited so far are learned books, and he has written many articles also for learned journals. They have been accepted with respect for the quality of his scholarship and the clarity of his reasoning. But they have been accepted in addition with gratitude for their attractive presentation and readability.

This welcome combination of good scholarship and good writing has proved effective not only for specialist readers but for nonspecialists as well. Publishers have urged Casson to write for a more general public, and fortunately he has done so, since he appreciates the value of communicating with intellectuals who are specialists in fields other than his own. He has written a number of books and articles just for them. And in addition he has done something harder and rarer. He has written books of original scholarship which have been accepted with enthusiasm by both

10

specialists and nonspecialists. These are *The Ancient Mariners* (1959) and *Travel in the Ancient World* (1974). Undoubtedly their success was helped by the straightforward clarity of ideas and words, since clarity functions equally well for all the categories of readers.

Lionel Casson has made his mark not only as a scholar-writer but also as an academic. From 1935 to 1979 he was on the faculty of the Classics Department at New York University, where he was a popular and beloved teacher. For some years he was chairman of his department. He was one of those reluctant academic administrators who would rather have gone to the library but who took on the job in order to keep things functioning calmly as well as efficiently in the department. He had no axes to grind nor political principles to prove. His idea was simply a fair, constructive solution of problems, and as a result he was greatly appreciated by his faculty. He was active in university affairs also, as participant in many committees. So outstanding was his presence in the academic community that he received a presidential citation from President Sawhill of New York University when he retired in 1979.

Living in one country was not enough for Lionel Casson. He chose to live in two countries, dividing each year between New York and Rome. Envy is what that practice evoked among his colleagues. His teaching also has been binational. At the American Academy in Rome, in addition to being a member of the Board of Trustees, he was director of the Summer Session in Classical Studies from 1963 to 1965, director of a National Endowment for the Humanities-funded Summer Seminar in 1978, and Mellon Professor from 1981 to 1982.

All the information given above is publicly known. What can be added here, in this personal note, to contribute further to the documentation of the life of Lionel Casson? Perhaps it would be interesting to present some information that is known only to his good friends, selecting such things as may serve to explain and enrich the account of his professional activities. For example:

When Lionel Casson was four years old, he came home from playing immies on a street in Brooklyn to announce to his family that henceforth his name would be Jimmy. And so it has been. Forever after he has preferred words of two syllables to those of three syllables, and plain to fancy.

11

When Jimmy was fourteen years old, he decided that he wanted to take up sailing. So he bought a small sloop called the *Viking* and a book called *How to Sail*. When he launched the *Viking* onto Long Island Sound, he was holding the main sheet in his right hand and the book in his left hand. Jimmy has always been a bookish person.

He learned to sail very well, and he loved it. Jimmy is a man of enthusiasm. How good and how enthusiastic a sailor he is the present writer discovered when Jimmy was first mate on John Dusenbery's beautiful 56-foot gaff-rigged schooner *Night Hawk*, and she was number 5 of a six-person crew (her husband being number 6). By that time Jimmy had begun his researches into ancient maritime matters. As he sailed he checked out questions about ships and seas. On other days, as he worked, his pleasure in ships and seas fed his researches. Living experience has infused his books, and enthusiasm has given them life.

Jimmy reads ancient literature as though he were reading about friends. There is no sense of the dim distances of time. The present writer is number 6 of a group of six, led by Bluma Trell and Jimmy, which has met once a week since 1945 to sight-read works of ancient Greek literature. When we are reading Thucydides or Arrian it is Jimmy who remembers what routes are taken or how the armies are drawn up. It is a feat of memory, of course, but he seems to remember it as though he thought of himself as being in the midst of it. When we read a play, he speaks the lines with expression, and gets up to act them out if necessary. He is especially good at doing old people, with croaky voice and halting gait. His performance as Tiresias brings down our small house (and has brought down many a classroom, we hear). No wonder his translations are lively.

Jimmy loves to laugh. He is a great audience for jokes, remembering them for years and asking for reruns. He claps at bons mots. This endears him greatly to his humorist-friends. It must also explain his special love for Menander, Plautus, Terence, and Lucian, and the appropriately lighthearted way in which he interprets them.

Jimmy's literary editor of the last version of his texts was his father, a lively, intelligent man in the lumber business who died recently at the age of ninety-two. If his father said that the manuscript was interesting and he could understand everything, then it went off to the publisher. No wonder his expositions are so sensible and lucid.

The present volume is a collection of articles written by Lionel Casson. They deal with a characteristically wide and interesting spectrum of subjects, culled from a characteristically diverse range of publications. The colleagues and friends of Lionel Casson feel that the reading community will be benefited by bringing these articles together in mutual context, and by making them more easily accessible. With this volume, also, they honor him by demonstrating why they honor him.

Blanche R. Brown

Introduction

When I was in my first year at graduate school, volume X of the magisterial *Cambridge Ancient History* arrived at the university library, fresh off the press. A chapter on Rome's commerce and industry, by an eminent specialist in ancient economic history, interested me particularly. As I flipped its pages my eye caught a line that brought me up short. In a section titled "The Quickening of Economic Life" I read that

> it was possible to reckon on being in Rome some eighteen days after leaving Alexandria, or, under favourable conditions, to be in Puteoli a mere nine days later (387).

Economic life may have quickened, but ships certainly hadn't: Nine days from Alexandria to Puteoli? That wasn't to come to pass till the days of steam! Pliny the Elder, I recalled, had included a nine-day run among his examples of unusually fast voyages, but he was talking about the opposite direction, from Puteoli to Alexandria. This was not hard to believe, even for the sluggish craft the ancients favored: in summer, when they did most of their travel on the sea, the prevailing winds over the waters between Italy and Egypt are strong northwesterlies; any vessel going from one to the other would have the wind on its heels all the way.

Suddenly the explanation came to me: the author must have

15

assumed that, if it took nine days to get from Puteoli to Alexandria as Pliny said, it took the same number to get back. A logical enough inference—but it overlooks the special way sailing craft behave: if prevailing winds make a voyage to a given destination exceptionally swift, the return necessarily will be exceptionally slow, since it involves a constant struggle against the wind. Nine days from Alexandria to Puteoli? Thirty-nine would be more like it.

Then and there I made up my mind that ancient maritime history was to be my field, starting with the exploration of just how the ships of the Greeks and Romans were built, manned, navigated, and so on. Once that was out of the way, I would move on to what they had been used for, to the story of maritime trade.

The first part of the program required many years. All the while the second part beckoned alluringly over the horizon. Every now and then I could not resist making forays into it. When I eventually finished my work on ships and seamanship—crowning it, I am pleased to add, with a contribution to the revised edition of the *Cambridge Ancient History* in which I had an opportunity to explain the nature of sailing and its effect on the speed of travel—I gave these my full attention. This book is largely a collection of such forays.

What concerned me was not so much broad economic considerations as the very fundamentals. What sort of men went into the business of trade and how did they operate? Did they make a lot of money? In "Traders and Trading in Ancient Athens" I tried to answer the first (at least for the fifth and fourth centuries B.C. for which, thanks largely to Demosthenes having defended a number of merchants and financiers, we enjoy some revealing insights), in "The Athenian Upper Class and New Comedy" the second (if New Comedy seems odd in the context remember that one of its standard plots has to do with the unexpected arrival of a father back from a trading voyage overseas to find his ne'er-do-well son squandering the family fortune).

Two of the articles treat aspects of what was far and away the most important trade in ancient times—grain. Grain was to the world of the Greeks and Romans what oil is to ours; their grain freighters were the greatest ships afloat, even as tankers are today. Five articles deal with, as it were, the very opposite, not the

16

shipping of a bulky and cheap commodity between relatively nearby points but of rare and expensive luxuries from distant lands—the trade between Rome and the Far East: the routes that led there ("Rome's Trade with the East," "The Location of Adulis"), the peoples with whom it was carried on ("Sakas versus Andhras in the *Periplus Maris Erythraei*"), what was brought back from there ("Cinnamon and Cassia in the Ancient World"), what social or economic effects, if any, resulted from the contact between two so very different regions ("China and the West").

I have included as well three articles which, though also dealing with socio-economic aspects of ancient life, leave the water for the land. Two concern a problem much in the headlines these days, unemployment. Did ancient governments ever do anything about it ("Unemployment, the Building Trade, and Suetonius, *Vesp.* 18")? Was it a factor in the ancients' general reluctance to use any form of power other than manpower ("Energy and Technology in the Ancient World")? Lastly, "The Scrap Paper of Egypt," plundering a source of information that became available no more than a century ago, throws light on an area that was long *terra incognita:* the day-to-day doings of ordinary people.

Some of the articles, published in professional journals, are inevitably more technical in tone than those I wrote for less scholarly media. Yet all are for readers with no more than an informed interest in the ancient world, none for specialists alone. All appear here as they did originally except for correction of an occasional error and updating of the documentation. To certain of them I have appended addenda in which I defend views that have come under attack, and I have provided full documentation for three that, being chapters in books of a nonscholarly nature, had lacked this.

The opportunity to pluck these pieces from a highly diverse miscellany of publications and bring them together between the covers of a book I owe to the initiative and devotion of a group of very dear friends and colleagues. I thank them with all my heart—no more for the opportunity than for the feelings that inspired them to provide it.

Abbreviations

For abbreviations of editions of papyri, see the list in Liddell-Scott-Jones, *Greek-English Lexicon*.

ABSA   *Annual of the British School at Athens*

AEpigr   *L'Année épigraphique*

AM   *Mitteilungen des deutschen archäologischen Instituts, Athenische Abteilung*

ANRW   *Aufstieg und Niedergang der römischen Welt*

BCH   *Bulletin de correspondance hellénique*

BIFAO   *Bulletin de l'Institut français d'archéologie orientale*

CAH   *Cambridge Ancient History*

CP   *Classical Philology*

CQ   *Classical Quarterly*

CIG   *Corpus Inscriptionum Graecarum*

CIL   *Corpus Inscriptionum Latinarum*

C & M   *Classica et Mediaevalia*

DarSag   C. Daremberg and E. Saglio, *Dictionnaire des anti-quités grecques et romaines*

Edmonds   J. Edmonds, *The Fragments of Attic Comedy* (Leiden 1957–61)

Eph.Arch.   *Ephemeris Archaiologikê*

ESAR   T. Frank et al., *An Economic Survey of Ancient Rome* (Baltimore 1933–40)

FHG   C. Muller, *Fragmenta Historicorum Graecorum*

IG   *Inscriptiones Graecae*

ILS   H. Dessau, *Inscriptiones Latinae Selectae*

JEA   *Journal of Egyptian Archaeology*

JHS   *Journal of Hellenic Studies*

JRS   *Journal of Roman Studies*

MAAR   *Memoirs of the American Academy in Rome*

Needham   J. Needham, *Science and Civilisation in China* (Cambridge 1954–)

OCT   *Oxford Classical Text*

OGIS   W. Dittenberger, *Orientis Graecae Inscriptiones Selectae*

ÖjhBeibl   *Jahreshefte der oesterreichischen archäologischen Instituts, Beiblatt*

PBA   *Proceedings of the British Academy*

Periplus   *Periplus Maris Erythraei*

RE   Pauly-Wissowa, *Real-Encyclopädie der klassischen Altertumswissenschaft*

REG   *Revue des études grecques*

RFIC   *Rivista di filologia e d'istruzione classica*

Schoff   W. Schoff, *The Periplus of the Erythraean Sea* (New York 1912)

SEG	*Supplementum Epigraphicum Graecum*
SEHHW	M. Rostovtzeff, *Social and Economic History of the Hellenistic World* (Oxford 1941)
Sel. Pap.	A. Hunt and C. Edgar, *Select Papyri* (Loeb Classical Library 1932–34)
SIG	W. Dittenberger, *Sylloge Inscriptionum Graecarum*
SSAW	L. Casson, *Ships and Seamanship in the Ancient World* (Princeton 1971)
TAPA	*Transactions of the American Philological Association*

1.
Traders and Trading in Classical Athens

In the fifth and fourth centuries B.C. Athens fed its population—150,000 by conservative estimates—chiefly on grain imported from south Russia, Sicily, and Egypt, and, to a lesser extent, on salt fish from Spain, the Black Sea, and elsewhere. Her formidable fleet of warships was built of timber from Macedon, Asia Minor, and the Levant, her altars burned incense from Arabia, her upper class enjoyed choice foods, textiles, and other luxuries from all over the Mediterranean.[1] This varied, wide-flung, and active commerce was carried on without any of the conveniences that seem so essential today: there were no financial instruments such as paper money, bank checks, letters of credit, or the like; there was no postal service nor other fixed channels of communication; there were no buoys nor lighthouses nor similar navigational aids to help a skipper off a dangerous coast, nor regular naval patrols to protect him against the ubiquitous pirates; and, in case of loss to either, no insurance to cushion the blow for the owners of the ship and cargo. Yet there never was a lack of volunteers for this hazardous way of earning a living.

Unfortunately our information about the merchants and their methods of doing business is scanty. Most of it comes from five courtroom speeches prepared by Demosthenes for clients who had gotten into trouble investing their money in commerce, and these show more of the seamier than the normal side of the

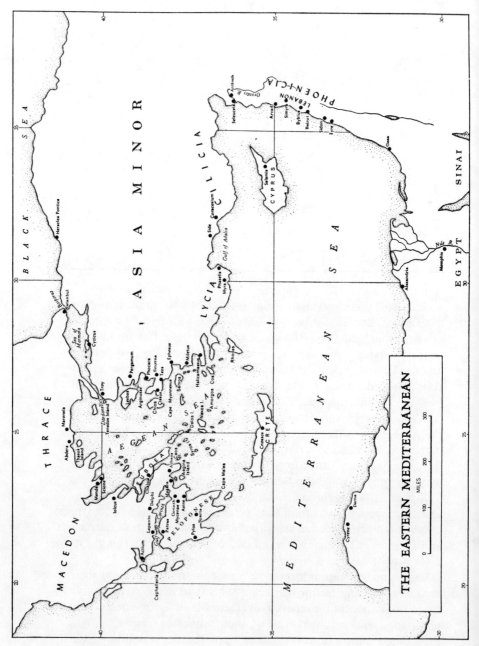

Fig. 1.

business. What follows is a brief summary of what we know about the operation of trade in Classical Athens, the roles involved, the men who assumed them, the risks they ran, and the rewards that prompted them to take such risks.

The ships and harbors posed no problem: they were by and large as good as any the world had until only a few centuries ago. The ships were beamy, sailing freighters powered by a broad and low mainsail amidships, sometimes with the addition of a smaller foresail in the bows set on a mast that raked slightly forward. They were under-rigged compared even with the likes of Columbus' clumsy *Santa Maria* and hence slow (their best speed with a favoring wind was no more than six knots), but in return they were safe. Their capacious hulls offered plenty of cargo space; vessels of 100 to 150 tons burden were common, and the biggest could hold as much as 400 (the average for western craft in the sixteenth cèntury was probably no more than 75). Ships of this size represented a considerable capital investment, for the price covered not only the hull, sail, spars, and rigging but also the crew since these, like most labor in the Greek world at this time, were usually slave, right up to and including the captain.

When a vessel put in at modest coast towns it often had to anchor in the open roads and be unloaded and loaded by barges shuttling from the shore, just as is still done today in parts of the Mediterranean. At Athens, however, and other major emporia, it entered a well-protected harbor, tied up to a stone quay to which it threw over gangplanks, and unloaded onto it; back of the quay were warehouses for storing cargo and porticoes where merchants, shipowners, and money changers could conduct business shielded from sun and rain.

Ancient maritime trade, with few exceptions, was carried on only during the summer, roughly from May to October. With the coming of fall, ships were put up for the winter, quays were abandoned, and ports, like summer resorts today, went into hibernation. This means that all activity had to be packed into five months. It also meant that ships, when sailing on the sea, were spared the perils of winter storms and, when loading or unloading in port, were spared delays caused by winter rains and profited from the long working days of summer. No outcries ever arose on account of those long summer working hours nor of the layoffs in winter, inasmuch as the personnel of the harbors—stevedores,

25

warehousemen, clerks, and the rest—like the sailors, were slave. It goes without saying that strikes were unheard of.[2]

One factor above all determined the way Athens' trade operated, what roles were played in it, and who filled those roles—the absence of large-scale sources of credit. The ancient trader, for reasons we will give in a moment, worked primarily with borrowed funds, and in Athens of the fifth and fourth centuries B.C. great accumulations of capital able to supply such funds simply did not exist. As a result, all business, industry as well as commerce, was small scale. The biggest manufacturer in Athens owned a shop with no more than one hundred employees. Of the dozen and a half loans to maritime traders whose size we know, the majority were 4,000 drachmas or less, enough to purchase, say, no more than forty or so tons of grain.

Later ages boasted men or families whose immense private wealth permitted them to lend money on the grand scale—Crassus in Rome of the first century B.C., the Medici in Renaissance Florence, the Fuggers in Augsburg of the fifteenth century, and so on. But the likes of these were completely unknown in Classical Athens. The richest man in town, the banker Pasion who figures in Demosthenes' courtroom speeches, was a multimillionaire by local standards but no more than moderately wealthy alongside a Cosimo di Medici or Ulrich Fugger.

Later ages boasted, too, massively capitalized banks that could grant lavish loans. Ancient Greece had its banks, to be sure, but they were small and, in any case, the furnishing of credit was a secondary operation. They began as money changers, and this forever remained a prime function. In those days it involved testing each coin tendered to make sure it was genuine and weighing it to make sure it was up to standard, a time-consuming and exacting procedure which justified the bankers' agio of 5 percent as against the minuscule fraction of today. We know that Greek banks took deposits on which they paid interest, usually about 10 percent, and then invested for their own account; however the deposits, small to begin with, were returnable on demand, and so bankers had to be wary about where they put such money, and maritime ventures, as we shall see, were far too speculative. Another service a Greek bank offered was safe-deposit; it regularly took care of clients' spare cash, gold and silver plate, jewelry, and other valuables when their owners left to go on journeys.[3]

With no big banks or wealthy moneylenders to turn to, a trader was reduced to garnering money from miscellaneous people who had funds to invest. Since the funds were never very ample and since the owners preferred to divide what they had among a number of debtors rather than trust all their eggs to one basket, commerce inevitably was a matter of multitudinous small shipments handled by a multitude of small traders. The 400-ton vessels mentioned above each carried the goods of numbers of men, never of one. A cargo of 400 tons of wheat would have required financing to the tune of 40,000 drachmas; the usual maritime loan was 4,000, as we indicated. The very largest we know of was 7,000 drachmas.[4]

The trader—or *emporos,* to give him his Greek name—needed money not only to purchase what he intended to import or export but also to rent space on a ship. Some were rich enough to own their own vessel—to be a *nauklêros,* to use the Greek expression, as well as *emporos*—but very few and, in any case, trading for them was a secondary pursuit: they filled a small area in the hold with their own goods and sold the better part of the space to others. Thus, ordinarily, there were three roles involved in a maritime venture: *emporos, nauklêros,* and moneylender. Often, on account of the scantiness of capital available, one or more of the roles was shared by a pair of partners.

The terms of maritime loans were such as to make them attractive strictly to investors strong of heart. To be sure, the traders had to put up security, but in the practice of the times this was either the ship or the cargo, and obviously such security had meaning only after a voyage came to a successful conclusion. At that time, if for some reason a trader dragged his feet about repaying, his creditors could foreclose and recoup their money. Since ships had a fixed and stable value, lenders were willing to lend right up to that value, but on a cargo whose value, being subject to the vagaries of the market, took wide swings, only up to half. In either case it was understood that the borrower was not to take out more than one loan on the same security, that to do so was a most serious offense. If a ship did not make it safely to port—went down in a storm or was captured by pirates or was made to disappear through some skullduggery—the lender lost all. This makes clear why traders operated with borrowed money rather than their own: disaster at sea might rob them of all they had with them, even of their life, but they or their heirs were spared the necessity of paying back a loan that had become purposeless. In return for accepting full responsibility for loss, lenders understandably charged a steep rate of interest. Bank deposits, as mentioned earlier, paid 10 percent, loans on gilt-edge security such as land 10 percent to 12 percent, less well-secured loans as much as 16 percent to 18 percent. But a maritime loan might bring 67.5 percent and often as much as 100 percent. In effect, the rate covered insurance as well as the use of the money.[5]

In one of the courtroom speeches of Demosthenes (35.10–13) the text of a maritime loan agreement is given in full. It is worth quoting, for it illustrates clearly and precisely the people involved, the rewards they stood to gain, and the risks they ran (I have added rubrics in italics and notes in brackets).

parties:	Androcles of Athens [this was Demosthenes' client] and Nausicrates of Carystus
	have lent to
	Artemo and Apollodorus of Phaselis [in Lycia, in Asia Minor]
amount:	3,000 drachmas,
purpose:	for a voyage from Athens to Mende or Scione [both in north Greece] and thence to Bosporus [in the Crimea], or, if they so desire, to the north shore of the Pontus [Black Sea] as far as the Borysthenes
interest:	[Dnieper], and thence back to Athens, on interest at the rate of 225 drachmas on the 1,000 [22.5 percent for four to five months = 67.5 percent per annum]—however, if they should leave the Pontus for the return voyage after the middle of September [that is, run the danger of hitting equinoctial storms], the interest is to be 300 drachmas on the 1,000 [30 percent for four to five months = 90 percent per annum]—on the security of 3,000 jars of
security:	wine of Mende which shall be conveyed from Mende or Scione in the ship of which Hyblesius is owner [that is, a chartered vessel].

They provide these goods as security, owing no money on them to any other person, nor will they make any additional loan on this security. They agree to bring back to Athens in the same vessel all the goods [certainly grain] put on board as a return cargo while in the Pontus.

time of
repayment
and
permissible
deductions:

If the return cargo is brought safely to Athens, the borrowers are to pay the lenders the money due in accordance with this agreement within twenty days after they shall have arrived at Athens, without deduction save for such jettison as the passengers shall have made by common agreement, or for money paid to enemies [the inevitable pirates], but without deduction for any other loss.

provisions
in the event
of
nonpayment:

They shall deliver to the lenders all the goods offered as security, to be under the latter's absolute control until such time as they themselves have paid the money due in accordance with the agreement. If they shall not pay back within the time stipulated the lenders have the right to pledge or even to sell the goods for whatever price they can get, and if the proceeds of the sale fall short of the sum the lenders are entitled to in accordance with the agreement, they have the right to collect [the difference] by proceeding, severally or jointly, against Artemo and Apollodorus and against all their property whether on land or sea, wherever it may be.

After several further stipulations the agreement closes with the signatures of the parties and witnesses.

As Demosthenes' brief reveals, the borrowers, Artemo and Apollodorus, managed to break every provision in the contract. First, they loaded aboard only 450 jars of wine instead of the specified 3,000. Next, they proceeded to float another loan on the same security. Then they left the Black Sea to go back to Athens without a return cargo. Finally, on arrival they put in not at the port but at the smugglers' cove, Thieves' Harbor as it was called. Time passed, and the creditors, seeing no sign either of their money or of any merchandise which they could attach, confronted the pair and were blandly told that the cargo had been lost in a storm and hence all obligations were off. Fortunately the

29

creditors were able to produce sworn depositions from passengers and crew that no cargo of wine or grain had been aboard.

Note that, of the four parties to the agreement, three—the trading partners and one of the lenders—were non-Athenians. So too was the shipowner, as we find out elsewhere, There was good reason for this. The form of investment that was safest and boasted the highest social tone was real estate. But ownership of real estate, whether land or houses, was open solely to Athenian citizens. This meant as well that only they could make loans secured by real estate. They turned to maritime ventures only when it suited them. Foreigners, on the other hand, had no alternative; however, since there was money to be made in the business, they were willing volunteers. Of the three roles involved, shipowning and trading and moneylending, they almost totally monopolized the first: practically all the vessels that carried products in and out of the Piraeus belonged to men from Marseilles, Byzantium, south Russia, Asia Minor, and so on. Athenians, with more attractive possibilities open to them, preferred to leave to others an investment that was of considerable size (remember that the shipowner laid out for the crew of slaves as well as the vessel), that stood idle for half the year, and that could be lost in the twinkling of an eye during the other half. In the second, trading, foreigners were easily in the majority, although there were plenty of Athenians taking part along with them. Indeed, in the comedies of this period, a standard character is the Athenian father who goes off overseas on business, leaving a ne'er-do-well son free to sow wild oats and start the wheels of the plot spinning. And, in the third, the financing of maritime ventures, Athenians outnumbered non-Athenians by a good margin.[6]

It was the size of the return that tempted them. Real estate was a fine form of investment, safe and prestigious, but it yielded no more than 8 percent. Keeping money on deposit in a bank or lending on good security brought, as we have seen, only 10 to 18 percent. Running a factory might net 20 percent or more—but even though factories were small they still forced an owner to tie up for life a considerable amount of capital in the work force of slaves. A maritime loan, on the other hand, could double a man's money within the few months of the sailing season; it was the one way in ancient Athens to make a quick financial killing.[7]

But to make such a killing one's ship had to come in. And so, prudent Athenians did not put all their spare funds in such ventures any more than investors today would put all theirs in speculative common stocks. We happen to know that Demosthenes' father, at the time of his death, had (27.9–11):

8,000 drachmas in cash
6,000 in small interest-free loans to friends
3,000 on deposit in banks, presumably at 10 percent
1,600 on loan, interest rate unknown
6,000 on loan at 12 percent
4,000 in a loan secured by a shop that yielded a profit of 1,200
annually = 30 percent (although probably only 20 percent
on the actual, and not the loan, value of the slaves involved)
7,000 in a maritime loan

Thus, 7,000 of 35,600 drachmas or 22.5 percent was in maritime loans.

To undertake these risky investments one had to be experienced as well as bold; they were not for the uninitiated. In the contract cited above we have seen the tricks and turns taken by the borrowers to evade paying back what they owed to Demosthenes' client. Another of his courtroom speeches (32) was on behalf of a relative of his who had the misfortune to get mixed up with a pair of rascals from Marseilles; they, after pledging the selfsame cargo for a whole series of loans, quietly sent off the boodle to their home town for safekeeping and then, since repayment had to be made only upon the ship's arrival, launched a scheme to scuttle it. Though they fumbled the attempt and the ship did reach port, and though the case against them was in the hands of Athens' most celebrated lawyer, the indications are that the poor lender never saw his money again. Even an old hand, one who "not quite seven years ago gave up voyaging myself and, having a fair amount of capital, try to put it to work in maritime loans" (Dem. 33.4), chose badly and found himself enmeshed in a lawsuit. It was a field for "those who have made a trade of the business," as Demosthenes puts it (37.53), an *emporos* or *nauklêros* (34.6) with spare cash, or someone like the Diodotus we hear of who "had made a lot of money out of trade" and at his death had 46,000 drachmas out of a liquid capital of 92,000—exactly 50 percent—in maritime loans.[8]

On top of all the dangers from acts of God and godless men

31

there was yet another, the need to deal in cash, to carry about large and heavy amounts of coin. A trader's method of procedure was more or less as follows. First he made his way to the waterfront to line up a shipowner with space available headed for the destination he had in mind. He then ranged up and down the porticoes back of the quay at the Piraeus, where men with money to invest or their agents gathered, until he found one or more willing to grant him a loan. The two parties, after drawing up a written agreement, repaired to the office—the same as his home—of some banker they knew and trusted. There, under his eyes, the lender or lenders passed over the coin, and the agreement was left with the banker for safekeeping. No writing accompanied the transfer of the money, no receipts were executed in duplicate or the like—something we feel so necessary. Greek businessmen of this age preferred to work orally before witnesses. The trader had a slave shoulder the sack or sacks of coin and accompany him to the ship. He either went aboard himself or entrusted cash and mission to an agent; the latter might be an Athenian employed by him as associate or a slave of his who served as his man of affairs and had full authority to act in his name. If the voyage ended successfully, the trader summoned his creditor(s) to a meeting at the banker's office and there, again with him as witness, handed over in cash the amount of the loan plus interest, and the parties wrote finis to the deal by tearing up the written agreement.[9]

A successful voyage meant not only that the ship had made it safely back but that the market price of the cargo had held up, permitting the trader to reap a very handsome gross profit. It took such a profit to leave a margin for himself after all the various costs had been covered—the massive interest charges, the freight, and the 5 percent agio if he had to change any money. In those days there were three currencies which, like the dollar today, enjoyed international circulation—Athens' silver fourdrachma pieces, Cyzicus' electrum staters, and Persia's gold darics. If a trader's cargo was, say, a load of grain from south Russia which annually shipped thousands of tons to Athens, no doubt the dealers there accepted his Athenian coins. But if he were operating where men preferred the local currency, he would have to pay the moneylenders their not inconsiderable due.[10]

No matter how carefully one drew up a contract, overlooked details or unforeseen circumstances could bring the parties into conflict, even though they both acted with all the goodwill in the world. And when one of them, as was so often true in maritime ventures, was a non-Athenian, adjudicating conflicts posed special problems. Since these foreigners were vitally important to Athens, links in the chain of grain imports that kept the city fed, Athens was concerned that they receive swift and efficient justice. She passed a law that cases involving traders had to go on no later than one month after the original complaint had been lodged; no trader was to be lured away to sell his grain at Corinth or Samos just because Athens had kept him waiting around for justice until his name came up on some overcrowded court calendar. And, whereas in other cases the penalty usually was a fine, those involving traders carried prison sentences. This helped both parties: if an Athenian won a case against a foreigner, the prison sentence guaranteed that the latter could not settle matters in his own way by taking off in his ship without paying the judgment; conversely, if the Athenian lost, fear of prison made him pay up promptly and not compel the foreigner, whose home might be hundreds of miles away, to hang around Athens and go through endless red tape collecting on the judgment.[11]

The foreign businessman had yet another source of help, his *proxenos*. A *proxenos* was the nearest thing to a consul to be found in the ancient world. He was usually a foreigner from another Greek city permanently residing at Athens who was officially acknowledged by the Athenian government to be the accredited representative of citizens of his home town. If, for example, a trader from Corinth needed advice about doing business at Athens or introductions to moneylenders or help with a law case, he sought out the Corinthian *proxenos*.[12]

"It would be an excellent idea," is Xenophon's advice to his countrymen (*Vect.* 3.4), "to honor traders and shipowners with front-row seats at the theatre and issue occasional invitations to dinner at City Hall to those of them who, through exceptional shipping and shipments, appear to be benefactors of the city." Xenophon knew on which side Athens' bread was buttered—or rather, that without the traders and shipowners there would be scant bread to butter.

33

Notes

1. H. Michell, *The Economics of Ancient Greece* (New York 1957²) 233–36, 258–83.

2. *SSAW* 65–70, 169–72 (ships); 228 (speed); 365 (harbors); 270–73 (sailing season); 328 (crews). Size of 16th c. craft, F. Braudel, *The Mediterranean and the Mediterranean World in the Age of Philip II* (New York 1972) 297.

3. Cash and credit, M. Finley, *The Ancient Economy* (Berkeley 1973) 141–45. Size of maritime loans, R. Bogaert, *Banques et banquiers dans les cités grecques* (Leyden 1968) 373. Twenty tons of grain: a *medimnus* = ca. 40 kg., and wheat at this time cost at least 4–5 drachmas a *medimnus* (A. Boeckh, *The Public Economy of Athens,* trans. G. Lewis [London 1842] 94). Banks and their operations, Bogaert 307–56.

4. Dem. 27.11, to a certain Xuthus. But if Xuthus was a broker, not a borrower, as has been argued (E. Erxleben in E. Welskopf, ed., *Hellenische Poleis* [Berlin 1974] 463, 493), then the figure represents more than one loan.

5. *Emporos* and *nauklêros,* H. Knorringa, *Emporos* (Amsterdam 1926) 96–98. Maritime loans, W. Ashburner, *The Rhodian Sea-Law* (Oxford 1909) ccxii–ccxvi; Boeckh (above, n. 3) 132–39. Amount of security, Knorringa 94–95. Rates of interest, Bogaert (above, n. 3) 290; Michell (above, n. 1) 342–43.

6. See below, chap. 2, n. 40.

7. Cf. below, p. 45.

8. Lysias 32.4–6, 13–15; cf. Bogaert (above, n. 3) 368.

9. Bogaert (above, n. 3) 336–45.

10. Bogaert (above, n. 3) 314.

11. J. Hasebroek, *Trade and Politics in Ancient Greece,* trans. L. Fraser and D. MacGregor (London 1933) 171–72.

12. L. Casson, *Travel in the Ancient World* (London 1974) 93–94.

2.
The Athenian Upper Class
and New Comedy

The upper class in Classical Athens, particularly during the fourth century B.C. when the evidence of the orators can be brought to bear, has received considerable attention, going back to a pioneering effort in 1840.[1] Today we are in a position to draw a more detailed picture, thanks in good part to the invaluable "social register" of Classical Athens compiled by J. K. Davies[2] and to the newly discovered plays of Menander,[3] which enable us to identify the class that figures most importantly in Greek New Comedy and properly apply its evidence. We can define with greater precision who were the wealthy, what their fortune consisted of, how much income they derived from it, and how this affected their style of life.

I

Ideally we ought to treat the whole of Athenian society and not just its upper levels. Unfortunately, the only members we know to any extent are, first, those who were affluent enough to hire the likes of Demosthenes, Lysias, and Isaeus for their incessant squabbling about money, and whose property, income, family relations, and the like emerge in the speeches written for their pleadings in court, and, second, those affluent enough to be reflected in Greek New Comedy, whose practitioners were no more

35

interested in Athens' poor than Molière or Feydeau in Paris'. These two sources provide a fairly broad spectrum that ranges from the invalid who engaged Lysias to defend his right to a state dole of an obol a day (Lysias 24) or the pennypinching protagonist of Menander's *Dyskolos* to Demosthenes' immensely rich client Phormio (Dem. 36). Within it are those to whom Davies by and large limits his register, namely the men the state felt free to call upon to subsidize its military and festival expenses; as Davies cogently demonstrates (xx–xxxi), the performing of liturgies provides an eminently workable criterion for distinguishing Athens' upper class.

So far as we can tell, a fortune of 3 or 4 talents made a man a liturgist,[4] marked him, in other words, as a well-to-do Athenian. How many such were there? And what percentage of the total population did they form? Fourth-century Athens probably had some 21,000 adult male citizens.[5] In 322 Antipater forced the city to adopt a property qualification for citizenship, and 12,000 who were worth 20 minae or less were dropped from the rolls.[6] Thus, in the thinking of the time, 20 minae was the poverty line: below it were the people too poor to be trusted with a share in running the state. Jones (76–84) reckons, and his figures cannot be far off, that the next highest bracket consisted of some 3,000 with property between 20 and 25 minae, a figure that meant, for a peasant, a small farm of perhaps six acres, for an artisan, a shop with perhaps five to six slave assistants, enough to ensure a living, but not very much more. Above these, Jones calculates, were some 6,000 whom the Athenians considered sufficiently well off to contribute to the *eisphora,* the sporadically imposed war tax.

A man worth 25 minae may have had the money to pay war tax, but, with a mere margin of 5 minae between him and the poverty line, he can hardly be considered well-to-do. We must now leave the lower brackets and start working down from the top. Here we have a most useful figure: the 1,200 who, by the naval law of 357/356, were required to undertake the trierarchy. This liturgy, the maintaining of a warship at sea for a year, even when split between a pair of syntrierarchs, ran to at least 20 minae and often a good deal more; thus it was one of the most expensive state burdens, and the 1,200 selected to bear it must have been Athens' wealthiest. As time went on it turned out to be too hard on many of them, so Demosthenes got the law changed to limit those liable to a select circle of 300.[7] These 300, then, were the topmost bracket, with the 900 others forming a bracket just below them; 5 talents put a man among the 900 (Isaeus 7.19, 31–32, 42), possibly somewhat less. Then there appears to have been a third bracket which included those with fortunes around the 3 to 4 talent minimum that qualified a man to be a liturgist; they would be called upon for less expensive burdens than the trierarchy, for a dithyrambic chorus at the Panathenaea, for example, which cost as little as 3 minae (Davies xxi). How many were in this bracket we have no idea; it necessarily numbered not more than 4,800 (the 6,000 eligible for the war tax less the 1,200 eligible for the trierarchy) and certainly very much fewer.

Even within the Three Hundred there was great variation. In its upper reaches were the Rockefellers and Onassises of the age. Lysias at one point (19.46–48) reels off examples of the reputedly greatest fortunes. There was Callias (the man who married Cimon's sister) who valued his property at 200 talents (we know from other sources—Andocides 1.130; Isocrates 16.31—that his son Hipponicus passed for the richest man in Greece). There was Nicias who was worth 100, and Ischomachus (the hero of Xenophon's *Oeconomicus;* see Davies 267), worth 70. Lysias quotes the figures only to throw doubt on them (and Jones [87] follows his lead), but there is no need for skepticism; such fortunes, no question about it, did exist. Oeonias, who fled when revealed to have been involved in the scandal of the Herms and Mysteries in 415 and whose properties as a result were confiscated and sold, owned lands in Euboea that alone brought the state 81 talents and 20 minae (*Hesperia* 22 [1953] 254, lines 311–14). Only the chance discovery of the inscription recording the sale has revealed that this obscure personage was one of Athens' wealthiest; there surely were others who have so far escaped history's notice. The estate of the banker Pasion was at least 65 talents (Dem. 36.5–6; cf. Davies 431–35). Lysias' family—he was a metic, but that is irrelevant in this context—had property worth 70 talents (*P. Oxy.* 1606.30; cf. Davies 589). Conon's earnings as a condottiere enabled him to leave an estate of 40 (Lysias 19.40). A Euthycrates mentioned by Hyperides (4.34) was worth more than 60, the Onetor who worked hand in glove with Demosthenes' guardian Aphobus over 30 (Dem. 30.10). Even 15 talents set a man well inside the Three Hundred, for this was the size of the estate alleged to have been left by Demosthenes' father, and the orator claimed that, for tax purposes, it put him in a class with such manifestly wealthy men as Conon's son Timotheus.[8] How much less than 15 talents was the minimum for inclusion in the charmed circle we cannot say, but, in view of the yield available from the normal openings for investment (see below), my guess is that it was at least 10. In summary, the picture that emerges is something like this:[9]

Upper Class, the liturgy payers, worth upward of 3–4 talents

Upper-Upper: 300 worth 10 talents or more, responsible for trierarchies after Demosthenes' reform

Middle-Upper: 900 worth some 5 to 10 talents, perhaps somewhat less, responsible for trierarchies before the reform

Lower-Upper: indeterminate number with at least 3–4 talents, responsible for lesser liturgies

Middle Class, 3 talents down to 20 minae

Upper-Middle ⎫

Middle-Middle ⎭ totaling, together with the Upper Class, 6,000, all liable for the war tax, i.e., worth 25 minae or more

Lower-Middle: 3,000 worth 25 to 20 minae

Lower Class, 12,000 worth less than 20 minae

II

The next question to deal with is: what did Athenians own and how much income did they derive from it?

In the early days, about the only form of property available was real estate, specifically agricultural or grazing land. As Athens and the Piraeus grew, real estate came to include houses for rent, both single-dwelling (*oikiai*) and multiple-dwelling, i.e., apartment houses (*synoikiai*).[10] Holdings for agriculture or grazing were almost always made up of scattered parcels rather than one great unit; the biggest single farm we know of could not have been much more than one hundred acres and most were considerably less.[11] And we have just recently become aware that any number of Athenians owned parcels overseas, not only in nearby places like

Euboea but as far away as Thrace and the Chersonese.[12] Others leased land overseas.[13]

Real estate remained throughout a favored form of investment, and for good reason. To begin with, there was an emotional component in owning land that overweighed economic considerations: it was a source of pride, status, family solidarity, as well as income.[14] Then it was less risky than any other form of investment (slaves had a discouraging tendency to die, debtors to default, ships to go down), and there was no competition from foreigners, since the right to own land was, except for special cases, limited to citizens. Moreover, it was a ready source of credit. The easiest way for an Athenian to raise cash was by hypothecating real estate; we not only have the numerous instances mentioned in the orators but the tangible evidence of over two hundred *horoi*, the stones inscribed with a brief statement which were placed on a property to indicate that it was encumbered by debt.[15]

But real estate had two drawbacks. For one, it was common practice among fourth-century Athenians to conceal the extent of their fortune in order to avoid or reduce their liability to liturgies and taxes or for other shady reasons, and land and buildings were all too visible, were *phanera ousia,* to use their term; loans, holdings overseas, and other forms of investment that they called *aphanes ousia* "invisible property" were safer from prying eyes.[16] For another, it yielded a return of only about 8 percent, far less than other easily available investments, and then only when the owner was able to find satisfactory tenants.[17] One way of increasing the yield and still retaining some of the safety of real estate was to go in for buildings that were used as baths, brothels, or inns.[18] This, of course, involved an additional investment in a staff of slaves to run the establishment.

Slaves, as a matter of fact, were the next favored form of investment after real estate. In Athens, all industry was carried on either by independent artisans, the poorer working alone and the more successful with one or more slave assistants, or by shops that were totally slave,[19] foreman and workers alike. Such shops were of all sizes to fit every investment purse, from a tiny establishment with but a few workers to the shield factory run by Lysias' family that was staffed by over one hundred. Timarchus' father owned a shoemaker's shop that employed 9 or 10, Demosthenes' father a couch-making establishment that employed 20 and a cutlery with 32 to 33; the cutlers cost for the most part 5 or 6 minae each, a very steep price, and must therefore have been highly skilled workmen.[20] Sometimes the shop, as Demosthenes' father's, was accommodated right in the owner's home, sometimes in a building all its own. If the latter, the foreman and workers might be totally independent, *chôris oikountes* "dwelling apart," responsible only for the payment of a fixed fee to their owner.[21] Sometimes no building at all was required, as in the case of the catering teams that turn up again and again in Greek New Comedy. At the head was a *mageiros,* which we traditionally translate "cook" but who was actually caterer and chef combined, and under him were a *trapezopoios* "waiter" and one or more scullions.[22] Our sources never mention the ownership of such teams, but this simply reflects the fragmentary state of our knowledge; they must have done a thriving business since, among Athens' upper crust, sacrifices, weddings, and similar celebrations seem usually to have been catered affairs.[23] Another active service was the supplying of courtesans, a term that covered everything from the equivalent of Cho-Cho-San to a hardworking call girl, but, as New Comedy clearly shows, a stigma attached to this and, despite the money to be made, it was left in the hands of none too savory foreigners.[24]

The great advantage of investing in slave workers was the yield—at least 16 to 20 percent as against the mere 8 percent to be gotten from land.[25] Moreover, for men ambitious to get ahead, it was a far surer path to follow than real estate, since ownership of land, as we have just mentioned, was based as much on emotional factors as economic, if not more, and parcels did not regularly come on the market; as has been acutely pointed out, though Greek has a word for the sellers of almost every conceivable object of exchange, there is none for "real estate broker."[26] In a well-known passage (Xenophon, *Mem.* 2.7.6), Socrates mentions four men who became comfortably wealthy from slave-manned workshops—a miller, a baker, and two cloakmakers; the miller actually made it into the ranks of the liturgy-payers. Praxiteles' sculpture studio was so successful that the family not only became liturgists but his son was able to undertake a formidable number of trierarchies (Davies 286–88).[27] The money that enabled Athens' best-known popular leaders to go into politics came from such shops: Cleon and Anytus owned tanneries, Hyperbolus was in lamp-making, Cleophon in lyre-making. Isocrates' expensive education was paid for out of the profits of his father's flute-making establishment. And many an Athenian must have made a tidy sum out of the shops that produced Athens' famed pottery.[28] The great disadvantage was that one's capital investment was subject to the whims of sickness and accident: the death or mutilation of a slave was that much money down the drain.[29]

Running a shop meant putting money not only into slaves but into materials as well; when Demosthenes' father died, his estate included an inventory of iron, copper, wood, ivory, and gall for his shops worth 2.5 talents (Dem. 27.10)—almost enough by itself to qualify a man for paying liturgies. A simpler and less expensive way of exploiting slaves was to acquire them merely for renting out. The best customers were the men who had digging concessions in the silver mines at Laurium; they needed thousands—far more than 10,000, to judge from Xenophon, *Vect.* 4.24—for work in the pits and galleries, and apparently preferred to hire rather than own, to let someone else stand the inevitable write-offs from the high mortality rate, worse in mining than in any other line of work. Nicias' fortune was reputedly based on 1,000 slaves whom he rented out to a single entrepreneur, and Hipponicus, son of the fabulously wealthy Callias and said to be, as we reported earlier, the richest Athenian of his time, owned 600 (Xenophon, *Vect.* 4.14–15). At the other end of the scale was the Diocleides who claimed to have witnessed the culprits forming up for the mutilation of the Herms; he saw them, he averred, when he was setting out for Laurium to pick up the earnings of a slave he had there (Andocides 1.38). The return was at least as high as 30 percent; it dazzled Xenophon into suggesting that the state invest in mine slaves in a big way and thereby put the whole citizen body in easy circumstances.[30]

Others than mine concessionaires also preferred to work with rented slaves, even as some of us today find it more expedient to lease a car than own one; "I want to buy a slave boy," says a banker in Plautus' *Curculio* (382–83), "but now let me get one to rent; I need my cash." Demosthenes, Sr.'s cutlery had three slaves on lease from one of Demosthenes' guardians (Dem. 27.20). The individual slaves whose names appear in the building

41

records were either *chôris oikountes* who contracted out their own services, or had been hired out directly by their owners.[31] People in all income brackets found the hiring out of slaves a useful way to supplement their income. Theophrastus' mean-minded miser, a man of considerable wealth—he traveled abroad on public business (30.7) and borrowed sums up to 30 minae (30.13)—not only regularly hired out slaves (30.15) but, when he went on a trip with acquaintances, used their slave attendants so he could leave his own at home to rent out (30.17). Arethusius, the *bête noir* of Pasion's son Apollodorus, had two slaves whom he hired out for agricultural labor or would allow to contract out their own services (Dem. 53.20–21). In Plautus' *Asinaria* there is a reference (441–43) to a slave hired out who has brought in half his pay and will bring the rest when the job contracted for is done. In Terence's *Adelphoe,* the friend of an indignant lady refers (481–82) to her lone male slave as the sole support of the family; he could only have been that by being hired out and bringing back enough to ensure them a living. There was a special area, the *Kolonos Agoraios* just west of the Agora, where slaves available for casual work shaped up awaiting potential employers. The cooks, all of whose employment was occasional, had their own "cook's market."[32]

When Socrates, during his visit to the lovely courtesan Theodote, noted the sumptuousness of her household, he asked her (Xenophon, *Mem.* 3.11.4), "Do you own land?" "Not I," she replied. "Well then, you own house property that brings in revenue?" "No house property." "Then don't you have some craftsmen?" "No craftsmen." "Then how do you manage the necessities of life?" Land, houses, craftsmen—these were what the wealthy Athenian ordinarily derived his income from. To them we may add lending money to responsible borrowers on good security. It brought at least 10 percent, commonly 12 percent, sometimes as high as 18 percent, more, in other words, than real estate but not as much as craftsmen.[33]

All the above were the equivalent of our "widows and orphans" grade of investment. There were any number of Athenians who were willing to try something more speculative for the better return it offered. They found it in mining, certain aspects of commerce, and tax-farming.

The silver mines of Laurium headed the list of the Athenian's preferred speculative ventures. For the lucky the profits could be enormous. Callias was one of the first beneficiaries: the mines were the basis of his fortune (Davies 260); people used to call his family the "pit-rich" (Plutarch, *Arist.* 5.6). There was one mine which, it was claimed (Hyperides 4.35), brought its owners 300 talents in three years. The speaker of Demosthenes 42, who embarked on a business career with the very modest inheritance of 45 minae (42.22), turned to mining and, beginning by wielding pick and shovel with his own hands (42.20), ended up a member of the select circle of the Three Hundred (42.3). Some people went in for the actual extracting of the ore, some for the running of a refinery, some for both.[34] The former involved the leasing of a concession from the state (mines were inalienable public property). Little investors as well as big could be accommodated, since the concessions were of various sizes and types (for starting of a new mine, continuation of work on an old one, reopening of an abandoned one). Some were so expensive that it took several people in a partnership to handle them, for few individuals had sufficient capital for the cost of the lease and the hire of the necessary number of mine slaves; the concession that yielded 300 talents was operated by a certain Epicrates who headed a syndicate "of just about the richest men in the city" (Hyperides 4.35). A speech of Demosthenes mentions (37.22) a concessionaire who paid the considerable sum of 1.5 talents, and in the inscriptions listing mining leases there is one that cost just short of 3 talents. But most in the inscriptions are far cheaper: a very common figure is 150 drachmae, and quite a few went for as little as 20, mere pits, no doubt, that a concessionaire, like the speaker of Demosthenes 42, could work with his own labor and no outlay save for a hammer, pick, and shovel.[35] On the other hand, investing in a refinery was solely for men with capital, inasmuch as it required the purchase of a good deal of expensive equipment—mortars, mills, washing tables, furnaces—as well as a gang of slaves to run it, for refinery slaves were not hired but owned, as in other manufactories.[36] Holders of small concessions no doubt worked out arrangements to have their ore processed by the nearest available facility.

Next, commerce. In the commercial ventures of the time, there were three roles to play: the *nauklêros,* the man who supplied the ship, either an owner or a charterer; the *emporos,* "merchant," who booked space on the ship and put cargoes into it; and the moneylender who supplied the *emporos* with the funds he needed to pay the freight and purchase the cargoes. Often, to spread the risk, one or more of the three roles were split up among partners. At times *nauklêros* and *emporos* were the same person, in which case he could borrow on the security of the ship; most often they were separate, and then the *emporos* borrowed on the security of the cargo he loaded aboard.[37]

Nauklêros	Emporos	Lender	Security
32 Hegestratus of Marseilles	Protus	Demon	cargo
33 Apaturius of Byzantium	Apaturius	Parmeno, Heraclides	ship
34 Lampis, Dio both of Cimmerian Bosporus	Phormio	1. Chrysippus, a partner 2. (illegitimate loan) Theodorus, Lampis	cargo cargo
35 Hyblesius of Phaselis, Apollonides of Halicarnassus	Artemo, Apollodorus	Androcles, Nausicrates	cargo
56 Dionysiodorus, Parmeniscus	Dionysiodorus, Parmeniscus	Dareius, Pamphilus	ship

In all three roles, the Athenian was competing with metics and aliens; barred from owning real estate, these found a natural outlet for their business energies in commerce. So many went into ship-owning that one has the impression Athenians deliberately avoided this form of enterprise. With more attractive opportunities open to them, they could well have preferred to leave to others an investment that was of considerable size (shipowners had to lay out for the crew of slaves as well as for the vessel) and that stood idle for over half the year and might be totally lost at any moment during the other half.[38] Andocides became a *nauklêros*—but only after exile had forced upon him a new role in life, turning him from soldier, diplomat, and politician to businessman (Andocides 1.137). Phormio, the wealthy client of Demosthenes to whom we have already referred, eventually added ship-owning to his business pursuits (Dem. 45.64), but he was a naturalized Athenian who had started life as a slave. A Micon of Cholleidai, mentioned

44

in one of Demosthenes' speeches, is the only instance besides Andocides of a native-born Athenian *nauklêros* in the orators, and there is but one possible example in New Comedy.[39] Athenians, however, were not at all reluctant to take on the other two roles. They competed with metics and aliens as merchants, either for their own account or as agents of commercial houses, either operating from Athens or voyaging abroad the way merchants in those days were wont to do, and far outnumbered them in the field of maritime loans.[40] This was a venturesome business: the risks were great, since there were acts of men—piracy and chicanery—to fear, as well as acts of god, and there was no such thing as insurance.[41] In compensation, the return was extraordinarily high. In the one contract that has been preserved (Dem. 35.10), the borrowers agreed to pay 225 drachmae on every 1,000 for the four to five months from the beginning of the sailing season to mid-September and 300 if delayed until after that—in other words, 22.5 and 30 percent for four to five months or 67.5 and 90.5 percent per annum. We hear of one merchant who invested 2 talents in a trading venture to the Adriatic and doubled his money (Lysias 32.25), and there is no reason to doubt the statement. Maritime loans were even a quicker way than the mines to make a fortune, but just as quick a way to lose one. Hence those who went in for them were generally experienced moneylenders and not just anybody looking for a good return on some spare cash.[42]

Lastly, there was tax farming. Athens, with its rudimentary bureaucracy, did not have the personnel to do its own collecting of taxes, so the practice was to farm them out, to auction off the right to collect them, whether it was the 2 percent customs duty on all cargoes going in and out of the Peiraeus or the tax on the city's prostitutes. The amounts involved were often too much for the resources of any one person—the winning bid for the customs duty in 402/401, for example, was 36 talents—so syndicates were formed to handle them. The head of a syndicate was generally a wealthy man, but the members could be people of very modest means.[43] We have no idea how much profit there was to be made, but it must have been generous, for there never seems to have been a shortage of bidders. Though metics were allowed to take part, most of the tax farmers we hear of were Athenian.[44]

Banking, like ship-owning, was left almost totally in the hands of metics and aliens. The Athenians, as we have seen, were not at all averse to moneylending, yet the other, equally important side of an ancient bank's business, money changing, pawnbroking, and safe-deposit, apparently did not attract them. Athens' largest banking house in the fourth century belonged to Pasion, who had started life as a slave; his successor was Phormio, also an ex-slave, and when Phormio gave it up it was entrusted to a management team of four slaves or metics (cf. Davies 433). There is actually only one certain instance of a native Athenian banker.[45]

III

So much for the sources of an Athenian's income and the return he might expect from them. The next problem is to reach some idea of the size of his family, for this, then as now, was a crucial factor in determining a man's cost of living.

Our information about family size comes not from birth registers or the like but almost wholly from the orators and inscriptions, from remarks made in court speeches or names included in lists of mine lessees *aut sim*. As a consequence it (a) refers only to adults, most often adult males; (b) with rare exceptions reveals merely that a family had at least so many children, for there may well have been others whose mention was irrelevant; (c) is so haphazard it cannot possibly be quantified.

Among the families in Davies' register there are innumerable instances of two children, most often sons, but this no doubt is a reflection of the nature of our information. There are plentiful instances of three children; though they lean heavily to sons, in 40 percent of them there is one daughter and in almost 10 percent two daughters against one son. There are quite a few instances of families with four, even five children; again the emphasis is on sons, but two daughters are common and there are two instances of four daughters.[46] The biggest family we know of is Themistocles': five sons by a first wife and five daughters by two others (Davies 217). The Euctemon of Isaeus 6, who live to be ninety-six, had three sons and two daughters by a first wife and two sons by a second (6.10, 13 and Davies 562–63). And a certain Nicarete in Demosthenes 57, whose family was so down on its luck that she had to hire herself out as a wet-nurse and sell ribbons in the Agora, managed to find time to give her first husband a son and daughter and her second five sons (57.28, 30–35, 42, 43).

46

The crucial point is: how many live births did it take to produce adult families this size? Here a significant parallel is of
help. A. R. Burn, using whatever vital statistics are available,
has revealed how closely the age distribution in Roman Africa
matches that of modern India. Jones demonstrates that the figures we have from fourth-century Athens make an equally good
match. What is even more to the point is that India's ideal
family size coincides in general with Athens', two grown sons
and a daughter. Now, demographic studies reveal that "an Indian couple must have six or seven children . . . in order to
have 95 percent certainty that one son will survive to the
father's sixty-fifth birthday."[47] It follows that something of the
same order must be true of fourth-century Athens: for the innumerable families with two sons who reached adulthood we must
assume five or six live births. The families of four or five children that we find were not the exception but those lucky
enough to have an above average survival rate. Athens, in a
word, was a city of young people, with a plethora of children
swarming about and of babes in arms (cf. Jones 78, 83).[48]

With this in mind, let us look at the basic living expenses an
Athenian faced. The building records of Eleusis, dating in the
320s B.C., indicate that the cost of food for a slave was then
reckoned at one-half drachma a day (Jones 135) = 180 a year.
One may argue that this is too high to be taken as an average, for
a hardworking slave needs to be well fueled, or that it is too low,
since it refers to the diet of a slave. No matter; it is a reasonable
figure, Jones uses it in his cost-of-living calculations (30), and
even if we discount it, the general conclusion will still be much
the same. For children we may reckon a cost of 100 drachmae a
year.[49] The speaker of Demosthenes 42 at one point says, "My
father left me . . . property of only 45 minae . . . and it is not
easy to live on that" (Dem. 42.22). It assuredly was not. Even if
invested at a generous return of 15 percent, his 45 minae would
bring him but 675 drachmae a year, not even enough for food for
himself, his wife and, say, four children—a conservative estimate
in view of India's experience—which would amount to 760 (180
× 2 + 100 × 4). The speaker in question solved his problem by
taking up a mining concession, hit it rich, and ended a very
wealthy man. But people without his luck, no question about it,
had to live frugally. Jones (84) points to a passage in Demos-

thenes which implies that some of those required to pay the war tax, i.e., anyone with an estate worth 25 minae or more, could not afford even a single slave. Indeed they could not, not those—and they would be the greater number—who were on the line or just over it.

Let us go further and take someone the Athenians considered unquestionably well-to-do, someone worth 3 talents and therefore in or near the ranks of the liturgy-payers. If it was all in rental property, the return, at 8 percent, would be 1,440 drachmae. He would certainly have one slave and most probably two. To feed himself, his wife, and the male slave would cost (180 × 3) 540 drachmae, four children and a female slave (100 × 5) 500 drachmae, leaving but 400 drachmae for all his other expenses, an amount that a single liturgy could gobble up. Or take the specific case of Stratocles in Isaeus 11. His yearly income was 2,200 drachmae (11.43). He had a son and four daughters (11.37; cf. Davies 84). One of the daughters had been left an inheritance of 2.5 talents by a childless uncle (11.41), so her upkeep and dowry presumably were taken care of from that source. That still left four other children and, as we have seen, a family that size might spend 1,040 drachmae a year on food alone. In his bracket Stratocles could hardly have given his daughters dowries of less than 3,000 drachmae (see below) or 9,000 for all three. Since girls married about age sixteen or even earlier, this would amount to a yearly charge of some 550 drachmae. Thus, out of his apparently handsome income, he would be left with no more than 600 drachmae (2,200 − 1,040 + 550) for all his other expenses. And Stratocles was worth not 3 talents but 5 (11.42; cf. Davies 88), and hence was liable for trierarchies, which, at the very least, would take 2,000 drachmae (Davies xxii). Stratocles' return on his capital was low because he was a *rentier*, with the bulk of his money in real estate at 8 percent. To maintain such a leisurely style of life he unquestionably must have drawn on the income of his daughter's 2.5 talents, custody of which had been left in his hands.

But how many could count on great expectations from generous childless uncles? The average family that boasted a wealth of as much as 5 talents simply could not afford to be *rentiers*. They either, like the protagonist of Menander's *Dyskolos*,[50] farmed their own land, which would ensure them a considerably greater yield than 8 percent, or put some of their capital into owning a shop or slave broking or moneylending. And at that they probably had to keep a sharp eye on disbursements; an estate of 5 talents was eligible for the trierarchy, which by itself could exhaust a whole year's income. To be sure, by living on the farm or in a city house which they owned, there was no outlay for rent, and clothing, made at home and made to last, was a negligible expense, but there would be sacrifices and parties on fixed annual occasions,[51] funerals and grave monuments for the dead, armor for the sons, dowries for the daughters, and the inevitable liturgies. And there were always years when the crops were poor or a key slave-worker died or a debtor defaulted. Theophrastus scoffs (*Char.* 22) at the pennypincher who has his sandals constantly resoled instead of buying a new pair, who stays in the house when his mantle is being washed because it is the only one he has, who makes the caterers he has hired for his daughter's wedding provide their own food; the jibes hit home because his target, a choregus and trierarch (22.2, 5), has no need to behave so, but there must have been many others for whom it was an unavoidable way of life. Even men worth a good deal more than 3 talents were constantly borrowing, hypothecating their lands, houses, slaves. It was not to raise money for business purposes but to cover some occasional large personal expense—a dowry, funeral, ransom, trierarchy, the cost of an adverse judgement in a lawsuit;[52] only the very rich had the reserves to fall back on for such contingencies. Scant wonder that there was so much wriggling and squirming to get out of being tapped for liturgies.[53]

Among the clients of the orators were two diverse groups. One consisted of men of moderate wealth, 1 to 5 talents,[54] those whose incomes and financial problems we have just discussed. The other consisted of men with at least 10 to 15 talents, the members of the Three Hundred. As a matter of fact, 15 talents marked the lower limits. The charmed circle included plutocrats with double that or more.[55]

These were the ones who were able to indulge in such conspicuous consumption as keeping horses (cf. Davies xxv–vi), even that extravagance par excellence, keeping them not for riding but for pulling a chariot (Dem. 42.24), who walked about with three slaves at heel and kept mistresses (Dem. 36.45), whose house in town boasted a garden (Isaeus 5.11) or a ball court and wrestling ring (Theophrastus, *Char.* 5.9), who went in for exotic pets and imported bric-a-brac (ibid.).[56] And of course they were able to lavish money on their children, no matter how many there were. Demosthenes' guardians laid out 700 drachmae a year for maintaining him along with his sister and mother (27.36). It was not considered excessive to pay 1,000 drachmae a year just for the upkeep of two boys and a girl. The cost of food and clothing was probably not much more than in families of lesser means, but children born with silver spoons in their mouths must have the costly services of the shoemaker, fuller, and hairdresser, and the sons must have their *paidagogos,* the daughters their maid.[57] Yet even these outlays were nothing compared with what had to be faced when the children grew up. And the expense that bulked larger than all the rest was the dowry that a girl in this elevated set required to attract a mate of appropriate financial standing; as a husband who had gotten a mere 20 minae with his bride re-marked (Isaeus 11.40), "a man with a lot of money wouldn't be given a dowry that small."

The size of the dowries is a sure gauge of a family's wealth. Yet, though often discussed, they have not been properly ex-ploited for a variety of reasons.[58] For one, our information de-rives from two quite different sources, the orators and inscrip-tions on the one hand and Greek New Comedy and its Roman adaptations on the other; the latter consistently provide a higher range of figures—the Roman adaptations many many times higher—and these figures have been both uncritically accepted and hypercritically rejected.[59] For another, no one has ever taken into account the crucial factor of family size. It makes all the difference how many daughters there were: a dowry of 20 minae may be the mark of a modest family if there was but one; if there were three, since the practice was to treat them equally,[60] the total outlay was 60, a talent no less, not at all the mark of a modest family. The number of brothers, too, has a bearing: a father of, say, three sons, aware that at his death each will have to live on but a third of the pie, will beware of cutting off overly large portions for his daughters.

Let us start off with the figures to be found in the orators (see chart).[61]

"His wife, who brought him a dowry worth talents, he gives a pittance for food," sneers Theophrastus' backbiter (*Char.* 28.4).

References	Size of Estate	Number receiving Dowries	Number of Brothers	Total Outlay
Dem. 45.28	65 t (Pasion)	wife		3 t, 40 m
Dem. 27.4–5, 28.15–16	14 t (n. 8)	wife, dau.	1	3 t, 20 m
Isaeus 5.5, 26	13 t (n. 55)	4 sisters	1	2 t, 40 m
Lysias 32.6; Davies 152	15 t (n. 55)	wife, dau.	2	2 t
Dem. 40.6, 24		2 dau.	3	2 t
Plato, *Ep.* 13, 361d–e		4 nieces		30 m for 1 = 2 t
Dem. 27.4; Davies 122, 141		2 dau.	0	for all 4 50 m for 1 = 1 t,
Dem. 40.8–12, 20; Davies 365		1 dau.	3	40 m for both 1 t, 40 m
Dem. 45.66		1 dau.		1 t, 40 m
Dem. 29.48, 31.6–9; Davies 422–23	30 t (n. 55)	1 dau.	2	1 t, 20 m
Dem. 41.3, 6, 29		2 dau.	0	1 t, 20 m
Lysias 19.16–17	5 t (n. 54)	2 dau.	1	1 t, 20 m
Dem. 42.27 and Davies 552, 554	5 t (n. 54)	1 dau.	0	over 1 t
Hyperides 1 (*pro Lyc.*) 13		wife		1 t
Lysias 16.10		2 dau.	2	1 t
Isaeus 2.3, 5	1.5 t (n. 54)	2 dau.	2	40 m
Dem. 59.50	meager (cf. 59.43)	1 dau.		30 m
Isaeus 8.7–8	1.5 t (n. 54)	1 dau.	2	25 m
Isaeus 11.40		1 dau.		20 m

As we can see from the evidence listed above, such dowries were by no means unusual. Families of even modest means gave as much as a talent, while those belonging to the Three Hundred, Athens' wealthiest, did not hesitate to lay out 2 talents and on occasion went as high as 4—higher, if we may believe Pasion's son, who rounds off to 5 the amount left in his father's will to his mother as a dowry upon her remarrying (Dem. 45.74).[62] Isaeus (3.51) has a speaker refer scornfully to the person who would dower a daughter with less than one-tenth of his property. On the basis of the figures known to us, no father or brother or husband was anywhere near that parsimonious.

Let us turn now to Greek Comedy. There is one instance of a dowry of 1 talent, three instances of 2 talents, two of 3, and even one of 4.[63] Is Menander, as has been claimed, going in for comic exaggeration?[64] Or are we in the milieu of the plutocrats, men who could lay out such sums without turning a hair?

An unequivocal answer is provided by one of the new plays, the *Aspis.* Chaerestratus, a fine and openhanded *senex,* gives his niece a dowry of 2 talents (135–36, 268–69). Since he has a daughter of his own, he will presumably deal at least as generously with her. His total outlay for dowries, then, will be a minimum of 4 talents. Now, his estate happens to be 60 talents (350)—almost exactly the same as Pasion's, Athens' richest banker, whose fortune has been estimated at 65 talents (Davies 434), and who, as we have seen, left in his will a dowry of just about 4 talents to his wife.

The sons' style of life no less than the daughters' dowries points in the same direction. Moschion in the *Samia* had his "dogs and horses . . . , cut a fine figure in the guards, was able to give a fair amount of help to friends in need" and, far from avoiding liturgies, eagerly took them on to improve his public image (13–16). The mention of horses is particularly significant: as has been pointed out, they were the mark of affluence par excellence, the Athenian equivalent of maintaining a chauffeur-driven Rolls-Royce. Another telltale feature is the calling in of caterers when there is a festival or family event to celebrate.[65] And, when these moguls of money contract debts, it is not for a mere sum in minae but for "many talents" (Menander, *Sicyon.* 135).

All this makes clear why the sons are in such a desperate quandary when they lose their heart to a "poor" girl. They are not the mere scions of well-to-do burghers; they are heirs apparent to a financial throne in an aristocracy of wealth, and it is their duty to marry an appropriate princess. In the two complete plays of Menander that we happen to have, the plot concerns young nobles of this sort who have betrayed their class by falling in love with, so to speak, the daughter of a commoner. We become so absorbed in Menander's world that we unthinkingly fall in with the values his characters express, unthinkingly accept the fathers of these girls as poor. They are poor the way a minor executive of General Motors is poor as compared with the chairman of the board. Cnemon, the father in the *Dyskolos*, a character informs us (604), is "the true Attic peasant"; with a peasantry of the like of Cnemon, Attica would have been unique in the annals of ancient agriculture![66] His land, of which he had so much he could afford for purely temperamental reasons to leave some uncultivated (162–65), was worth no less than 2 talents (327–28); Athenians paid the orators good money to help them go to court and battle for estates that size (Isaeus 2.34–35, 4.7, 8.35). The father in the *Samia*, Niceratus, far from coming from across the tracks, lived right alongside Demeas, father of the boy involved, was Demeas' close personal friend, and accompanied him on trips abroad (96–112). Both Cnemon and Niceratus were parsimonious, the first clearly by choice (cf. *Dyskolos* 328–31), the other perhaps by necessity, since, as we have seen, even men worth several talents could often find it hard to make ends meet. But either of them would have been the envy of any of the 12,000 Athenians who, having less than 20 minae of property to their name, were in 322 B.C. dropped from the citizenship rolls. The contretemps in New Comedy are not between rich and poor but between the very very rich and those some cuts below them.

Now that the recent finds of Greek New Comedy have supplied a fair sampling of figures for dowries and property, it has become clear that these are of a different order from the figures long known from the Roman adaptations. The latter are so consistently higher one is driven to the conclusion that the Roman poets as a general practice inflated the numbers they found in their originals, perhaps as much as four or five times. A generous dowry in Menander is 2 talents; in Plautus and Terence it is 10 (Terence, *And.* 950–51; Plautus, *Merc.* 703; cf. *Truc.* 845, well in excess of 6) while 2 is but minimal (Terence, *H.T.* 838, 937–40).

53

The biggest dowry known from Greek New Comedy is 4 talents, from Roman comedy 20 (Plautus, *Cist.* 561–62).[67] Cnemon in the *Dyskolos* has an estate of 2 talents (327–28), while Menedemus in Terence's *H.T.*, a comparable character, has one worth 15 (145–46).[68] In Plautus' *Mostellaria,* the clever slave claims (648) to have bought the house next door for 2 talents, a price that delights the man who thinks he has acquired it (904–15) and who asserts (912–14) he would not sell it back for 6; we have no prices for houses from New Comedy, but in the orators Demosthenes' father's house was worth only half a talent (Dem. 27.10) and the house of the wealthy Aristophanes (cf. n. 55), the highest priced private dwelling mentioned in the orators (cf. Pritchett in *Hesperia* 25 [1956] 271), only 50 minae. In Terence's *Phormio,* property in Lemnos brings a return of 2 talents (789–91), which, at 8 percent, would make the holding worth 25; the most expensive property we hear of in the orators, also belonging to Aristophanes, was worth a little over 4 (Lysias 19.29, 42 and Davies 202; cf. Pritchett, ibid. 271–73). Very likely, as has been suggested, the figures were inflated to put them in line with what Plautus' and Terence's audiences were used to, for rich Roman senators of their day could have bought and sold many times over even the wealthiest Athenians.[69]

The "typical citizen . . . Menander . . . portrayed . . . is a middle-class landowner, a businessman, or a *rentier,* well-to-do but not extremely rich. . . . Millionaires of the day (if there were any) are not accepted as typical Athenians and therefore do not appear in Menander's comedies." So wrote Rostovtzeff (*SEHHW* 163) before the recent spectacular additions to the corpus of Menander. We now know that it is precisely the "millionaires" who figure most prominently in his plays. We see reflected there the ancient equivalent of the society of Molière's *Misanthrope* or Oscar Wilde's *Importance of Being Ernest,* not the comfortable suburbanites of American television comedy.[70]

IV

Let us summarize. Athens' upper and middle classes together numbered some 9,000 out of 21,000. We may consider as the upper class those who paid liturgies, men worth at least 3–4 talents. Among them was an upper bracket of 1,200 liable for the trierarchy and, within these, the Three Hundred, the city's wealthiest, boasting at least 10 to 15 talents and in some cases much more. Men of means owned, either wholly or with partners, land, slave-manned workshops, slaves for hire, mining concessions and refineries or both; they invested in commerce, tax farming, moneylending. Perhaps a majority had the bulk of their money in land with some representation in other areas, but there were not a few who eschewed land, with its modest return, for one or more of the other areas. The lower levels of the upper class, people with 3 to 5 talents, were in easy circumstances only if the family was small—and small families were the exception. Only the very rich, the members of the Three Hundred, had no financial worries: they could afford to go in for horses and other forms of conspicuous consumption and provide their women with handsome dowries. Greek New Comedy, contrary to what has been thought, concentrates on this particular class, hence the size of the dowries mentioned in the plays. This must be kept carefully in mind when using the plays as sources of socioeconomic information.

Notes

1. The following abbreviations have been used:

   Davies = J. Davies, *Athenian Propertied Families, 600–300 B.C.* (Oxford 1971)

   Finley = M. Finley, *Studies in Land and Credit in Ancient Athens, 500–200 B.C.* (New Brunswick 1952)

   Jones = A. H. M. Jones, "The Social Structure of Athens in the Fourth-Century B.C.," first published in *Economic History Review* 8 (1955) 141–55 and reprinted in *Athenian Democracy* (Oxford 1957) 75–96

   A. Boeckh, *Die Staatshaushaltung der Athener* (Berlin 1886³) i 560–623, first published in 1840, still has much useful information to offer.

2. Aside from the orators, Davies' chief source of information is epigraphy. For the 5th c. the most illuminating inscriptions are the group that records the sale of property confiscated from Alcibiades and others condemned in 415/414 for mutilating the Herms and profaning the Eleusinian mysteries. They have been published by W. K. Pritchett: "The Attic Stelai," pt. i (texts) *Hesperia* 22 (1953) 225–99; pt. ii (analysis and commentary) *Hesperia* 25 (1956) 178–317. For the 4th c. the most illuminating are those that list leases of mining properties in the Laurium area. They have been published and

analyzed by M. Crosby: "The Leases of the Laureion Mines," *Hesperia* 19 (1950) 189–312 and "More Fragments of Mining Leases from the Athenian Agora," *Hesperia* 26 (1957) 1–23.

3. *Menandri reliquiae selectae*, ed. F. Sandbach (OCT 1972); *The Plays of Menander*, trans. L. Casson (New York 1971).

4. Davies xxiv. Jones (86) suggests 2 talents or even less, but, as we shall see, that is impossibly low. One talent = 6,000 drachmae or 60 minae (1 mina = 100 drachmae).

5. The census taken by Demetrius of Phalerum (317–307 B.C.) produced this figure (Athenaeus 6.272c), and it squares with whatever other evidence can be brought to bear; see Jones 76.

6. Plutarch, *Phocion* 28.7 and Diodorus 18.18.4–5; cf. Jones 77.

7. Naval law, Dem. 14.16–17; cost of liturgies, Davies, xxi–xxii; Demosthenes' amended law, Jones 88 and 151, n. 53.

8. Demosthenes' father's estate, Dem. 27.9, 28.11, 29.59 and Davies 126–33; actually it was slightly under 14 (Davies 127). In the same class as Timotheus, Dem. 27.7 and cf. G. de Ste. Croix, "Demosthenes' *Timema* and the Athenian *Eisphora* in the Fourth Century B.C.," *C & M* 14 (1953) 30–70, esp. 65–66; cf. Davies 130–31.

9. Jones points out (90–93) that, aside from the upper crust, there was a gentle gradation in the distribution of wealth—over 40% of the population were upper and middle class—and suggests that this contributed greatly to Athen's political stability.

10. The wealthy Dicaeogenes of Isaeus 5—his property was worth perhaps 13 talents (below, n. 55)—owned an apartment house in the Ceramicus (5.26–27). Pasion had 2 apartment houses (Dem. 36.34, 45.28). Hagnias' family property in Isaeus 11 included 2 *oikiai* which were rented out (11.42), and Ciron's modest estate in Isaeus 8 included one (Isaeus 8.35). The holdings of Aphobus, Demosthenes' guardian, included an apartment house (Dem. 29.3), and there were both *oikiai* and *synoikiai* in the properties confiscated from those involved in the scandal of the Herms and Mysteries (*Hesperia* 25 [1956] 265, 268).

11. Pasion's property included 3 farms in 3 different demes (Davies 431). Hagnias' family property included 2 farms (Davies 87), as did the estate of Timarchus' father (Aeschines 1.97). The speaker of Lysias' "On the Olive Stump" refers to his "other lands . . . in the plain" (7.24). The biggest single farm property we know of, described as having a boundary 40 stades long and often taken to be 750 or so acres in extent, was perhaps no more than 100;

see G. de Ste. Croix, "The Estate of Phaenippus (Ps.–Dem. xlii)," *Ancient Society and Institutions, Studies Presented to Victor Ehrenberg on his Seventy-fifth Birthday* (Oxford 1966) 109–14. The other properties whose size is known were considerably smaller: 70 acres (300 plethra, Lysias 19.29; Plato, *Alc.* i, 123c), 22.5 or 45 acres (100 or 200 plethra, Plutarch, *Arist.* 27.1–2; Dem. 20.115), 14 acres (60 plethra, Isaeus 5.22).

12. The evidence for the 5th c. has most recently been collected and discussed by P. Gauthier in M. Finley, ed., *Problèmes de la terre en Grèce ancienne*, Centre de recherches comparées sur les sociétés anciennes, civilisations et sociétés 33 (Paris 1973) 163–78. Overseas holdings were so numerous that, in the inscription recording the sale of what had been confiscated from the men involved in the scandal of the Herms and Mysteries in 415, a special section was given over to them (*Hesperia* 22 [1953] 263); there were properties in Thasos and Abydos, and of other owners besides Oeonias in Euboea (cf. Pritchett in *Hesperia* 25 [1956] 276). Jones (167) sees the acquiring of such properties as starting under the empire, when Athens exploited its dominance to gain for its citizens the right of owning land in Allied territories. He also suggests (175–76) that cleruchs did not necessarily take up residence on their overseas properties but could remain in Athens as *rentiers*, which, if true, would make ownership of overseas property an everyday matter. The view has commended itself to P. Brunt (*Studies Ehrenberg* [above, n. 11] 81–84), but not to Gauthier (163).

Gauthier does not include overseas properties that Athenians received as gifts from potentates grateful for services rendered. This is how Gylon, Demosthenes, Sr.'s father-in-law, was able to settle down in Cepi Milesiorum in the Cimmerian Bosporus and presumably acquire the funds that enabled him to dower his daughter so handsomely (Aeschines 3.171–72 and Davies 121–22) and perhaps how Alcibiades got his holdings in Thrace (cf. J. Hatzfeld, *Alcibiade* [Paris 1951²] 319–20).

In the 4th c., with the privileges of empire gone, Athenians still went in for owning lands wherever they could. Lemnos remained an Athenian possession, and an inscription (*Hesperia* 29 [1960] 25, no. 33, lines 7–8) records an orchard, other land, and a farmhouse there confiscated in 370/369 from an Athenian owner, while Terence in the *Phormio*, based on an original by Apollodorus, assigns to a *matrona* resident at Athens properties on the island whither her husband repairs periodically to collect the rents (679–80, 789–91). In Menander's *Heros*, the master is away on "private business in Lemnos" (45–46); it may well be the same sort of thing. Gifts from Philip put property in Boeotia in Demades' hands and in Pydna in Aeschines' (Davies 100, 547). Aeschines too had lands in Boeotia and probably elsewhere as well (Davies 547). And Athens' freewheeling generals, who between pay and loot amassed fortunes, in order to indulge in conspicuous consumption that would have raised too many eyebrows back home, "chose to live outside the city, Iphicrates in Thrace, Conon in Cyprus, Timotheus in Lesbos, Chares in Sigeum, . . . Chabrias in Egypt" (Theopompus ap. Athenaeus 12.532b).

57

13. See Davies 469 for an Athenian lessee of temple property on Delos.

14. Cf. M. Finley, *The Ancient Economy* (Berkeley 1973) 116–22.

15. Published by Finley in *Studies in Land and Credit* (above, n. 1).

16. References in de Ste. Croix (above, n. 8) 34. Cf. Finley 54–55.

17. Isaeus 11.42: a farm worth 15,000 drachmae rented for 1,200 = exactly 8%, and 2 houses, one worth 3,000 and the other 500, together produced 300 = 8.57%. In *IG* ii–iii^2 2496.9–28, buildings and a workshop in the Peiraeus, assessed for war tax at 700 drachmae, rented for 54; if assessed at their worth, the return was 7.71%. Cf. de Ste. Croix (above, n. 8) 38–39.

    On the difficulties in finding tenants, cf. Lysias 7.9–10: a vineyard (7.14) was rented to 4 different tenants in 7 years; 2 held it for only a year apiece. And there is no reason for thinking that Athenian landlords were spared the sort of troubles Pliny the Younger laments (*Epist.* 9.37).

18. Dicaeogenes (above, n. 10) owned a bath (Isaeus 5.22), Euctemon in Isaeus 6 a *synoikia* in the Ceramicus (6.20) which he turned into a brothel, a *synoikia* in the Peiraeus (6.19), and a bath (6.33) in the Peiraeus (whose location has been identified; see *Hesperia* 34 [1965] 78). The *synoikia* in the Peiraeus, being next to the wine market, may have had a bar, along with rooms for guests, for the two usually went together. There certainly were inns at the time (see L. Casson, *Travel in the Ancient World* [London 1974] 87–91) and somebody had to own them.

19. Free labor, never very important in the ancient world, at Athens was limited to seasonal agricultural help and other casual employment. Free men in industry were almost always independent artisans or self-employed workers. On this important point, see Finley (above, n. 14) 73–74.

20. Building inscriptions reveal numerous instances of an artisan working with a handful of slave assistants. Cf., e.g., *IG* i^2 374.202–207, 238–44, 308–11 (408/407–407/406): certain columns of the Erechtheum were fluted by a team of 7 stonecutters, Simias "resident in Alopeke" (i.e., a metic) with 4 slaves of his own and 2, no doubt hired, belonging to someone else. Lysias' father, Lysias 12.8, 12, 19; the 120 slaves mentioned very likely included a number of domestics employed in the family homes (Davies 589). Timarchus' father, Aeschines 1.97. Demosthenes', Dem. 27.9; 5 to 6 minae is high even for skilled labor (cf. the prices gathered by Pritchett in *Hesperia* 25 [1956] 276–78). Leocrates owned a bronze foundry whose slaves were sold off for 35 minae (Lycurgus, *Leoc.* 22–23, 58); if they were worth as much as Demosthenes, Sr.'s expensive cutlers, his shop had 5 or 6. The shoemaker in Herondas' seventh mime, head of a thriving establishment that specialized in expensive footwear, had a staff of 13 slaves (7.44).

21. Demosthenes, Sr.'s shops on the premises, Dem. 27.24–25 and Finley 67. The property of Comon, which was at issue in Dem. 48, consisted of a team of sailmakers and of color grinders; the first was housed in his own home, the other in another building he owned (48.12). On the *chôris oikountes*, see W. Westermann in M. Finley, ed., *Slavery in Classical Antiquity* (Cambridge 1960) 20–23. Timarchus' shoemakers belong to this category: they ran the shop by themselves, paying Timarchus 2 obols a day for each worker and 3 for the foreman and keeping what was left to live on and presumably put aside for eventual purchase of their freedom. Timarchus' father's slave woman who was "trained in working fine linen and offered it for sale in the agora" (Aeschines 1.97) may well have lived apart and operated independently. Syriscus, the charcoal burner in Menander's *Epitrepontes*, is another case in point: he turned up at intervals to render the required payments (*apophora*) to his master (cf. line 204). For *chôris oikountes* in the building trade, see below.

22. The team in Menander's *Aspis* consisted of the cook, a waiter, and a scullion (221–33). There were always the household slaves to call upon if additional hands were needed; cf. *Dyskolos* 403–404, 430–37, 456–63.

    Athenaeus makes the statement that there is no example of "the slave cook except in Poseidippus alone" (14.658f), and this has led to much wrangling over the status of cooks, whether they were slave or free; see, e.g., H. Dohm, *Mageiros: Die Rolle des Kochs in der griechisch-römischen Komödie,* Zetemata 32 (Munich 1964) 19–22. In New Comedy they consistently have names that elsewhere are borne by slaves (A. Gomme and F. Sandbach, *Menander, A Commentary* [Oxford 1973] 131), wear masks that Pollux lists (4.148) under slave masks, associate with slaves (Menander, *Dyskolos* 393 ff.), commit the sort of acts typical of slaves (*Dyskolos* 888 ff.), fear whippings just like slaves (*Dyskolos* 900–901; cf. Gomme and Sandbach's note ad loc.)—in short, though in real life the profession included freedmen and the occasional citizen who would stoop to any disreputable line of work (Theophrastus, *Char.* 6.5), on the comic stage they were slave (cf. Gomme and Sandbach 290). I suspect Athenaeus had in mind the cook who was a slave in a household (cf. Plautus, *Men.* 219–25, 273–75) as against the professional hired from outside.

23. Menander, *Dyskolos* 393 ff. (sacrifice), *Samia* 286 ff. and *Aspis* 216 ff. (wedding), *Epit.* 206–208 (party); cf. Dohm (above, n. 22) 76–80.

24. For the attitude, cf., e.g., Terence, *Adelphoe* 177–89; other references in W. Headlam, *Herodas, The Mimes and Fragments* (Cambridge 1922) xxxviii. Habrotonon, the slave courtesan in Menander's *Epitrepontes,* was getting 12 drachmae a day (136–37); the average skilled laborer at this time made no more than 2 to 2.5 (Jones 135). To be sure, a girl as accomplished as she must have cost her owner a tidy sum. The notorious Neaera, who had been raised and trained in the same house as the courtesan patronized by no less a personage than Lysias (Dem. 59.18–21), cost 30 minae (Dem. 59.29).

25. Demosthenes, Sr.'s cutlery yielded just short of 16% per annum. The annual income was 3,000 drachmae on a capital of 19,000 (Dem. 27.9–10; the total value of the cutlers plus couch-makers plus money out at interest was 29,000, and the last two items totaled 10,000—6,000 out at interest and 4,000 down on the books for the couch-makers). The 20 couch-makers, taken over as security for a loan of 4,000 drachmae, produced 1,200 per annum = 30%; they were almost certainly worth more than book value, since security was usually much more than the amount of a loan and might run twice as high (cf. Finley 80–81, Prichett in *Hesperia* 25 [1956] 274). Davies (129) is very tempted by the textual emendation in Dem. 27.9 which transfers the clause "and these were none of them worth less than 3 minae" from the description of the cutlers, where it now stands and makes difficult sense, to the description of the couch-makers, where it would make excellent sense. However, he is reluctant to accept it on the grounds that a capital value for the couch-makers of 6,000 drachmae (20 × 300) instead of 4,000, when deducted from the total figure of 29,000, would leave too low a valuation for the cutlers. Actually, no such deduction is necessary. So far as the valuation of the estate was concerned, the value of the couch-makers was the amount of money for which they were security, 4,000 drachmae. The clause would represent Demosthenes' estimate of their value on the open market, viz. 6,000. On this basis the annual yield from the couch-making shop, 1,200 on a capital of 6,000, would work out to 20%.

Timarchus' father collected from each of his shoemakers 2 obols a day or 120 drachmae a year; if they were worth 600 apiece, like Demosthenes, Sr.'s most expensive cutlers, the yield was 20%; if they were worth less, as is quite likely (cf. Pritchett in *Hesperia* 25 [1956] 277–78), the yield was proportionately higher.

26. See Finley (above, n. 14) 118.

27. Other possible instances of successful movement up the socioeconomic ladder are a sculptor and a carpenter who worked on the Erectheum (Davies 242, 280).

28. Davies 41 (Anytus), 246 (Isocrates), 318 (Cleon), 517 (Hyperbolus); Andocides 1.146 (Cleophon). J. Beazley, "Potter and Painter in Ancient Athens," *PBA* 30 (1944) 87–125, points out (111–12) that the shop of the Penthesilea Painter came close to a form of mass production; in the half century or so of its existence, a score of different painters can be distinguished, and we can identify cups whose inside was painted by one hand and the outside by another. See also T. Webster, *Potter and Patron in Classical Athens* (London 1972) chap. 1 and especially p. 41, where he estimates the staff of the average shop turning out fine pottery at 10 to 20 potters and painters.

29. This I suspect is why we are told that Demosthenes, Sr.'s cutlery had "32 or 33" slaves (Dem. 27.9) or that Timarchus' father had "9 or 10" shoemakers

(Aeschines 1.97); the complement of a shop was not always up to full strength.

30. Xenophon, *Vect.* 4. The slaves, he states (4.14–15), brought their owners a return of an obol a day (= 60 drachmae per annum; he uses a 360-day year). In *Vect.* 4.23–24 he cites figures that offer a basis for estimating the cost of mine slaves, but they are somewhat imprecise, so the results derived from them vary: Boeckh (above, n. 1) i 86 offers 125–50 drachmae as the cost of a single slave, E. Ardaillon (*Les mines de Laurion dans l'antiquité* [Paris 1897] 104) 122 or 194, J. Thiel (*Xenophontos Poroi* [Vienna 1922] 52–53) 158 or 195. The 30% yield in the text is a minimum based on a cost in round numbers of 200. The lower figures—Jones (in Finley [above, n. 21] 5) uses Boeckh's—bring the yield up to 40% and 50%.

31. In *IG* i² 374, the records of the Erechtheum, Kerdon, slave of Axiopeithes, put in a day's work taking down scaffolding (line 71) and another day's work, along with another slave of the same owner, fluting columns with Simias' gang (above, n. 20).

32. On the *Kolonos Agoraios,* see A. Fuks in *Eranos* 49 (1951) 171–73, who has collected all the references. For its location, see J. Travlos, *Bildlexikon zur Topographie des antiken Athen* (Tübingen 1971) 169, no. 218. The *mistharnountes* who lined up there included, to be sure, free men, but my feeling is that most were slave. For the "cook's market," see Plautus, *Pseud.* 790–807, and Dohm (above, n. 22) 70–71; Pollux (9.48) calls it the *mageireia.* Theophrastus' pennypincher, instead of buying his wife a lady's maid, hired one from the "woman's market" to accompany her everytime she wanted to go out (*Char.* 22.10); according to Pollux (10.18) this was where household gear was sold but apparently it was also where female labor shaped up.

33. In Isaeus 8, Ciron's modest estate of between 1 and 2 talents, chiefly in land and houses, included some money out on loan (8.35). The wealthy estate at issue in Isaeus 11 included 40 minae out on loan at 18% (11.42). A certain Arcesas lent 16 minae to Pasion's son Apollodorus on the security of an apartment house at 16% (Dem. 53.13). Demosthenes, Sr., who, as we have noted, disliked real estate, had a talent out at 12% (Dem. 27.9), and Timarchus' father, who shared the dislike, also had money out on loan (Aeschines 1.97). Onetor and Timocrates, two extremely wealthy men—Demosthenes (30.10) estimated their fortunes at 30 and 10 talents respectively—were in the habit of "lending no small sums to others." On interest rates see R. Bogaert, *Banques et banquiers dans les cités grecques* (Leiden 1968) 347.

34. In Davies' register there are almost 30 certain or probable instances of men or families who invested in mining leases (35, 42, 70, 111, 156, 158, 161, 162, 163, 167, 178, 186, 187, 189, 192, 205, 221, 238, 279, 320, 341, 386, 424, 518, 525, 531, 533, 591). Half a dozen also had money in refineries (42, 70, 163, 385–86, 531, 533). Timarchus' father invested only in refineries; the listing of

his property (Aeschines 1.97–101) includes two but makes no mention of mining concessions. There are a few in Davies' register whose known investments include only refineries (139, 143), but these may have held concessions as well.

Pantaenetus, the speaker's opponent in Dem. 37, owned both a refinery and a mining lease. The case involves only his refinery (*ergasterion*, 37.4 and throughout) and the loan for which he had hypothecated it, a loan in the form of a *prasis epi lysei*, i.e., with "security in the form of conditional sale"; see Finley 32–35. His mining lease (*metallon*, 37.22), which cost him 1.5 talents, is a thing apart; it is mentioned only because, when he sent his slave to the state treasury with the cash for a part payment, his creditors highhandedly stopped the man and took the money away. Many have confused the two properties: F. Paley and J. Sandys in their *Select Private Orations of Demosthenes* i (Cambridge 1898³) 98–100; the Loeb translator; H. Michell, *The Economics of Ancient Greece* (New York 1957²) 106; Westermann in Finley (above, n. 21) 90. L. Gernet, the Budé translator, renders the relevant passages properly.

For a convenient account of what is known about the technique of mining and refining, see Michell 98–112, and for the leasing R. Hopper, "The Attic Silver Mines in the Fourth Century B.C.," *ABSA* 48 (1953) 200–254.

35. M. Crosby in *Hesperia* 19 (1950) 202 collected the prices known up to that time: of 76 leases where the price is preserved, 22 cost 20 drachmae and 30 cost 150. The highest price that occurs in the inscriptions is 17,550—450 drachmae short of 3 talents (*Hesperia* 26 [1957] 13, no. S5, line 15), the next highest 6,100 (*Hesperia* 5 [1936] 404, line 299), the third highest 2,000 (*Hesperia* 19 [1950] 255, line 3). Hopper (above, n. 34) argues (238–39) that all the figures most probably represent the payment for a prytany; thus a 20-drachmae lease cost the lessee 200 per annum, a 150-drachmae lease 1,500 per annum, and the one for 17,550 would come to 29 talents, 15 minae. He also discusses (234–37) the length of the leases—most were for 7 years, certain renewals for 3—and the prices: 20 drachmae was the fee set by the state for opening a new mine or continuing work on one of unknown quality; 150 the fee for continuing work on a promising mine; 20 for reworking of abandoned sites by an original lessee; 150 by a new; still higher figures, probably set by auction, for sites of proven quality.

Despite the fragmentary and haphazard nature of our information, there is a demonstrable correlation between wealth and cost of concession. Of the more expensive leases, 150 drachmae and higher, there are some 16 instances in which the lessee's name has been preserved. At least half of the names appear in Davies' register: Euthycrates, who held the lease of 2,000 mentioned above (Davies 71); Thrasylochus, Meidias' brother, who held two, one of 1,550 and another of 150 (Davies 385); Leukios (Davies 341) and Epicrates (Davies 162), both with leases of 200; Euetion (Davies 189), Cleonymus (Davies 556), Onetor (Davies 424), possibly Euthycrates (Davies 35), all with leases of 150. (The seven that do not appear are: *Hesperia* 10 [1941] 16, no. 1, lines 50–51 [lease of 1550], 83 [lease of 150]; 19 [1950] 261, no. 19, line 18, and 264, no. 20, lines 12–13, 16–17 [two leases of 150, one of 160]; *IG* ii^2 1582.75, 82–83 [two leases of 150]). Of the cheapest leases, those for 20 drachmae, there are some 20 instances in which the lessee's name is preserved; of these, only 4 are in Davies' register, and of these 4, 2 held two such leases simultaneously, Callias (Davies 525) and Pheidippus (Davies 533). The 2 others are Aismides (Davies 42) and Diotimus (Davies 163). (The 16 that do not appear are: *Hesperia* 10 [1941] 16–17, no. 1, lines 44, 56–57, 58–59, 60, 67, 71, 76, 78–79; 19 [1950] 251, no. 16, line 10; 26 [1957] 4, no. S2, lines 24, 27–28, 29, 33, 35, 36–37, 41; *IG* ii^2 1582.122–23.)

36. An *ergasterion* usually consisted of a crushing mill and washing tables placed as near as possible to the mine or mines it served to keep transportation to a minimum. The refinery proper, the furnace for smelting, was called a *kaminos*, and there were considerably fewer of these, presumably strategically located. In the inscriptions, 83 *ergasteria*, sc. crushing and washing facilities, are mentioned as against 6 *kaminoi;* cf. Crosby in *Hesperia* 19 (1950) 194–95. The *ergasterion* in Dem. 37 was probably a full-scale affair with both a furnace (37.28) and crushing mill (*kenchreôn* in 37.26 is probably the facility for crushing the ore, though the evidence is inconclusive; see Ardaillon [above, n. 30] 62, Paley and Sandys [above, n. 34] note ad loc., Hopper [above, n. 34] 204). The work force consisted of 30 slaves (37.4; Jones [14] mistakenly took them as the crew of a mining concession). It was sold, slaves included, for 3 talents, 26 minae (37.31).

37. Our information comes chiefly from 5 speeches of Demosthenes dealing with bottomry loans, 32–35, and 56. Demon, the lender in 32, and Androcles, one of the lenders in 35, were the only citizens; all the others were either certainly or probably metics or aliens.

38. The sailing season was roughly April into October; see *SSAW* 270–73; slave crews, 328.

39. Micon, Dem. 58.6, 9, 15; cf. Davies 57–58. The title figure of Plautus' *Mercator* had sold his farm to become a *nauklêros-emporos* (74–77, 87–89), but we cannot be certain that Plautus found this in his original. Pataecus in Menander's *Perik.*, who lost his fortune when "the ship which used to furnish my livelihood" (378) sank and thus was either a *nauklêros* or *nauklêros-emporos,* was a native of Corinth.

40. Lysias 32.4 (Diodotus had made his considerable fortune—over 15 talents [Davies 152–53]—in commerce); Dem. 52.20 (2 brothers from Eleusis prepare to borrow money for a business trip to Acê in Phoenicia, perhaps—cf. Herondas 2.16–17 with Headlam's note ad loc.—to purchase wheat). Nicobulus in Dem. 37 sailed off on business to the Pontus (37.6, 10, 25), very likely to trade in wheat, for the area was Athens' major supplier; he also went in for moneylending to keep his spare cash at work (37.54), and, since one of his loans was on the security of real property, the silver refinery mentioned in nn. 34 and 36

above, he must have been a citizen (as Gernet, the Budé translator assumed [225, n. 3]; the arguments of Erxleben [see below] to the contrary are unconvincing). The Athenian father who goes abroad on business—thereby leaving a son free to sow wild oats and thus start the wheels of the plot spinning—is a common figure in Greek New Comedy. In Menander's *Samia*, Demeas and Niceratus have just returned from the Pontus (96–112), and in his *Dis Exapatôn* two brothers have gone off to Ephesus to collect a debt owed to their father (cf. Gomme and Sandbach [above, n. 22] 118). For examples from Roman comedy see Terence, *Phormio* 66–68 (business trip to Cilicia); Plautus, *Most.* 440, 971 (to Egypt); *Stichus* 366–83 (Asia); *Trin.* 771 (Seleucia).

We find the Athenian Pythodorus acting as agent for Pasion (Davies 430), the Athenians Stephanus and Timosthenes acting as agents, including voyaging abroad, for his successor Phormio (Dem. 45.64, 49.31), and the Athenian Antiphanes representing abroad a certain Philip who, being a *nauklêros*, was most probably a metic or alien (Dem. 49.14–15). Bogaert (above, n. 33, 68–69) along with the Loeb translator assumes that Antiphanes and Philip were abroad together; Gernet in the Budé translation renders the phrase describing Antiphanes properly: "Antiphanès de Lamptra, qui naviguait comme intendant de l'armateur Philippe." E. Erxleben, "Die Rolle der Bevölkerungsklassen im Aussenhandel Athens im 4. Jahrhundert v. u. Z" in E. Welskopf, ed., *Hellenische Poleis* (Berlin 1974) i, 460–520, claims (473–75, 501) that there are far more examples of non-Athenian *emporoi* than Athenian. Very likely they were in the majority, but the evidence available is too haphazard to yield hard and fast conclusions. Moreover, aside from a reference (468–69) to a fragment from Diphilus, he takes no cognizance of New Comedy; yet the Athenian merchant was obviously common enough to be used as a standard character.

Erxleben has analyzed the nationality of the moneylenders who went in for maritime loans. His summary (502) shows 41 Athenians as against 11 metics, 16 aliens, and 1 slave. The Diodotus of Lysias 32, who had made his fortune in commerce (32.4), left at his death 7 talents and 40 minae in maritime loans (32.6). Demosthenes, Sr., who put all his money into manufacturing and moneylending, had a maritime loan of 70 minae on the books when he died (Dem. 27.11), and his son seems to have gone in for such loans as well (Plutarch, *Comp. of Dem. and Cic.* 3.6; cf. Erxleben 467). Nausicrates and Xenopeithes in Dem. 38, who had most of their capital in moneylending (38.7), had 100 staters, perhaps 2,800 drachmae (cf. Dem. 34.23), out on loan to a trader in the Cimmerian Bosporus (38.11–12).

41. For piracy, cf. Dem. 52, a case that grew out of the death of a merchant in a pirate attack (52.5); cf. also Lysias 32.29. For chicanery, cf. Dem. 32, involving a pair of rascals from Marseilles who borrowed sizable sums in Syracuse on the security of their ship, sent the money off for safekeeping in their home town, and then, since repayment was contingent upon safe arrival, tried to scuttle the vessel.

42. The Demon of Dem. 32 (see above, n. 37) was a relative of Demosthenes, and he may have been out of his depth when he went in for a maritime loan,

for he seems to have been so neatly swindled out of his money (cf. the previous note and Davies 117) that even his gifted relative's help may not have gotten it back for him; cf. above, p. 31.

43. The winning bid in 402/401 B.C. was made by a syndicate headed by Andocides which nosed out Agyrrhius' syndicate (Andocides 1.133–34); Andocides was a very rich man, and Agyrrhius came from a well-known family of liturgical status (Davies 31, 278–79). On the other hand, Leocrates, whose estate was a mere talent, was once a partner in a syndicate farming the customs duty (Lycurgus, *Leoc.* 19, 22–23, 58).

44. See the previous note. There is also Xenocleides, mentioned by Demosthenes (59.26–28) as tax farmer of the customs duty in 369 B.C. In the story of Alcibiades' tricking of a syndicate into buying out the successful bidder (Plutarch, *Alc.* 5), the latter was a metic.

45. On ancient banking, see Bogaert (above, n. 33) 315–56 and, on the bankers of Athens, 62–86. The earliest banker in Athens that we know of was a certain Antimachus mentioned by Eupolis (frg. 127 K = Edmonds i 342); his nationality is unknown. The next are the Antisthenes and Archestratus who turned their bank over to their ex-slave Pasion and thereby launched him on his spectacular financial career. Bogaert (62) feels that both were metics, though we cannot be sure. The only certain native Athenian banker is the Aristolochus mentioned in Dem. 36.50 and 45.63–64 (cf. Davies 60).

46. Three children: there are 29 instances of 3 sons (Davies 32, 44, 65, 80, 93, 161, 163, 179, 194, 197, 209, 247, 283, 306, 338, 351, 399, 403, 415, 423, 456, 467, 498, 545, 566, 571, Dem. 54.14, Lysias 17.3, Aeschines 1.102), 24 of 2 sons and 1 daughter (Davies 16–17, 24 [two instances], 61, 85, 115, 142, 148, 152, 229–30, 250, 253, 267, 313, 319–20, 361, 422–23, 456–57, 477–78, 481–82, 544, 547, Dem. 59.38, Isoc. 19.9), 5 of 1 son and 2 daughters (Davies 45, 200–201, 437, Isaeus 10.25, Lycurgus, *Leoc.* 22–23).

Four children: 6 instances of 4 sons (Davies 26, 94, 363, 365–66, 417, Lysias 13.65), 8 of 3 sons and 1 daughter (Davies 82–83, 177, 194–95, 275, 332–34, 365, 590, Isaeus 3.26, 30), 4 of 2 sons and 2 daughters (Davies 93–94, Lysias 16.10, Isaeus 2.3, 10.4), 3 of 1 son and 3 daughters (Davies 297, 315, 319).

Five children: 1 instance of 5 sons (Davies 79), 2 of 4 sons and 1 daughter (Davies 80, 246), 2 of 3 sons and 2 daughters (Davies 461–64, Isaeus 12.2–5), 2 of 1 son and 4 daughters (Davies 84, 145–48).

47. A. R. Burn, "Hic breve vivitur," *Past and Present* (1952–53) 2–31. Jones 82–83, where he reproduces Burn's chart. Indian family size, D. Mandelbaum, *Human Fertility in India* (Berkeley and Los Angeles 1974) 15, 18.

48. Rostovtzeff, *SEHHW* 163, assumes families of one or two children, which is impossibly low. W. Lacey, *The Family in Classical Greece* (London 1968) 165, tends to allow more than two only to families with "sources"; as it

happens, the only families we know about were those with "resources," one or more of whose members had the wherewithal to hire lawyers and hence appear in the corpus of the orators. There is no reason to exempt ancient Athens from the time-honored conjunction of poverty and children.

49. Cf. Lysias 32.20: "[Their guardian] reckoned, on the one hand, the food for two boys and their sister at 5 obols per day [= 100 drachmae per annum per child], but, on the other hand, for shoes and cleaning and hairdressing he put down neither a monthly nor yearly amount but a lump sum for the whole period [8 years] of more than a talent [i.e., over 750 drachmae per annum]." The speaker's complaint is leveled not so much at the amount reckoned for food as at that for the three luxury items and the cavalier bookkeeping.

50. His estate was 2 talents (327–28).

51. Cf. Menander, *Epit.* 749–50, reference to the annually recurring expenses of the women's festivals.

52. Cf. Finley 81–87. He points out (83) the number of *horoi* that record hypothecating of real estate to raise money for a dowry. See also Dem. 40.52 (loan to pay funeral expenses), 53.10 (loan to pay off a ransom), 50.7 (for a trierarchy), 47.49–51 (for paying off a judgement).

53. The orators' clients frequently claim that their opponents are trying to avoid liturgies (e.g., Dem. 42.3–4, 21; Isaeus 5.36, 11.47, 11.49); there must have been fire behind the smoke.

54. 1 talent (Lycurgus, *Leoc.* 22), 1–2 talents (Isaeus 2.34–35 and cf. Davies xxiii; 4.7 and Davies 237; probably 8.35 and Davies 314), 2–3 talents (Isaeus 11.41; 3.2 and Davies xxiii; Dem. 38.20 and Davies 416–18), 3–5 talents (Isaeus 7.19, 31 and Davies 45; 11.42, 44 and Davies 87–88; 6.19, 20, 23, 33 and Davies 562; Lysias 19.9, 59 and Davies 200; 17.2, 5 [real estate hypothecated for 2 talents and presumably worth much more; see note 25 above]; Dem. 42.28 and Davies 554 [real estate hypothecated for ca. 3 talents]).

55. Demosthenes, Sr.'s estate was worth almost 14 talents (above, n. 8); Aristophanes, who made money campaigning for Evagoras, had at least 15 (Lysias 19.29, 42–43 and Davies 202); Diodotus, a merchant, left over 15 (Lysias 32.4–6, 13–15 and Davies 152–53). The estate of Dicaeogenes produced an income of 80 minae (Isaeus 5.11, 35; for its components, see also 5.22, 26 and Davies 146); at, say, 10% this implies a worth of over 13 talents. Davies (593) estimates the worth of the speaker of Lysias 21 between 20 and 30 talents. A certain Timocrates was worth over 10 talents and his brother-in-law Onetor over 30 (Dem. 30.10 and Davies 423), Conon at least 40 (Lysias 19.40 and Davies 508), Pasion 65 (Dem. 36.5–6, 11, 34 and Davies 431–35), Lysias' family 70 (*P. Oxy.* 1606.30 and Davies 589).

66

56. This is the class Xenophon had in mind when (*Vect.* 4.8) he speaks of people's need for cash in prosperous times, "the men for fine armor, good horses, a magnificent house and furnishings . . . , the women for expensive clothes and gold jewelry."

57. The speaker in Lysias 32.28 reckons 1,000 drachmae a year as a generous but reasonable amount for the upkeep of 2 boys and their sister along with a *paidagogos* and maid, and in 32.20 he indicates the principal items of expense. If we allow 500 for food (cf. n. 49 above), that would leave 500 for shoes, cleaning, hairdressing, and similar services.

58. See, e.g., W. Erdmann, *Die Ehe im alten Griechenland,* Münchener Beiträge zur Papyrusforschung und antiken Rechtsgeschichte 20 (Munich 1934) 319–21 and Finley's justifiable criticism (above, n. 1, 266); H. Wolff, *RE* 23 (1957) 139–41.

59. Rostovtzeff, *SEHHW* 163: "To the girls he [the Athenian *bourgeois*] gives a decent but not excessive dowry, usually of one, two, three, or four talents of silver, 16 being the maximum"; Finley 79: "Roughly, 3,000–6,000 drachmas seems to have been the accepted standard for the wealthiest people. A dowry of more than 6,000 drachmas could be grounds for gossip, even suspicion." Rostovtzeff's figure of 16 is now read as 10 (Menander, ed. Koerte, frg. 333.11) and, though the text is uncertain, some sort of exaggeration seems intended ("don't marry an ugly old women even with a dowry of 10 talents"). For dowries in Roman comedy, see below. Finley arrives at his low maximum by ad hoc explanations for any that run higher; in one important instance the explanation is based on an error: the 1 talent and 40 minae (10,000 drachmae) which Stephanus of Acharnae gave his daughter (Dem. 45.66; cf. Davies 438), Finley attributes to Phormio and explains as an ex-slave's bravura gesture. Bogaert (above, n. 33, 390) has already pointed out the mistake.

60. Dem. 40.24, 1 talent each to 2 daughters; Dem. 41.3, 29, 40 minae each to 2 daughters; Lysias 16.10, 30 minae each to 2 sisters; Isaeus 2.3, 5, 20 minae each to 2 sisters. In Lysias 19.16–17, 1 daughter received 40 minae and there is a clear implication that a sister received at least as much.

61. The figures found in inscriptions coincide nicely in the middle range but do not run quite as high as those in the orators and descend a good deal lower. There are 18 dotal *horoi* with the amount indicated (Finley, nos. 132–37, 141–43, 146–50, 153, 156; *Hesperia* 41 [1972] 275); they range from 1 talent, 20 minae (8,000 drachmae) down to 3 minae (300 drachmae), with 8 clustered between 10 and 20 minae. In an inscription from Tenos (*IG* xii.5.873, end of 4th or beginning of 3rd c. B.C.), 3 sisters receive 20 minae each. An inscription from Mykonos (Dittenberger, *Syll.*[3] 1215, probably 3rd c. B.C.) lists 8 that range from 2 talents, 2 minae, to 7 minae, with 4 clustered between 10 and 20.

62. Alcibiades received 10 talents when he married Hipponicus' granddaughter, with a promise of 10 more upon the birth of their first child (Plutarch, *Alc.* 8.2; Andocides 4.13–14), but this was so exceptional the story "went the rounds of the Greek world for centuries" (Finley 79).

63. 1 talent, Kock, *Frag. com. graec.* iii 430, no. 117 = Edmonds iiiA 378; 2 talents, *Aspis* 135–36, Thrasonides 446 (= C. Austin, *Comicorum graecorum fragmenta in papyris reperta* [Berlin 1973] no. 151), *P. Oxy.* 2533 (= Austin no. 251); 3 talents, *Dyskolos* 844, *Perik.* 1015; 4 talents, *Epit.* 134.

64. Finley, 267, conformable with his view that the wealthiest families rarely gave more than a talent (cf. above, n. 59). To consider the figures exaggerated not only is unnecessary but blunts the point of Menander's portrayals. E.g., when Smicrines in the *Epitrepontes,* a sharp businessman for whom money talks, bemoans (134) the dowry of 4 talents he bestowed upon a son-in-law who forthwith proceeds to behave abominably toward his daughter, Menander is not showing us his weakness for exaggerating financial losses but his anguish at not getting what he paid for, particularly when he paid, as it were, the top of the market.

65. See above, n. 23. The caterer in Menander's *Aspis* expected to be paid 3 drachmae (223–24). It was the menu that was expensive, little short of a talent for an elaborate spread (Menander, ed. Koerte, frg. 264).

66. B. Mieczysław ("Menanders Dyskolos und Athen" in *Menanders Dyskolos als Zeugnis seiner Epoche,* Deutsche Akad. der Wiss. zu Berlin, Schriften der Sektion für Altertumswissenschaft 50 [Berlin 1965] 13–14) takes Menander's word absolutely literally: "Er ist arm," he says repeatedly of Cnemon and describes him as leading "das Leben eines echten attischen Bauern" and his stepson Gorgias as "ein wirklich armer junger Bauer." Really poor peasants did not do their farming, as Gorgias did, with a slave at their side; cf. Jones 13–14.

67. In *Trin.* 1158 the dowry is 1,000 gold Philippi. Since the Philippus was worth about 25 denarii and there were 6,000 denarii to the talent (*ESAR* 1.127), this works out to over 4 talents.

68. Thus, when in Terence's *Phormio* (392–95), Phormio sneers that Demeas would certainly remember the name and total ancestry of a relative who had left him 10 talents, the implication is a mere 10 talents, the equivalent of a 2-talent estate in the orators, which, as we have seen, is modest. In Demeas' circle fortunes were over three times that size at least: his neighbor's wife had the land on Lemnos described below that was worth 25 talents, and the text makes clear that this was by no means all the family's holdings.

69. In Plautus' *Trinummus* a house is sold for 40 minae (125–26), but this was an absurdly low price (cf. 1081–82). Suggestion that figures are inflated, in

Gomme and Sandbach (above, n. 22) 297. Wealth of Roman senators, cf. Finley 101.

70. The Roman adaptations naturally reflect the same social class, families whose sons keep dogs and horses (Terence, *And.* 56–57), who have their parties catered (Plautus, *Aul.* 280, *Casina* 719–23, *Merc.* 578–80 and 741–43, *Pseud.* 790–94), who can produce sizable sums in cash at a moment's notice (Plautus, *Bacch.* 1050, *Epid.* 296–305), and who give their daughters handsome dowries; they are not merely "a well-to-do upper middle class Greek society . . . not necessarily one of extreme or even great wealth" (G. Duckworth, *The Nature of Roman Comedy* [Princeton 1952] 273).

3.
The Grain Trade of the Hellenistic World

Throughout the course of ancient history, the Mediterranean came to know one type of ship above all others: the plodding merchantmen that carried thousands of sacks of grain from port to port. They unloaded on the beaches of tiny islands or the battered docks of minor towns or the spacious wharves of huge ports. At one time they formed an organized fleet that, surpassing England's East Indiamen or our China clippers, did not see a peer until the days of steam. Let us trace the history of this vast effort during one of the crucial periods of its development.[1]

For the time before the great changes that followed in the wake of Alexander, our information is limited chiefly to Athens. Yet it is enough to reveal a significant part of the basic pattern. In the fifth century B.C. we can observe Athens importing grain from the three great centers which we shall see were the major sources of supply during the whole of the Hellenistic period: Sicily, Egypt with Cyprus and Cyrene, and the Black Sea region.[2] A century later, when our information gets fuller, we can see, too, that the handling of this commerce was not in Athenian hands. A shipment of grain generally involved two or three distinct personages: the owner of the ship (*nauklêros*), the merchant or entrepreneur who raised the capital to purchase the cargo and rent the cargo space (*emporos*), and the moneylender who supplied him with the funds.[3] Often a merchant owned his own ship,[4] thereby reducing

70

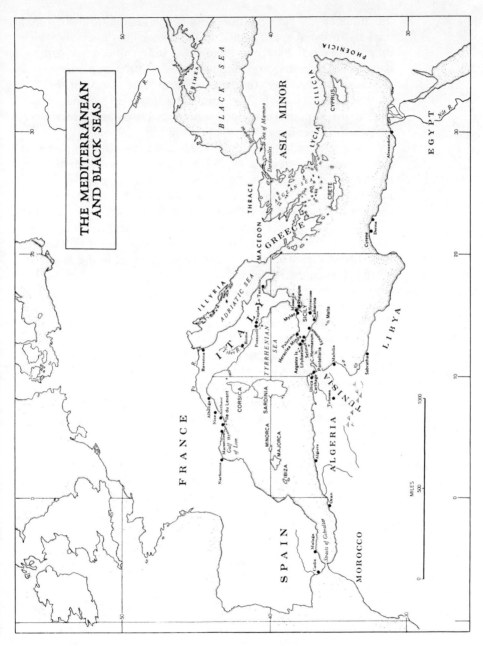

THE MEDITERRANEAN
AND BLACK SEAS

BLACK SEA

CRIMEA

Dnieper R.

THRACE

MACEDON

GREECE

ILLYRIA

ADRIATIC SEA

ITALY

Po R.

Ravenna

Rome

Tiber R.

Puteoli

Naples

Tarentum

TYRRHENIAN SEA

AEGEAN SEA

Sea of Marmara

Byzantium

Dardanelles

ASIA MINOR

LYCIA

CILICIA

PHOENICIA

CYPRUS

CRETE

Cyrene

Derna

EGYPT

Nile R.

Alexandria

Messina

Mylae

Rhegium

SICILY

Syracuse

Catarina

Palermo

Heraclia Minoa

Selinus

Lilybaeum

C. Hermaeum

Pantellaria Is.

Malta

Aegates Is.

Utica

Carthage

Mahdia

Sabratha

Tripolis

LIBYA

TUNISIA

ALGERIA

Oran

Algiers

MOROCCO

Straits of Gibraltar

Malaga

Cadiz

SPAIN

FRANCE

Narbonne

Marseille

Gulf
of Lion

Ile du Levant

Hyères Is.

Antibes

Nice

Albenga

CORSICA

SARDINIA

MINORCA

MAJORCA

IBIZA

MILES

0

500

1000

Fig. 2.

71

the number of personalities in the transaction to two; often bankers invested spare capital in the ownership of vessels[5] which they then could charter to merchants. In fourth-century Athens, bankers, merchants, and shipowners very often were not native Athenians.[6] This was common in the ancient world: in the succeeding centuries we shall see foreign businessmen playing a major role in the commerce of such centers as Delos and Alexandria.

With the opening of the Hellenistic age, our information, although less detailed, becomes wider in scope. Thanks partly to some casual references in Polybius and other historians but mostly to the inscriptions on Delos and other Aegean islands, we now have access to the picture beyond the shores of Athens. Of the numerous modern writers who have attempted to describe the grain trade of this period, practically all agree on two points: that the islands of Rhodes and Delos were the twin grain markets that served the eastern Mediterranean[7] and that in the later part of the Hellenistic period the West stepped in to bolster the supply.[8] Despite the almost universal agreement, a complete survey of the problem will show, I think, that this view is a distortion: Delos' role was much smaller than she has consistently been given credit for, and the West was very likely receiving grain rather than shipping it eastward in late Hellenistic times. The first step we must take is to establish the broad outlines of the picture: which areas needed grain and which supplied it? whose ships carried it? whose bankers supplied the capital? Some of the answers can be given with certitude; others we can merely suggest.

Who needed the grain? As in the fourth century, Athens was still a great importer,[9] along with certain other areas of Greece.[10] To these we must add just about all the Aegean islands[11] and many of the large coastal cities of Asia Minor.[12] The chief sources were the same as in the preceding century: Sicily, the Crimea, and Egypt with its dependencies Cyprus and Cyrene.[13] Though the suppliers always had a favorable balance of trade, many of their customers could defray at least part of their purchases with exports of their own: Athens with olive oil, honey, pottery and similar manufactures,[14] other parts of Greece with wine,[15] Macedon with lumber and pitch,[16] Ionia with wine, oil and wool.[17] Rhodes, Samos, and Chios matched the grain they took in with export of wine of all qualities, the other islands with a miscellany of products: marble from Paros, fuller's earth from Cimolus,[18] raddle from Ceos,[19] cheese from Cythnus and Rhenaea.[20] Delos had no exports to offer, but she could pay her way from her harbor receipts and the profits made at her famous festival, which was as much a commercial fair as a religious occasion.[21]

Of one point we can be absolutely certain: Rhodes was the greatest figure in the international grain trade of the Hellenistic world. We first see her importance therein about 330 B.C. At that time the notorious Cleomenes, whom Alexander had left behind as ruler of Egypt, through some sharp practices artificially drove up the price of grain on the international market. The important point is that Rhodes was the center of his operations.[22] When Poliorcetes besieged the island in 306/305, Ptolemy Soter of Egypt, the bulk of whose trade was carried on through Rhodes, rushed in supplies of grain, as did Cassander and Lysimachus.[23] After the disastrous earthquake about the year 227/226 that overthrew the famous colossus, Hiero II, Seleucus II, Antigonus Doson, and Ptolemy Euergetes all sent extravagant free gifts to help the island recover.[24] The last actually donated well over a million artabs of grain, better than thirty thousand tons, the second largest single shipment recorded in antiquity. This alone is ample evidence of Rhodes' commercial importance—a gift of these proportions from a member of the hardest-fisted, most business-like family known to the history of the ancient world.

At the heart of Rhodes' commercial importance lay her geographical position, far better in some respects than that of Delos which has been so highly praised:[25] she lay between two of the three great suppliers of grain, Egypt and the Crimea, and within easy distance of many of their best customers, the Cyclades and the coastal cities of Asia Minor. She had her own bankers with ample capital for investment in maritime enterprises.[26] Even more important, she was the possessor of a great merchant marine. Athens was an important commercial city, but the ships that served her were rarely Athenian.[27] Corinth, another trade center, had a celebrated ship-building industry and must have had a large merchant fleet, but we hear little about it.[28] Rhodian vessels as early as the fourth century B.C. "sail for trade all over the inhabited earth."[29] They are available for charter.[30] We find them in the harbors of Syria, Phoenicia, Cilicia, and Pamphylia.[31] They were to be seen along the wharves of Syracuse.[32] It was to protect this merchant marine and her financial commitment in maritime commerce that Rhodes took upon herself the policing of the seas and pioneered in the creation of a code of maritime law.

Rhodes' geographical position and her merchant marine clarify the precise place she held in the grain trade. Her ships traveled to Egypt and the Black Sea, carrying wine from her own vineyards and those of her neighbors, to return laden with grain. The Egyptian traffic was largely in her hands,[33] and, though Pontic supplies were sold to customers all over the Aegean, it is certain that a substantial portion of them went to Rhodes.[34] Part of the grain that came to her wharves was used to feed her own population and her neighbors, since the islands' farms were largely given over to viticulture, but much was transshipped to Athens, to the cities of coastal Asia Minor, and to the Aegean islands.[35] There is an inscription[36] which reveals that at least in the late third century Egypt was having some difficulty disposing of her surplus, presumably because of competition with Pontic supplies. Such a situation would explain the respect that the Ptolemies consistently evinced towards Rhodes. The island's merchants patronized all sources;[37] in a buyer's market such as the inscription reveals, Egypt's sales could very well depend on their good will.

It is difficult to see what part can be assigned to Delos in this picture. She could hardly have been a center for Egyptian grain, except on a small scale, since the bulk of that trade, as we have seen, was in Rhodian hands.[38] She imported grain from the Black Sea area for her own needs,[39] but there is no ground for assuming that she took in significant quantities for re-export. The customers for Black Sea grain were Athens and other parts of Greece and of Asia Minor, and a glance at the map will show how Delos is far from being well located as a distribution point for these areas. Yet it has been repeatedly said[40] that Delos was a center for the international grain trade. Let us examine the evidence in detail.

There is always cited an inscription dated in the early part of the third century B.C. which honors a merchant of Byzantium who sold the island 500 *medimni* at a price below the current rate.[41] Alongside this are adduced a number of honorary decrees in favor of various personages who stem from the Hellespont-Bosporus-Black Sea area; no reasons for the bestowal of the honor are recorded on any.[42] These inscriptions tell us at most only the source of the grain Delos consumed; nothing in them reveals her as a great distribution point. Five hundred *medimni* are intended certainly for the local population; it is the bonus a seller gives to a good customer. The amount is absurdly small, 750 bushels, probably enough to feed the inhabitants for just one day. The other honorary decrees—if they concern grain at all— could very well be for the same sort of thing, gifts from merchants who sold the island the grain needed locally. Honorary decrees were cheap in a small place like Delos; it took almost 2,500 *medimni* to get one at Ephesus[43] and at least 3,000 at Athens.[44]

A second inscription invariably cited is more illuminating.[45] It was erected on Delos by Histiaea, in northern Euboea, honoring a certain Rhodian. The city had sent its *sitônai* to Delos to purchase grain, and the recipient of the decree, clearly in business on the island, by lending them the necessary capital, interest-free, had expedited the transaction. It is curious to find Histiaea sending to Delos for grain. The nearest source were the shippers in the Hellespont or, if an international market was preferred, there was Athens. The clue to the inscription lies in the presence of the Rhodian and the fact that he lent the city the necessary funds without charging interest. This well explains, I think, why her *sitônai* came all the way to Delos for their supplies: they got credit there, the cheapest credit possible, as a matter of fact. And, if we ask why a Rhodian was willing to lend money without interest, a very reasonable answer can be put forth: the grain was to be shipped in a Rhodian bottom; one gave up the interest to be gained from capital in favor of the profit to be made on freight. Moreover, after discharging at Histiaea the vessel could push on just a bit further to Macedon and pick up a return cargo of lumber and pitch. The inscription thus reveals Delos as a grain market, to be sure, but one that was serving as an adjunct to that of Rhodes.

The third piece of evidence is again an honorary decree, dating between 239 and 230, in favor of Antigonus Doson's grain-purchasing agent, who, the document records, resided at Delos for a considerable period.[46] Again we must search for the reason why Doson preferred to buy at Delos rather than from Hellespontine or Bosporan shippers who were located so much nearer. And again, an answer is forthcoming: Delos was a steady customer for

Macedonian lumber and pitch,[47] products which had no sale in the Hellespont-Bosporus-Black Sea area. Nor is there any reason to believe that Doson's purchases were very extensive; certainly a half-century or so earlier, Macedon was giving away grain rather than buying it.[48]

The harbor of Delos was poor; even today when northerlies blow—the prevailing summer winds—the caïques avoid the site of the ancient port and put in at a tiny landing place on the opposite shore of the island.[49] But because of the festival which gathered pilgrims from all over, the harbor had been improved by artificial means at a very early date and was made into the best available in the Cyclades.[50] It could not handle large-sized ships,[51] but it was no doubt perfectly adequate for the island trading vessels which probably were not very different from those that ply the Aegean today. Delos, then, was a natural choice as center for the trade of the nearby islands and, since they all were importers of grain, she very likely became the focus of a local traffic,[52] servicing her neighbors' needs as well as her own. The supplies came to her certainly from the Black Sea,[53] and very probably from Egypt via Rhodes who may have used her as a more westerly distribution point. So much can be said for the island's role. To consider it a major center, one that could compete with Rhodes in its own right, is to distort the facts.[54] Where grain was concerned, Rhodes called the tune.

There is one phase of Delos' activity in the grain trade that I have not yet taken up, namely her connections with the West. I have shown above that Sicily supplied grain to the eastern market, and it is *a priori* likely that some of this was sold to Delos and, through her, to neighboring islands.[55] In 179 B.C. Massinissa gave Delos a gift of grain, and this has been consistently used as evidence that Numidia now became a major factor in the eastern market and that Delos was her outlet.[56] Here again the economic picture on closer examination will show a quite different aspect.

The evidence comes from five lines of the Delian temple accounts.[57] In January and April of 179 B.C., the *sitônai* and, interestingly enough, a Rhodian ambassador (*presbeutês*) deposited funds collected from the sale of grain "from Massinissa." The figures reveal that the shipment came to the modest total of just about 2,800 *medimni,* or 4,200 bushels. Since it was sold at the incongruously low price of three and four drachmae per

76

medimnus[58] it has properly been assumed that the king had given it as a gift. What was the reason that lay behind it and why was a Rhodian ambassador involved?

In 204 B.C. the struggle between Rome and Carthage had ended. The kingdom of Syracuse lost its independence, and the grain that Hiero had formerly placed for sale on the eastern market was now in Roman hands. A few years later, Numidia appears on the scene with surpluses to dispose of. In 200 and 198 B.C. Massinissa sent considerable quantities to feed the Roman armies in Macedon and Greece.[59] In 191 and again in 170 he dispatched large amounts to the same places.[60] These were the factors that led to Massinissa's gift to Delos. During the Macedonian Wars the king found a customer for his surplus grain in Rome's armies. However, once the latter's wartime needs came to an end, since her peacetime requirements were now satisfied by Sicilian grain, Massinissa was forced to search for new outlets. The most natural move was to turn to Hiero's old customers: since Sicilian grain had now supplanted African in the Roman market, why should the latter not replace Sicilian in the East? The gift to Delos makes excellent sense as Massinissa's first move in this direction.[61] But, we must remember, a Rhodian ambassador is somehow involved. Rostovtzeff[62] suggests that he played the role of the banker. This cannot be—the 2,800 *medimni* were a gift; there was no need for a banker. But there was a need for something which the Rhodians were the best fitted to supply, viz. ships, for Numidia had none of her own.[63] The most reasonable hypothesis is that the Rhodian conducted the negotiations in order to ensure that this shipment—and future ones if there turned out to be any—would travel in Rhodian bottoms rather than, say, Carthaginian. Delos was to be the center for local distribution of Numidian grain as she probably had been for Sicilian before. And, as before, it was to be carried out under the watchful eye of Rhodes. We do not know whether Massinissa was successful or not in his attempt. Save for the shipment in 170 to the Roman armies in Macedon, there is not a scrap of evidence to prove the presence of Numidian grain thereafter in the eastern Mediterranean.[64] The indications are rather, as we shall see, that within a few decades all that the West had to offer fell short of Rome's growing needs.

The evidence discussed so far belongs to the third century B.C.

and the early part of the second. For the next 130-odd years, from 167/166 when Rome made Delos a free port under Athenian control to the taking over of Egypt by Augustus, we know practically nothing of the history of the grain trade in the East. It was during this period that Delos became a great entrepôt, a truly international center of trade. In the second half of the second century B.C. and the early part of the first, the island reached the peak of its prosperity. Before this time one anchorage basin, the Sacred Port, had with various improvements fulfilled all needs; now five others equipped with moles, quays, and warehousing facilities were added.[65] Communities of merchants from all quarters settled on the island permanently. Some impact was felt upon Rhodes almost immediately. Just twelve years or so after Delos was declared a free port, a Rhodian embassy appealed to the Roman Senate: their harbor revenues, they respectfully submitted, had dropped from 1,000,000 to 150,000 drachmae a year (Polybius 30.31.10–12). Does this mean that the large part of the eastern grain trade which Rhodes had controlled so successfully for so long had slipped from her grasp? A brief analysis of even our scanty information will reveal that this was not so.

There are a number of certain facts that must be borne in mind at the outset. For one, Rhodes never became a poor city. Her continental possessions were taken away, and with the loss of revenue from that source (Polybius 30.31.7) and from the drop in harbor dues, she no longer had the funds to finance a navy that could patrol the seas as before, with results known to every schoolboy who has read the *Pro lege Manilia*. But when Strabo visited the city in the time of Augustus he was profoundly impressed by its well-being (14.2.5), as were many who subsequently wrote of her (e.g., Dio Chrysostomus 31.55). Delos, however, did become a ghost town and very quickly. The nature of her newly found prosperity was such that it could come to an abrupt end; had she been a key link in a basic service such as the grain supply this, of course, would not have been the case.

The wealth of Delos at this time lay in two directions, neither of which had much to do with grain: in slaves[66] and as a transshipment point for the products of Arabia, India, and the Far East. Her harbor was not nearly so good as, for example, that of Rhodes, but for the cargoes she specialized in this was a minor consideration: the slavers—fast, light oar-driven pirate vessels—could put in anywhere, and it took only a modest-sized vessel to carry thousands of dollars worth of silks, spices and perfumes.[67] Very little of this valuable merchandise was kept on the island; by far the greater part was destined for forwarding to Rome. The national origin of the vast numbers of merchants now established on Delos makes all this abundantly clear.[68] There was, first, a great number of South Italian businessmen.[69] Some had settled on the island before it became a free port and were perhaps instrumental in having it declared so, but the majority arrived on the scene in the ensuing decades. They came to Delos in preference to Rhodes for a number of reasons. Although there were unquestionably shipowners among the South Italians, those who settled on the sacred island were for the most part bankers and merchandisers,[70] men who preferred the greater, albeit more speculative, profits of financial maritime adventures to the smaller, stabler income to be derived from freight, as well as the comforts of living on shore to the rigors of life aboard ship. At Rhodes, a wealthy state where there was ample local capital available, there was no place for such men. Again, Rhodes was traditionally hostile to foreigners. And last but by no means least, a dealer would not be hampered by the law in the frank commercial atmosphere of Delos as he would in the well-policed city of Rhodes, the giver of maritime law to the world.[71] It was the difference between doing business, say, in Tangiers as against London. So the South Italians came to Delos and made their fortunes forwarding goods to their homeland.

A second large group of inhabitants on the island came from the Levant, from Tyre, Sidon, Beirut, and other Syrian ports.[72] Clearly their function was to load at their home ports goods that had come by camel, or combination of ship and camel, from India and the Far East and to deliver them to Delos for transshipment to Italy. An Alexandrian community[73] did the same for the portion of this traffic that was routed via the Red Sea, as well as for the Arabian and Somaliland specialities whose trade the Ptolemies monopolized. Merchants from Pontus and Bithynia[74] were very likely connected with the commerce in slaves.

What of the grain trade? Probably it was slightly larger than in the previous century, to take care of the island's swollen population. But there is no reason to suppose that the center of this traffic ever ceased to be Rhodes. She still had her merchant marine and she still was prosperous; her harbor was still far more suitable for the larger carriers that were necessary to transport bulky cargoes. The easiest explanation is that Rhodian bottoms carried Egyptian and Pontic wheat as well as other products just as they had for centuries. But, whereas before 166 traders from the Levant had put in at Rhodes as a convenient stopping place[75] or, for that matter, as the nearest market, and slave traders had disposed of their merchandise on her blocks,[76] now they bypass her, quite willing to forego her advantages in return for the free harbor privileges as well as the freer atmosphere of Delos.[77] But if traders could push on past Rhodes to Delos there was no reason why they could not go the whole hog and push on to Puteoli, since that was becoming more and more the ultimate destination of their cargoes, and cut out the profit of the Delian middlemen. There were meteorological as well as economic reasons for bypassing Delos: the prevailing winds in the Aegean, the well-known Etesians, are northerly; a vessel from the Levant to make Delos had to drive right into their eye, the worst possible course for a sailing ship. It was far easier to load cargo aboard a larger craft that could stay at sea a considerable length of time and, shaping the most direct course that the wind would permit, sail south of Crete and head for the straits of Messina.[78] So Delos in the course of time lost her lucrative transient trade, while Rhodes, though the removal of the contributions of the Levantine traders to the total of her harbor dues had caused it to drop drastically, still maintained her large carrying trade and stayed prosperous.[79] Delos might have reverted to the role she played in the third century B.C. and carried on again as the focal point of local maritime traffic, but circumstances willed otherwise: in 88 B.C. one of Mithridates' generals ravaged the island horribly; recovery had just gotten under way when, in 69, a sack by the pirates delivered the death blow.

Information about the suppliers of grain in this period is very scanty. Polybius mentions (28.2.17) that in 169 B.C. Rhodes petitioned the Senate for permission to purchase 100,000 *medimni* (= 150,000 bushels) of Sicilian grain. The passage thus confirms the inference we drew earlier that supplies from Sicily were no longer available for general sale on the eastern market. At the same time it makes it clear that some special circumstances must

have arisen to prevent Rhodes from importing from her usual
source. These are not far to seek. In 169, for the first time in over
a century and a half, Egypt had been invaded. Antiochus IV
dispersed the Egyptian army at the frontier, captured the port of
Pelusium, established headquarters at Memphis, and set about
laying siege to Alexandria.[80] It is no surprise to find Rhodes
casting about elsewhere at this moment for grain.

Thus Rhodes, we may be sure, under normal conditions, still
drew her supplies from Egypt. As a matter of fact, the latter so
far as one can judge even increased in importance in this period
as a source of grain for the eastern market. Sicily, as we have
seen, had been obliged to withdraw, and there is no evidence for
Numidia. The Pontic area because of wars and disturbances was
not the rich source it had been hitherto,[81] although some grain
certainly was being shipped out of it. Egypt is thus left as the
East's major supplier. This raises a problem that, so far as I
know, has never been formulated by any writer on the subject.
Yet it is a basic one, the solution to which affects seriously the
whole political as well as economic history of the times. In 30 B.C.
Egypt, which long before had been *de facto* under Rome's control, now becomes officially a part of the empire and takes her
place as one of the key sources of grain for the capital, a role she
held until her seemingly limitless flow was diverted to Constanti-
nople. Vespasian, in his struggle with his rivals, made the taking
of Egypt and Alexandria one of his first moves: with these in his
grasp he was able to starve Rome into submission.[82] Under Augustus, Egypt provided Rome annually with 5,000,000 bushels,
ca. 135,000 tons, an enormous amount that filled fully one-third
of the city's needs[83] and required the services of a merchant fleet
larger probably than any we hear of until the nineteenth century.
What happened to this grain before Augustus' annexation, during
the time of the Republic? Did any of it go to Rome in those
years?

The implications of the problem are far reaching. If we assume
that during the Republic this much grain—or perhaps somewhat
less, since Augustus thoroughly revamped the slovenly administration of the later Ptolemies—was kept on the eastern market,
the ineluctable conclusion is that the conversion of Egypt into a
Roman province brought in its wake a tremendous economic
dislocation in both the East and the West. It would mean the loss

81

to the former of its chief source of supply. And if the Roman Republic had subsisted up to this time solely on the Sicilian, Sardinian, and North African grain—the only suppliers that the ancient sources mention—then, with the sudden influx of huge amounts from Egypt, there should conversely be a sudden glut of grain in the West. Yet clearly this did not happen. The East did not starve. Rome itself under the emperors appears to have absorbed the grain of Egypt without diminishing what she drew from her traditional sources of Republican days, and that despite the fact that the number of recipients of the corn dole was significantly less under Augustus and his followers than before.[84] It would certainly seem that no profound dislocation had taken place.

If this is so, we are forced to conclude that, even under the Republic, Rome had been eking out her western supplies with grain from Egypt—if not the 135,000 tons that Augustus drew from the new province, then at least an amount sufficiently large so that its increase led to no wide-scale economic disturbance. In the light of this, let us review what we know of the commercial relations between Rome and Egypt down to the time of the latter's annexation.

Economic contact between the two countries may perhaps go as far back as 273 B.C. In that year Philadelphus sent a commission to Rome, and it has been vigorously argued by some—while others have preferred to reserve opinion—that the purpose of the embassy was to discuss trade.[85] Numismatic evidence has been used to prove that commerce between the two existed in the third century B.C.[86] But we cannot state conclusively that grain played any part; there were a number of other things that Egypt could export in return for iron or sulphur, the Italian products she had most need of.[87] In 210 B.C. Rome sent envoys to Egypt to negotiate the purchase of grain (Polybius 9.44); this, of course, was during an emergency, in the midst of a terribly destructive war. The grain was probably delivered, for the Senate sent a handsome set of presents to Ptolemy Philopator (Livy 27.4). Immediately after peace was restored, however, supplies in Rome were so plentiful that Sicilian and Sardinian dealers were letting cargoes go to the shipowners to pay for the freight (Livy 30.38). In 191 Ptolemy Epiphanes sent an embassy to Rome offering both money and grain, but neither was accepted (Livy 36.4). In 168, hard upon Antiochus IV's voluntary departure from Egypt after his successful invasion, Ptolemy Philometor sent a cargo of grain to the Roman troops stationed at Chalcis for the war with Perseus; the gift was one of Philometor's maneuvers in rounding up allies to strengthen his hand against his recent conqueror.[88]

After the battle of Pydna the trade contacts between Egypt and Rome were close and constant. There were South Italian businessmen in Alexandria, and others in Delos who worked with them, engaged in the forwarding of Egyptian products to Rome.[89] After the famous Popilius Laenas incident, Egypt became in a very real sense a protectorate of Rome, and the effect of this change must have been felt economically no less than politically. In 80 B.C. Ptolemy Alexander II willed her to the Roman people,[90] and from that moment on she hovered on the brink of annexation.[91] She would have lost her independence a full half-century earlier than she did were it not for tense struggles that were going on in Rome itself, involving forces so complex that, in spite of a good deal of contemporary information, we can only with difficulty trace the political movements entailed, while the economic are almost completely beyond our ken.[92] Yet one thing is certain: during the whole of this period ships left Alexandria continuously for the shores of Italy.[93] It has always been assumed that they carried in their holds either the luxury products that Egypt forwarded from the Far East, India, and Arabia or the miscellaneous articles that were manufactured at Alexandria.[94] Why not grain as well? The institution of public distribution of grain and the constant increase in the list of recipients that followed in its wake had certainly caused Rome's needs to mount precipitously. The extra freight charges involved in bolstering her supply with Egyptian grain would not have stood in her way any more than in 210 B.C. Moreover, the Ptolemies were dependent upon Rome for their very existence; a little pressure judiciously applied could easily have secured for her the best possible price.

A little judicious pressure as a matter of fact might even do more, it might succeed in lining a few pockets. In the early part of 57 B.C. Ptolemy Auletes, who had been chased off his throne by the Alexandrian mob, turned up at Rome.[95] He was immediately welcomed most warmly by Pompey, who carried him off to his Alban villa to install him as house guest there. A very short time later a scarcity of grain came to pass in the city, and although it seems to have subsided for a month or so, it reappeared in serious form in September. To meet it, Pompey was placed in complete control of Rome's grain supply, with virtually unlimited powers, for a period of five years.[96] Were Ptolemy's presence and the shortage connected? The events—the king's arrival, his welcome by Pompey, the scarcity, Pompey's appointment as buyer-in-chief of grain—follow suspiciously close on the heels of one another. We are told that, during 56, Pompey met the immediate emergency with shipments from Sardinia, Sicily and North Africa.[97] This is what we would expect to hear: supplies from those areas could arrive within a matter of weeks.[98] But the very next year at the opening of spring,[99] the grain czar turned his attention to Egypt. He had his man Gabinius put Auletes back on the throne, and, just to make sure that everything was airtight, he presented the king with a Roman businessman to serve as Egypt's finance minister. A neater combination for making a financial killing in Egyptian grain simply cannot be conceived.

All this, to be sure, is speculative. But there is even a direct bit of evidence that can be adduced. In describing the conditions caused in 39 B.C. by Sextus Pompey's blockade, Appian (*B.C.* 5.67) says: "Famine now fell upon Rome since neither the merchants of the East (ἑῴων ἐμπόρων) could put to sea for fear of (Sextus) Pompey and his control of Sicily, nor those of the West because his lieutenants held Sardinia and Corsica, nor those of Africa opposite since the same forces ruled the seas off those shores, too. There was consequently a great rise in prices." Who were these "merchants of the East"? They could only have been shippers of Egyptian grain.

Let us summarize our findings. From the time of Alexander to the middle of the second century B.C. the key figure in the grain trade of the eastern Mediterranean was Rhodes. It was she who distributed most of the supply from Egypt, and her share of that from the Black Sea area, to the coastal cities of Asia Minor and the Aegean islands and Greece. She employed Delos as a convenient distribution point for shipment to the neighboring islands and as a more convenient receiving point for grain from the West. Financing was done with her own capital, and much of the grain traveled in her own bottoms. Athens and Greece, as in the fourth century, received in addition substantial supplies directly from the Pontus. From the middle of the second century B.C. to the annexation of

Egypt, Rhodes does not lose her position in the grain trade although other forms of her commerce suffer. Whereas in the previous period there had been enough grain available to produce competition at times, the situation now changes. Sicilian supplies are now diverted to Rome. Numidian grain attempts to replace it but is soon swallowed up by Rome as well. The amount available from the Black Sea is somewhat reduced. The burden thus falls upon Egypt. In the first century B.C., because of the growing needs of the public distribution of grain, Rome too must seek Egyptian supplies to such a point that, once annexed, the latter furnishes her with no less than 150,000 tons a year, a third of her requirements.

Addendum

R. Meiggs, in his *Roman Ostia* (Oxford 1973[2]), devotes a short note (472–73) to the above article. "Casson," he states there, "concludes that Egypt was already one of Rome's main suppliers in the late Republic. . . . The main objection to this thesis is the silence of Cicero. Had Rome depended on Egyptian corn we should expect some clear reference in the public speeches or correspondence."

Meiggs' objection would certainly be valid had I come to the conclusion he says I did. But, far from calling Egypt a "main supplier," I merely suggested that, in late Republican times, "Rome had been eking out her western supplies with grain from Egypt—if not the 135,000 tons that Augustus drew from the new province, then at least an amount sufficiently large so that its increase led to no wide-scale economic disturbance"—an amount, let me willingly add, sufficiently small in most years not to qualify for mention by Cicero.

P. Fraser (below, n. 33), in a footnote (ii 270, n. 187), expresses his agreement with Meiggs; for him, too, Cicero's silence is decisive. His text, however, tells a different story: there he reveals that he sees the very same development I do, save on a lesser scale. Discussing the trade relations between Egypt and Republican Rome, he writes (i 155): "the intermittent significance of Alexandria for Rome as a source of cereals foreshadows the organized traffic of the Empire." I would change but a single word in this formulation, replacing "intermittent" with "frequent." By assuming frequent shipments of Egypt's grain to Republican Rome we can explain why no serious economic dislocation took place when Augustus converted the land into a major supplier. This consideration, I hold, is of more weight than any *argumentum ex silentio*—always a treacherous form of reasoning—from Cicero.

G. Rickman, *The Corn Supply of Ancient Rome* (Oxford 1980) 233, also agrees with Meiggs. Indeed, for him there is no need to explain the absence of any economic dislocation through Augustus' taking over Egypt's grain since he is convinced that, "with the development of Africa, Rome's claim on Egyptian corn rapidly lessened." He offers no evidence to support this statement, and indeed there is none to offer. In fact, some business documents newly discovered at Pompeii point just the other way. These reveal that, around A.D. 40, but a few decades before the time when Africa had been so developed that 6 Romans alone owned half of it (Pliny, *N.H.* 18.35), dealers at Puteoli were handling large amounts of grain from Egypt (see below, chap. 4, Appendix). African grain is nowhere mentioned.

Notes

1. The following abbreviations have been used:

Durrbach, *Choix*	=	F. Durrbach, *Choix d'inscriptions de Délos* (Paris 1921)
Heichelheim	=	F. Heichelheim, s.v. "Sitos" *RE* Suppl. 6.819–91 (1935)
Maiuri, *Nuov. Sill.*	=	A. Maiuri, *Nuova silloge epigrafica di Rodi e Cos* (Florence 1925)
Roussel	=	P. Roussel, *Délos colonie athénienne,* Bibl. des écoles françaises d'Athènes et de Rome 111 (Paris 1916)
Tarn	=	W. W. Tarn and G. T. Griffith, *Hellenistic Civilization* (London 1952³)

The ships I refer to were heavy, slow, beamy sailing ships, the workhorses of ancient commerce that carried not only grain but other cheap and bulky commodities such as wine and oil, which were transported in massive clay jars (*SSAW* 157–68). They were a world apart from the light, swift, slender galleys, driven by multiple oarsmen, that were used as warcraft or official dispatch vessels. The distinction seems obvious, yet it has been overlooked. See, for example, J. D'Arms in *MAAR* 36 (1980) 83 (repeated in his *Commerce and Social Standing in Ancient Rome* [Cambridge, Mass. 1981] 59); E. Will in *CP* 77 (1982) 242 (who informs me she now shares my opinion). They cite Cicero, *ad Att.* 16.4.4. as evidence that a certain Sestius, owner of extensive potteries for the manufacture of shipping jars, possessed ships of his own for transporting his products. In the passage in question Cicero remarks on the vessels Brutus and Domitius have at their disposal—vessels which were to carry Brutus and his staff to his proconsular assignment in Crete (cf. *CAH* x 9, n. 3; D. Shackleton Bailey, *Cicero's Letters to Atticus* vi [Cambridge 1967] 265, n. to 394.2.9) and no doubt, when the need would arise, form the nucleus of a naval force. These include *bona dicrota* as well as some *navigia luculenta* belonging to Sestius and other notables. The *bona dicrota* were two-banked galleys of a type standard in Hellenistic navies (cf. *SSAW* 133), and Sestius' "nice craft" can only be galleys of more or less the same sort. Sestius may well have had a fleet of his own vessels for transporting his jars,

THE GRAIN TRADE OF THE HELLENISTIC WORLD

but this passage says nothing at all about them, only about his contribution to
Brutus' force of warships and dispatch boats.

2. For references to the sources see H. Knorringa, *Emporos* (Amsterdam 1926)
   77–78, 98–101. Knorringa tries to argue (78–79) that Black Sea grain played
   an important role in supplying Athens only during the 4th c., but this is not
   the case; cf. Rostovtzeff, *CAH* viii 563–64, and A. Jardé, *Les céréales dans
   l'antiquité grecque,* Bibl. des écoles françaises d'Athènes et de Rome 130
   (Paris 1925) 141, n. 3.

3. See above, p. 27.

4. E.g., Dionysiodorus and Parmeniscus in Dem. 56 seem to have carried the
   cargo involved in the dispute in their own ship. They subsequently chartered
   others in addition (56.21).

5. As, for example, the well-known Phormio who inherited Pasion's bank; cf.
   Dem. 45.64. Some of the bankers were retired *emporoi* like the defendant in
   Dem. 33.4.

6. See above, pp. 44–45.

7. Durrbach, *Choix,* pp. 57–58: "Délos put . . . devenir un des gros entrepôts
   de céréales"; Tarn 264: "a great corn-market"; Rostovtzeff, *SEHHW* 217:
   "Delos . . . was competing with Athens in the grain trade at this time," cf.
   231–33, 692; W. A. Laidlaw, *A History of Delos* (Oxford 1933) 128: "she
   was fast becoming an international grain-market"; Larsen, *ESAR* 4.350: "a
   center for the grain trade."

8. See below, n. 56.

9. Pontic grain: *IG* ii^2 653 (289/288 B.C.), 657 (299/298), 903 (176/175); Egyptian
   grain: 650 (290/289), 682 (296–291), 845 (ca. 220; cf. *REG* 51 [1938] 428);
   Sicilian grain: *SEG* 3.92 (3rd B.C.), Athen. 5.209B (time of Hiero II); Macedonian grain: *IG* ii^2 654–55 (289/288).

10. Histiaea: *IG* xi 4.1055 (230–220 B.C.); Oropus: vii 4262 (end of 3rd); Sicyon:
    Livy 32.40.9 (197, gift of Attalus of Pergamum); Corinth: Lycurgus, *In Leoc.*
    26 (330, grain from Epirus); Chalcis: *IG* xii 9.900a,c (mid-2nd). Cf. *SEG* 9.2
    (ca. 330), grain from Cyrene for numerous places in Greece during a year of
    shortage.

11. Andros: *IG* xii 5.714 (cf. *AM* 36 [1911] 1–20; mid-4th to 318). Amorgos: xii
    7.11 (end of 4th or beginning of 3rd); xii 7.40 (2nd). Cos: M. Segrè, "Grano
    di Thessaglia a Coo," *RFIC* 62 (1934) 169–93 (ca. 260, Thessalian grain);
    Herondas 2.16–17 (ca. 270, Phoenician grain); Maiuri, *Nuov. Sill.* 433 (3rd,

87

Cypriot grain). Ios: *IG* xii 5.1011 (end of 3rd). Mitylene: *SIG*[3] 212 (mid-4th, Pontic grain). Samos: *SEG* 1.361 (end of 4th); 366 (247/246), cf. E. Ziebarth, "Zum samischen Finanz- und Getreidewesen," *Zeitschrift f. Numismatik* 34 (1923–24) 356–63; *SIG*[3] 976 (beginning of 2nd); *AM* 38 (1913) 51–59 (ca. 100, probably Pontic grain); Samos had a standing organization for the import of grain. Samothrace: *SIG*[3] 502 (228–25, Egyptian and probably Pontic grain are involved). "Islanders" (found on Moschonesi): *IG* xii 2.645 (time of Antipater and Polyperchon). The League of the Islands: xii 5.817 (beginning of 2nd). Cf. *SEG* 9.2 (ca. 330), grain from Cyrene for numerous islands during a year of shortage.

12. Ephesus: *SIG*[3] 354 (ca. 300 B.C.). Heraclea: *FHG* 3.538 (probably time of Philadelphus, Egyptian grain). Evidence for other places dates from the imperial period (cf. *ESAR* 4.877–79) but there is no reason to think that conditions were very different during the Hellenistic age.

13. See the previous 4 notes. Tarn (254, n. 7) is wrong in thinking that Cyprus was not self-sufficient; cf. Andocides 2.20 (ca. 410, 14 shiploads from Cyprus to Athens and more to come); *OGIS* 56.17–18 (239/238, grain from Cyprus to Egypt during a shortage there); Maiuri, *Nuov. Sill.* 433 (3rd, grain from Cyprus to Cos). There were other suppliers who appear occasionally. Syria and Phoenicia could send grain to Egypt during one of the latter's rare emergencies (*OGIS* 56.17–18). Gifts of grain from Pergamum are recorded (10,000 *medimni* from Attalus to Sicyon, Livy 32.40.9; 280,000 from Eumenes II to Rhodes, Polybius 31.25). For grain from Macedon see above, n. 9, from Epirus see n. 10. Even Thessaly apparently could at times ship out grain (see n. 11) although at others she suffered shortages herself (*Eph. Arch.* [1912] 61–64, nos. 89–90, ca. 200; *IG* ix 2.1104, 1st B.C.).

14. Oil: *IG* ii² 1100 (124 A.D., but no doubt true of the earlier period; cf. Rostovtzeff, *SEHHW* 744–45). Honey: *P. Cairo Zen.* 59012, 59426; *P. Mich. Zen.* 3, all 3rd B.C.

15. Dem. 35.35.

16. G. Glotz, "L'histoire de Délos d'après les prix d'une denrée," *REG* 29 (1916) 280–90 (pitch), 290–94 (lumber).

17. References to the sources in Tarn 255–56. For the distribution of Rhodian wine amphora handles see Rostovtzeff, *SEHHW* 680 and 1486; Fraser cited in n. 33 below.

18. *P. Cairo Zen.* 59704.18 (3rd).

19. *IG* ii² 1128 (mid-4th).

20. *P. Cairo Zen.* 59110 (257 B.C.).

21. Strabo 10.5.4.

22. Dem. 56.7–10, 16–17; Ps. Arist., *Oec.* 1352a–b.

23. Diodorus 20.96.1–3: 300,000 artabs of grain (over 300,000 bushels) from Ptolemy, 10,000 *medimni* (= 15,000 bushels) of barley from Cassander, 40,000 *medimni* (= 60,000 bushels) of wheat and 40,000 of barley from Lysimachus.

24. Polybius 5.88–89.

25. Vessels headed for Italy from Egypt, the Levant, or the south coast of Asia Minor had to go out of their way and travel against unfavorable winds to make Delos. Because of the wind conditions in the Mediterranean, the course for Italy went south of Crete; cf. *TAPA* 81 (1950) 43–51. Moreover, Rhodes-Egypt was one of the few runs that could be made all year, even in winter (Dem. 56.30). Only the west coast of Asia Minor was better served by Delos; cf. Strabo 10.5.4.

26. *IG* xi 4.1055 (= Durrbach, *Choix* 50, 230–220 b.c.): a Rhodian banker operating on Delos; Maiuri, *Nuov. Sill.* 19 (ca. 200): a family of bankers. Cf. Rostovtzeff, *CAH* 8.623 for instances of the city itself making substantial loans.

27. See above, nn. 3, 6.

28. Cf. Tarn, "The Dedicated Ship of Antigonus Gonatas," *JHS* 30 (1910) 218–20.

29. Lycurgus, *In Leoc.* 15 (330 b.c.).

30. Dem. 56.21.

31. Polyaenus 4.6.16 (306 b.c.). They were to be found in whatever ports Seleucus II held ca. 227/226 (Polybius 5.89).

32. Hiero II and Gelon granted free port privileges to Rhodian vessels after the earthquake in ca. 227/226 (Polybius 5.88; Diodorus 26.8).

33. Diodorus states (20.81): "They [the Rhodians] derived most of their revenues from merchants who sailed to Egypt; the city, by and large, lived off this kingdom." The period referred to is 306 b.c. When Cleomenes was indulging in his manipulations of Egyptian grain ca. 330, he used Rhodes as his center of operations and his agents chartered Rhodian vessels (Dem. 56.7–10, 21). The huge gifts of grain given the island by the Ptolemies show eloquently how important they considered it to be. A papyrus document (*P. Ryl.* 554, 258 b.c.) has turned up which provides a concrete illustration of the way in which Rhodes served as a transit point for goods destined for Egypt; cf. Rostov-

89

tzeff's extended discussion of the piece in *SEHHW* 226–28. On Delos in the 2nd c. B.C., Alexandria maintained an association of warehousemen (*egdocheis*) only, although those of other cities included "merchants, shippers, and warehousemen" (references cited and discussed by Roussel, 89–93). The clear inference is that Egypt's cargoes traveled in foreign bottoms, a large number of which we may safely assume were Rhodian.

The tangible proof of Rhodes' commercial ties with Egypt are the multitudinous handles of her shipping jars that have been found there, some 80,000 of them, over 10 times the number from any other export center; for details and references, see P. Fraser, *Ptolemaic Alexandria* (Oxford 1972) i 164–68. They are unmistakably Rhodian, for they have stamped upon them Rhodes' official device as well as the name of an annual Rhodian magistrate to indicate date of manufacture. Fraser argues that only a small percentage of the jars arrived filled with Rhodian wine. A somewhat larger percentage may have carried wine from Laodicea shipped through Rhodian merchants, but the great majority, he insists, were empties; Egypt, he believes, had urgent need of such. He leaves totally unexplained why empties would bear not only an official device but an official date to boot. In any event, empty or full, they are eloquent witness to the volume of the island's trade with Egypt.

34. The Black Sea region imported wine from Rhodes, as we know from the thousands of amphora handles discovered there (references in Rostovtzeff, *CAH* 8.629. n. 2), and unquestionably sent the island grain in return. The importance of this region to Rhodes is shown by her immediate reaction to Byzantium's attempt in 220 B.C. to levy a toll on ships passing through the Bosporus (Polybius 4.47) and her prompt dispatch about the same time of war matériel to Sinope when the latter was threatened by Mithridates III of Pontus (Polybius 4.56); cf. Rostovtzeff, *SEHHW* 675.

35. Dem. 56: Egyptian grain via Rhodes to Athens; cf. Lycurgus, *In Leoc.* 18 (grain shippers with cargoes for Athens at Rhodes). *SIG*³ 354 (ca. 300 B.C.): Agathocles, son of Agemon, a Rhodian, supplies grain to Ephesus. The same merchant was honored by Arcesine on Amorgos, very likely also for help with the grain supply (*IG* xii 7.9; cf. E. Ziebarth, "Zur Handelsgeschichte der Insels Rhodos," *Mélanges Glotz* [Paris 1932] 916). *IG* xii 5.1010 (3rd B.C.): Ios honors a Rhodian; the fact that his crown is to be paid for out of whatever funds were left from the amount allotted for purchase of grain indicates that his services lay in that direction.

36. *SIG*³ 502 (228–225 B.C.): Samothrace requests permission of Euergetes to purchase grain duty-free from the Chersonese or anywhere else it appears advantageous to do so. Egypt had apparently set a tariff on imports of foreign grain; cf. C. Préaux. *L'économie royale des Lagides* (Brussels 1938) 149.

37. See above, nn. 32–34.

38. See above, n. 33. Wind conditions made it practically imperative for any ship bound from Egypt to Delos to go by way of Rhodes; cf. *TAPA* 81 (1950) 43–51.

39. Jardé (above, n. 2) 170–71, by acutely showing the effect of events in the Hellespont and Bosporus upon grain prices on Delos in 282 B.C., revealed thereby that the island was chiefly supplied from the Black Sea area.

40. See above, n. 7.

41. *IG* xi 4.627 = Durrbach, *Choix* 46.

42. Listed by Durrbach, *Choix*, p. 57.

43. See above, n. 35.

44. *IG* ii² 360 (3000 *medimni*), 363 (3,000), 398 (3,000? XXX seems a most likely restoration in line 13), 408 (at least 4,000), 400 (4,000 and 8,000), 845 (8,000).

45. *IG* xi 4.1055 (230–20 B.C.) = Durrbach, *Choix* 50.

46. *IG* xi 4.666 = Durrbach, *Choix* 48.

47. Both products were purchased regularly by the temple at Delos; see above, n. 16.

48. *IG* ii² 654–55 (289–288): 7500 *medimni* to Athens from Audoleon, king of the Paeonians; Diodorus 20.96.1–3: 10,000 to Rhodes from Cassander in 306–305.

49. This was my experience on two occasions when I visited the island. Others have noted the poorness of the harbor; see Tarn 264, Rostovtzeff, *SEHHW* 230.

50. J. Paris, "Contributions à l'étude des ports antiques du monde grec," *BCH* 40 (1916) 5–30; K. Lehmann-Hartleben, *Die antiken Hafenanlagen des Mittelmeeres, Klio* Beiheft 14 (1923) 50–51, 152–61.

51. Hiero II of Syracuse built a great ship about 240 B.C. (see Dittenberger's note to *OGIS* 56.17) to serve as a grain carrier but had to give it up because it was too large for many of the harbors (Athen. 5.206E, 209B). Almost certainly Delos was one such.

52. *IG* xii 5.817 (ca. 188 B.C.): The League of the Islands honors Timon the Delian banker (cf. Durrbach, *Choix*, pp. 86–87) for helping its *sitônai* by not charging an agio. The terms of the sale had been set in Rhodian currency and

91

the merchants wanted a 5% premium for accepting Tenian or some other; cf. Larsen, *ESAR* 4.360.

53. See above, n. 39.

54. Rostovtzeff (*SEHHW* 676, 692) states that in the 3rd c. B.C. Delos controlled the Black Sea grain trade but lost it to Rhodes when the latter reached the peak of her prosperity in the first half of the succeeding century. The evidence he presents boils down to the mention of gifts on the part of Bosporan kings to the temple at Delos or other participation in the island's religious affairs, plus a handful of 3rd century honorary decrees—no specific reason for the bestowal is recorded on any of them—in favor of natives of the Chersonese, South Russia, Byzantium, and other towns of the Hellespont-Bosporus-Black Sea region (*SEHHW* 232 and nn. 60, 61, 676 and n. 89). Yet there are just as many similar decrees for people who stem from the same area that belong to the early second century: *IG* xi 4.778–80 (Byzantium), 813–14 (Olbia), 844 (Chersonese). Moreover, participation or the absence of it in Delos' religious activities is no certain evidence for economic relationships.

55. Cf. above, n. 51.

56. Heichelheim 855: "tritt im 2. Jhdt. v. Chr. in unseren Nachrichten überhaupt das Westmittelmeergebiet als Kornlieferant gegenüber den alten Märkten ausgeprägt hervor"; Rostovtzeff, *SEHHW* 692: "Massinissa . . . the great new purveyor of corn to the ancient world," cf. 630 and *CAH* 8.630; Tarn 254–55.

57. Durrbach, *Inscriptions de Délos* 442A, 100–105.

58. The market price was probably in the neighborhood of 10 drachmae; cf. Larsen, *ESAR* 4.384.

59. Livy 31.19.4; 32.27.2.

60. Livy 36.4.8; 43.6.

61. The gift has been described as large (Heichelheim 855; Larsen, *ESAR* 4.351) but to do so distorts it and makes one misunderstand its purpose. It was a little gift scaled, like the Byzantian merchant's 500 *medimni,* to a little is-land's modest needs. It simply is not to be compared with other royal gifts such as those recorded for Athens: 7,500 *medimni* from the king of the Paeonians in 289/288 (*IG* ii^2 654), 10,000 from Lysimachus in 299/298 (*IG* ii^2 657), 15,000 from Spartocus, the Bosporan ruler, in 289/288 (*IG* ii^2 653). Even a private citizen once gave her 8000 (*IG* ii^2 845, ca. 220) and Hiero II of Syracuse is rumored to have bestowed 1,000 on a single Athenian (Athen. 5.209B). Really large gifts ran into tens of thousands of *medimni;* see above, nn. 13, 23, 24; Diodorus 20.46.4.

62. *SEHHW* 1485–86, n. 95.

63. When Masgaba, the king's own son, visited Rome to congratulate the Senate on the victory over Perseus, 2 ships had to be chartered to bring him and his entourage back (Livy 45.14).

64. Rostovtzeff states (*SEHHW* 1462, n. 20) that Numidia exported grain to Delos, Athens, and Rhodes and cites Heichelheim (856) as authority. Heichelheim, however, merely cites secondary sources (one of which is an earlier work by Rostovtzeff). Except for Massinissa's gift to Delos there is no ancient evidence to support this statement. We hear nothing of African grain in the east beyond the handful of passages in Livy that refer to the supplies furnished by Carthage and Numidia for the Roman armies during the Macedonian wars. Rostovtzeff further cites an inscription from Istrus (2nd B.C.) that honors a Carthaginian for import of grain. He mentions the possibility that the merchant in question may not have been dealing in Carthaginian grain but dismisses it as highly improbable. On the contrary, it is highly probable. P. Walsh, "Massinissa," *JRS* 55 (1965) 149–60 at 154–55, concludes that Massinissa's Numidia played no very important role in international commerce.

65. Paris (above, n. 50) 64–69.

66. Strabo 14.5.2; cf. Roussel 19–20.

67. Venice at the height of her prosperity ca. 1500 needed only 30 to 40 ships for her inter-regional trade (Frederic C. Lane, *Venetian Ships and Shipbuilders of the Renaissance* [Baltimore 1934] 107). The average size was about 250 tons burden; the largest was not over 440 (ibid. 39–48). In its palmiest days the city imported a total of 2,500,000 pounds of spices from Alexandria every winter (ibid. 26); it would take just five 250-tonners to carry the whole shipment.

68. Cf. Larsen, *ESAR* 4.350; Rostovtzeff, *SEHHW* 795–98.

69. Roussel 75–84.

70. Roussel 12 and n. 7, 75, 82 and n. 6; cf. Rostovtzeff, *SEHHW* 795–98.

71. This was one of Rostovtzeff's typically acute observations (*CAH* viii 644).

72. Roussel 87–92, 93–94.

73. Roussel 92–93.

74. Roussel 88.

75. Cf. *P. Ryl.* 554 and Rostovtzeff's discussion, *SEHHW* 226–28.

76. Mysta, the inamorata of Seleucus II, and a batch of prisoners captured by the Galatians in 240 B.C. wound up at Rhodes (Polyaenus 8.61; Athenaeus 13.593E).

77. Cf. Rostovtzeff, *SEHHW* 776–78.

78. Cf. *TAPA* 81 (1950) 43–51, esp. 47.

79. The account in Ferguson's *Hellenistic Athens* (London 1911) 330–33 which portrays three ports of the Aegean—Athens, Rhodes, Delos—as succeeding each other in that order is highly oversimplified.

80. Cf. *CAH* viii 505–6. E. G. Turner has taken the date of *P. Ryl.* 583 to mean that the events connected with Antiochus fall in 170 (*Bull. John Ryland's Library* 31 [1948] 149–51), but the traditional date is based on incontrovertible evidence. The date of the papyrus can be explained in other ways; cf., e.g., E. Bikerman, *Chronique d'Égypte* 54 (1952) 398–99.

81. Strabo 7.4.6.

82. Tacitus, *Hist.* 3.48; 4.52.

83. Aurelius Victor, *Brev.* 1.6; Josephus, *B.J.* 2.386. Cf. below, p. 96–97.

84. The number rose constantly until it reached 320,000. Caesar in 46 B.C. reduced it to 150,000, but Augustus raised it again to 200,000, where it seems to have more or less stayed; cf. D. van Berchem, *Les distributions de blé et d'argent à la plèbe romaine sous l'empire* (Geneva 1939) 21, 27–30.

85. Tarn, "Ptolemy II," *JEA* 14 (1928) 251, Rostovtzeff, *SEHHW* 394–97, both for; Holleaux, *CAH* vii 823, reserves judgement. For other references see the article cited in the next note, pp. 89–91.

86. L. Neatby, "Romano-Egyptian Relations During the Third Century B.C.," *TAPA* 81 (1950) 89–98.

87. Rostovtzeff, *SEHHW* 396.

88. *OGIS* 760; cf. J. Swain in *CP* 39 (1944) 91 and n. 83.

89. The references are listed and discussed by Rostovtzeff, *SEHHW* 920–22.

90. G. I. Luzzato, *Epigrafica giuridica greca e romana,* R. Università di Roma. Pubbl. del Istituto di Diritto Romano, dei Diritti dell'Oriente Mediterraneo, e di Storia del Diritto 19 (Milan 1942) 203–5. As Luzzato points out, the

recently discovered epigraphical evidence confirming the authenticity of similar wills should dispel all doubts about the genuineness of this one.

91. Proposed by Crassus in 65 B.C. (cf. Luzzato [above, n. 90] 205), by Caesar in the Rullian Laws of 63.

92. Why, for example, was Egypt not annexed before Augustus' time? Pompey chose not to do it in 63. Caesar proposed it in the same year but permitted Ptolemy Auletes to be restored in 59 and again in 55, and deliberately refrained from doing it in 47. It is fascinating, yet completely baffling, to attempt to work out the motives that lay behind these decisions. Modern writers offer a wide choice of reasons for the delay at any given time: legal (how could a Roman official play Pharaoh?—Luzzato), economic (Caesar wanted to save Egypt from the clutches of the Equites—Syme), political (save Egypt from the clutches of Caesar—Mommsen), and romantic (Cleopatra's good looks—Frank). The various cross-currents of interest—political, economic, social—reach a veritable crescendo of complexity in the notorious Auletes affair of 57–55 B.C. (see below, n. 95).

93. Cf. Cicero, *In Verr.* 5.145, 157.

94. Cf. the goods Rabirius Postumus brought back from Alexandria after his year as *dioikêtês* (Cicero, *Pro Rab. Post.* 40).

95. A convenient summary of the Auletes affair with references to all the sources can be found in R. Tyrrell and L. Purser, *The Correspondence of M. Tullius Cicero* ii (London 1906[2]) xxix–1.

96. The shortage first appeared at the beginning of July 57 (Asconius, *In Milon.* 38). Cicero reports that it ended abruptly upon his recall from exile (*De domo sua* 6.14) and that his return to Rome in September was marked by ample supplies of food (*Post red. ad Quir.* 8.18). However that may be, just a few days later the shortage was considered so serious that the Senate passed the resolution that made Pompey grain czar for 5 years (*ad Att.* 4.1.6–7).

97. Plutarch, *Pompey* 50.

98. On 11 April 56 Pompey left for Sardinia (*Q.fr.* 2.5.3.); he had been preceded by his lieutenant who left in December (*Q.fr.* 2.1.3.). He probably was back in Rome in September; cf. M. Gelzer, *Pompeius* (Munich 1949) 164. Had he gone to Egypt he would have consumed most of the summer sailing season in just getting there and back; cf. *TAPA* 81 (1950) 50–51.

99. On 22 May 55 Cicero writes to Atticus (4.10.1): *Puteolis magnus est rumor Ptolomaeum esse in regno.*

4.
The Role of the State in Rome's Grain Trade

G rain was to antiquity what oil is to the world of today. Few of the larger cities of the Mediterranean could rely solely on what was grown locally; most were compelled to eke this out with purchases from those favored lands that had a surplus to dispose of. The two centers that figure so importantly in ancient history, Classical Athens and Imperial Rome, are notable cases in point. So dependent were they on a supply from elsewhere that, if for any reason it was cut off, they faced hardship and even famine.[1] A service so vital could not be left totally to private enterprise; the government had to mix in. At Athens, for example, the state passed stringent regulations limiting the activities of traders in grain and on occasion would send its warships out to escort the freighters carrying the precious cargo.[2] At Rome Augustus created the service headed by the *praefectus annonae* which some scholars credit with well-nigh total control over the city's imports of grain. In this paper I shall review the evidence for the period when Rome's commerce was at its height, the first two centuries A.D., bringing in some new material of great significance that has just recently come to light (Appendix).

The city of Rome in these centuries was in its heyday, and its sizable population was fed almost wholly on grain from overseas, mostly from North Africa and Egypt. Our best indication of the amount involved has been gained by combining statements made by two different ancient authors: Aurelius Victor reports (*Caes.* 1.6) that, under Augustus, Rome annually received 20,000,000 modii (ca. 135,000 tons) from Egypt, and Josephus (*B.J.* 2.383, 386) puts into the mouth of Agrippa II a remark to the effect that North Africa satisfied Rome's needs for eight months of the year and Egypt for four; the arithmetic works out to a total of 60,000,000 modii (400,000 tons in round numbers). Though there is no certain way of verifying the statements, they could well be based on respectable sources and are not in themselves unreasonable.[3]

Some, however, have preferred to put their faith in another pair of passages. Aelius Spartianus in his life of Septimius Severus mentions (23; cf. 8) that the emperor "at his death left the *canon* of seven years, such that 75,000 modii could be issued daily" (*moriens septem annorum canonem, ita ut cotidiana septuaginta quinque milia modium expendi possent, reliquit*), in other words, close to 28,000,000 annually. And a scholium on Lucan 1.319, a line alluding to Pompey's control of the overseas sources of grain and his consequent ability to use famine as a weapon, explains that "Rome desired 80,000 modii of *annona* for every day" (*Roma volebat omni die LXXX milia modiorum annonae*).

An initial stumbling block, of course, is the exact sense of *canon* and *annona* in these contexts, and in the literature on the passages we find a wide variety of suggestions with scant agreement on any one.[4] Yet putting aside this difficulty, there are two features shared by the figures as cited that raise grave doubts about their usefulness, features that, so far as I can tell, have never been commented on. First, in both passages the figures are merely hypothetical, not actual, the one an amount that "could be issued," the other an amount that Rome "desired." Second, both figures are artificial: they refer to a daily issue, whereas the distributions, whether of the dole or of rations to personnel, were monthly.[5] They could not possibly have come from official sources.

Thus we are back to 60,000,000 modii as the most likely figure for the amount of grain that Rome consumed annually. Of this the state, through the organization built around the office of the *praefectus annonae*, assumed responsibility for the procuring of 12,000,000; this covered the five modii a month distributed free of charge to 200,000 families, the notorious dole that the emperors inherited from the Republic and which they never dared give up, although they managed to slim down considerably the list of eligibles.[6] The state also took care, presumably again through the office of the *praefectus annonae,* of feeding the imperial bureaucracy and the military units stationed in and around Rome; how much this required is anybody's guess.[7] All things being equal, i.e., when the even tenor of trade was undisturbed by storms on the sea or in politics, we assume that these obligations were met from the State's own grain, that which came to Rome either as tribute or from the yield of the emperors' properties; these, big to begin with, constantly increased in size.[8]

But not every family living in Rome had a right to the dole; far from it. Moreover, even those who did have a right received from this source at best only half the sustenance they required.[9] The rest of Rome's needs was taken care of by the *negotiatores* or *mercatores frumentarii,* the private grain dealers, who turn up so frequently in inscriptions and not infrequently in literature.[10] Did the state also assume a responsibility for the grain they handled? Did it, for example, set up machinery, or even just take steps, to keep the private grain dealers under enough control to ensure that the whole population would have ample supplies at reasonable prices?

I

For long the view has been promulgated that such was the case, that Rome's entire grain trade was under tight government control. We find it stated a century ago in G. Humbert's article "Annona" in the *Dictionnaire des antiquités* and in J. Marquardt's treatment in his *Römische Staatsverwaltung.*[11] Hirschfeld in his fundamental study of the imperial administration dismissed the private dealers as being of scant consequence for the supplying of Rome; the state, he felt, basically handled the grain trade. He pointed to a passage in Josephus which, as he saw it, implied that all shipments of Egyptian grain were so carefully regulated by the prefect of Egypt that his permission was required for exports to any place other than Rome.[12]

Rostovtzeff explored the question in detail in his article "Frumentum" in the *Real-Encyclopädie.* Against Hirschfeld he held that the lion's share of the trade was in the hands of private dealers—although he agreed with Hirschfeld on the state's control of Egyptian grain, the requiring of official sanction for any shipments going elsewhere than to Rome.[13] In fact, to the passage from Josephus he added a number of Asia Minor inscriptions which presumably put the point beyond doubt. However, by the time he came to write his *Social and Economic History of the Roman Empire* he had changed his mind. What he has to say on the matter is not entirely consistent, but there emerges clearly his conviction that the state exercised very close control; he of course repeats the point about the prefect's regulation of Egypt's exports.[14] Subsequent writers put the case even more strongly;[15] J. Schwartz, for example, in an article devoted to "Le Nil et le ravitaillement de Rome," concluded that, so far as the grain trade of Rome was concerned, "Nous sommes, pour le moins, en pleine 'économie dirigée.'. . . Il n'y avait plus de liberté au Ier siècle."[16] A recent full-scale treatment of the subject echoes not only Schwartz' sentiments but even his language: H. Pavis d'Escurac too talks of "dirigisme" (253, 296–97), tells us that the private sector of the grain trade "n'est-il libre qu'en théorie" (257), assures us that the *praefectus annonae* had as one of his duties "contrôler les prix de ventes des blés" (169).

To be sure, some voices were raised on the other side. A long and detailed case for assigning a large share of the trade to private enterprise was made by G. Cardinali in his entry "Frumentatio" in the *Dizionario epigrafico*. Cardinali based it chiefly on the overall figures discussed above and on his estimate of the population of Rome. Most recently G. Rickman, on the same basis, has argued for private participation on a sizable scale.[17]

There is a fundamental difficulty in this approach: the almost total lack of agreement on what numbers to use. The estimates of Rome's population, for example, range from 600,000 to almost three times that many, and the latest writers on the subject consider it hopeless even to try to make an estimate.[18] The figure of 60,000,000 I mentioned earlier has been widely accepted as reasonable for the total of the city's imported grain—yet there are some who regard it as too high and some who regard it as representing merely the amount that came in as tribute.[19] Like Cardinali and Rickman, I am convinced that private enterprise played a prime role, that the state did not exercise tight control over the trade. I think it can be demonstrated without recourse to estimates of Rome's imports or its population.

II

Let us start by reexamining Hirschfeld's example of close state control, the presumed forbidding of shipments of Egyptian grain to any place other than Rome without specific approval. He cited in support a passage from Josephus (*A.J.* 15.307) which tells how, when Herod and his backers were troubled by drought in Palestine, the prefect of Egypt "allowed them to be the first to export grain and helped in every way, both in the purchasing and the shipping." These words do not necessarily imply official authorization; they can easily mean nothing more than that the prefect did Herod a favor, used his office to help a friend through a difficult moment. Rostovtzeff adduced as further proof Epictetus 1.10.2 and 9–10, where mention is made of requests for permission to export grain as one of the matters that keep the *praefectus annonae* busy. This, however, has nothing to do with exports from Egypt or anywhere else overseas: the *praefectus* was stationed in Rome; hence what Epictetus characterizes as "a piddling request" (*enteuxidion*) for "a bit of grain" (*sitarion*) had to be from Italian communities desiring to draw on what was available under his jurisdiction in the capital.

Rostovtzeff and other scholars have adduced as well a number of inscriptions. Most are honorary decrees, lauding a citizen for multitudinous civic services, among them the import of grain from Egypt. But that is all they mention, the import of such grain; there is not the slightest reference to the obtaining of any official authorization to do so. One, honoring a citizen of Tralles, adds the detail that the shipment, 60,000 modii, was "permitted" (*synchōrethenta*) by Hadrian. A newly discovered inscription, found at Ephesus, throws light on what is meant by this. It is a reply from some emperor of the second century in answer to what seem to have been complaints from the local grain dealers. "You will use," he tells them, "such permission (*synchōresis, sc.* to buy Egyptian wheat) with consideration (*eugnōmonōs*), keeping in mind that the first necessity is that the ruling city have abundant supplies of the wheat that is prepared for the market and collected from everywhere, and, after that, all the other cities are similarly to fill their needs. If it appears that the Nile, answering our prayers, will furnish a flood of the usual measure and the Egyptian farmers have a good crop, you among the first"—and here the text breaks off. It is enough, however, to reveal what the state did about the marketing of Egyptian grain. The emperor's reply makes no reference whatsoever to any legislation on the matter, but merely reminds the dealers of the way things are; he lays down no rules, but simply makes a polite request. In other words, there was no fixed tight regulation, just an informal allocation of access to would-be buyers: first those from Rome, and then those from all the other cities in some sort of order. The plain implication of the inscription is that Egyptian wheat was regularly available on the free market, so much so that, when it was not, explanations were forthcoming. And, indeed, the honorary decrees mentioned above are just so many examples of purchases of such wheat. Only during a year when the Nile did not answer everybody's prayers and furnish a flood of the usual measure did limitations have to be introduced, as when Hadrian "permitted" 60,000 modii to the people of Tralles.[20]

Lastly, thanks to the new evidence I mentioned earlier, we are now aware that not all the grain that left Alexandria and arrived at the port of Puteoli went on to Rome. Sizable amounts stayed at Puteoli, not to relieve the local population from hunger, but to be warehoused for the greater profit of the local dealers (see section IV below).

There is, then, no evidence of strict state controls at the source, at the point of export. Is there any at the other end, evidence of regulation of the grain dealers of Rome? If the state did exercise such control, we should expect to find at least traces of it, indications of the existence of some plan, some system, some administrative machinery. We have only a handful of allusions to Rome's grain supplies, all casual and haphazard, but in one key respect they agree unanimously: they reveal the total absence of any planning, system, or machinery. They concern those moments in the city's history when, because of a shortage of grain, an emergency developed, at the worst raising fears of famine, at the least raising outcries against exorbitant prices. In every case—and this is a point that, so far as I know, has never been properly emphasized—the emperor responded with a measure that was not only ad hoc but different from any tried by his predecessors, in one instance different even from what he had himself tried earlier. The first crisis we hear of was in A.D. 6 when the shortage was serious enough to threaten the city with starva-

101

tion. Augustus' answer (Dio 55.26.2–3) was to reduce the number of mouths that had to be fed by evacuating peripheral elements of the population (slaves being held for sale, gladiators),[21] by thinning the ranks of the imperial servants, and by introducing rationing—the first and last time we hear of this, the solution par excellence in our own age for food shortages. In A.D. 19 a public outcry arose over the high cost of grain. Tiberius' solution (Tacitus, *Ann.* 2.87) was to set a maximum sales price that must have been well below the going price, since he subsidized the grain dealers two sesterces per modius, presumably to enable them to meet it and still stay solvent; this is the first and last time we hear of subsidies. In A.D. 32 the cries went up again over the high price of grain, louder and more violent than ever before; Tiberius handled this occasion (Tacitus, *Ann.* 6.13) by simply giving the Senate and magistrates a tongue-lashing for not cracking down on such goings on. Under Claudius prices got so out of hand that an irate populace pelted him with crusts of bread as he walked through the Forum. His answer was to try an entirely new approach (Suetonius, *Claud.* 18).

Claudius resolved to adopt a long-range solution and not stagger from crisis to crisis. In the measures he took there is not the slightest trace of government control or even supervision; he had recourse not to the stick, only to the carrot. The answer to the problem, he felt, was to increase Rome's regular supply of grain by bringing in shipments all year round, during the winter as well as the official summer sailing season. And his method for achieving this was to offer incentives to merchants, including guarantees against loss. The clear implication is that the trade was so effectively in the hands of private enterprise that the only solution the emperor could conceive of was to induce them to increase their efforts. What he started long continued; incentives were still being offered at the beginning of the third century.[22]

III

If, then, the state did not control the grain trade by regulation of the dealers, were there other ways in which it accomplished the same end?

I cited a passage above referring to the large amounts of grain Severus succeeded in stockpiling. Presumably he was able to do so because Rome's share of tribute grain and the yield of the imperial estates came to more than was needed for the dole and the feeding of government personnel. If this was regularly the case, if the state regularly had reserves at its disposal, could it not, by releasing given amounts at appropriate times, exercise leverage on the market and thereby control prices? Many have suggested that it did.[23]

We have evidence that emperors other than Severus were able to hoard grain.[24] Yet there is just as much evidence that the feeding of the city, or at least the price of grain, depended by and large on the safe and prompt arrival of the grain ships. Delays or rumors of delay caused anxiety and unrest, even panic[25]—which would not have been so had there been a cushion of reserves in the warehouses. Stockpiling of ample supplies must have been the exception, not the rule. It could not have furnished the state a mechanism for steady control over prices. Pliny in his *Panegyric* devotes many words to Trajan's handling of the grain supply (29–32), but nowhere does he include glowing descriptions of any reserves his hero had built up; the best he can say (29) is that forced requisitions are a thing of the past and yet people still have plenty to eat. The scholars who so confidently assert that the state sold grain cannot document the statement with a single concrete instance.

There is yet another way in which the state may have manipulated the grain market to serve its ends, by large scale purchases. Does not Pliny, after declaring that there are no more requisitions, tell us that *emit fiscus quidquid videtur emere?* The question, however, is: did it see fit to buy with a view to influencing price? Not at all, as we learn from Pliny's very next sentence: *Inde copiae, inde annona, de qua inter licentem et vendentem conveniat* "Hence our provisions, hence our grain supply, arranged by agreement between bidder and seller." Prices, in other words, were set by the market.

Although state purchase of grain is assumed by a number of scholars,[26] there is scant evidence for it outside of Pliny's statement. Officials charged with securing grain appear in inscriptions from North Africa, but they are dealing with local needs, not Rome's. One sole inscription mentions purchasing for Rome, and it is surely to be connected with some emergency.[27]

There are even those who would have it both ways: that the

state had plentiful reserves which it threw on the market and thereby exercised control over prices, and that it also was a large-scale buyer, even negotiating long-term contracts with private grain dealers for the regular purchase of the amounts needed to satisfy Rome's requirements.[28]

The evidence, of course, is perfectly clear: we hear far more often of shortages than surpluses, and in meeting the shortages the emperors consistently used but one approach: blandishment—not regulation—of the private grain dealers. As for controlling prices, which we are assured was one of the functions of the *praefectus annonae*,[29] the evidence shows if anything just the opposite, that prices kept getting out of hand to the point where the emperor had to do something about it.[30]

IV

Let us turn, finally, to the new evidence that I have several times alluded to.

In 1959, during the construction of a highway near Murecine, site of an eastern suburb of Pompeii, the remains of a Roman villa came to light. From it was recovered a basket that, on the day of the disaster, had been left on a triclinium. In it was a precious find, almost seventy wax tablets, business documents mostly concerned in one way or another with moneylending carried on by two freedmen of the same family, C. Sulpicius Cinnamus and C. Sulpicius Faustus.[31] Six of the tablets (Appendix) involve, directly or indirectly, grain from Egypt. They demonstrate beyond a shadow of doubt that, at least up to A.D. 40, the date of the latest piece, individual private dealers were very much involved in the trade.

Five of the six concern a series of related loans to a certain C. Novius Eunus, a large-scale dealer in foodstuffs. The earliest, dated 28 June 37, is an agreement covering 10,000 sesterces, payable on demand, that Novius borrows from an imperial freedman, Ti. Iulius, Augusti libertus, Evenus Primianus; the transaction was actually handled by Evenus' agent, a slave of his named Hesychus. As collateral Novius pledges "7,000 modii, more or less, of Alexandrian wheat and 4,000 modii, more or less, of chickpea, emmer (?), and lentil in 200 sacks, all of which I have in deposit under my name in the public warehouse, the Horrea

Bassiana, at Puteoli." The interest is not stated but, as we shall see, it was the standard 1 percent a month.

The next document is dated 2 July, four days later. It is a lease. A certain C. Novius Cypaerus, through his agent, a slave of his named Diognetus, rents to Hesychus, the agent who handled the loan to Novius, "storage unit no. 12 in the Horrea Bassiana, the public warehouse in Puteoli, central area, where there is stored the Alexandrian wheat which he today accepted as collateral from C. Novius Eunus, likewise in the same warehouse, rear area, the *intercolumnia* space where he has in storage the 200 sacks of vegetables which he accepted as collateral from the same Eunus, from the first of July for 1 sesterce per month."[32]

C. Novius Eunus, then, was a trader who handled grains and vegetables in substantial amounts (7,000 modii of Alexandrian wheat would be about 45 tons, and the addition of the vegetables would bring the whole up close to 75). The date is significant: May and June were precisely the months when the first shipments of grain from Alexandria arrived at Puteoli.[33] The storage charges are ridiculously low, nominal in fact. Though the space was let to Hesychus, the creditor's agent, it was for storing Eunus' security and the charges would probably eventually be for Eunus' account.[34] The holder of the space, C. Novius Cypaerus, could well be a fellow freedman who may either have been in partnership with Eunus or may simply have been doing him a favor.

The third document is dated 2 July—exactly the same day the lease was drawn up and the security made over. It is a second loan agreement, but this time with Hesychus alone; he is himself identified as the creditor and not as agent for his master. Novius states that he "has accepted from Hesychus, slave of Evenus Primianus, freedman of Tiberius Caesar Augustus, on loan and owes to him 3,000 sesterces over and above the 10,000 which I owe to the same [i.e., Evenus] by virtue of my other note of hand. . . . For which total sum I have given him as collateral 7,000 modii of Alexandrian wheat deposited in the Horrea Bassiana, public warehouse of Puteoli, central storehouse . . . and 200 sacks of lentil, chickpea, and emmer (?) and jars in which are 4,000 modii, which are deposited in the same warehouse."

The listing of the security differs in one slight respect in this document from the previous two. There the legumes, 4,000 modii in all, are said to be in 200 sacks; here they are said to be in 200

105

sacks and an unspecified number of jars. This solves a crux; 4,000 modii in 200 sacks would require sacks of 300 pounds apiece—far too heavy to be handled by one man. But if some of the legumes was stored in the jars—and it was not uncommon to do so—then we can assume sacks of a reasonable 100 pounds apiece.[35]

Why a second loan on the same security? For the same reason that a creditor will issue a second mortgage on the same real property today: the security was worth it. In A.D. 64, after the great fire, Nero held down the price of grain to 3 sesterces a modius (Tacitus, *Ann.* 15.39). This was a minimum price; in 37 grain must have been worth at least that much and very likely more. In other words, the Alexandrian wheat alone had a value on the retail market of 21,000 sesterces, and the legumes would surely send the total value far beyond that—an ample margin to cover a creditor in case of default. It looks as if Novius, after making the first loan, discovered he could use more cash and Hesychus, seeing a foolproof opportunity, ventured some of his own funds.[36]

I have stated that the second loan was made by Hesychus himself, and not for the account of his master, on the basis of the wording, which is distinctly different from that of the first loan. The next document puts the matter beyond any doubt. It is dated 29 August 38. In other words, thirteen full months have passed. It is yet another loan, a renewal, as we shall see, of an unpaid balance on the second, smaller loan. Evenus is not even mentioned, making it clear that the creditor in that loan had been Hesychus and Hesychus alone. In fact, Evenus is no longer Hesychus' master, for Hesychus now styles himself "Hesychus, C. Caesaris Augusti Germanici servus, Evenianus," indicating that Evenus had in the interim ceded him to the imperial service. The loan is payable either to Hesychus or to C. Sulpicius Faustus, one of the two men who figure prominently as moneylenders in the archive. There is no mention of security; either it was taken for granted or perhaps by now Novius had so demonstrated his good faith that none was required. The amount lent to him is 1,130 sesterces. Now, the amount he had originally borrowed from Hesychus was 3,000. This with interest at the standard rate of 1 percent a month for thirteen months would come to 3,390—in other words, exactly three times 1,130. The obvious conclusion is that the interest indeed was the standard rate and that Novius had paid off two-thirds of the loan and was renewing for the remaining third. He must have paid off the first loan of 10,000 to Hesychus' former master since it had priority.[37]

The last document is yet another renewal of the balance of the small loan. It is dated 15 September 39—a second year has passed. It is for 1,250 sesterces payable, as before, either to Hesychus or C. Sulpicius Faustus, but not on demand as before—it must be paid by October 31 or a penalty of 20 sesterces a day will apply. The unpaid third of the loan, 1,130 sesterces plus interest for twelve months (135 sesterces and a little over) comes out to 1,265 rather than 1,250; perhaps Novius had paid a bit on account to round the figure off.

V

Seven thousand modii of grain, the amount Novius owned, is not inconsiderable. Others handled even more. The last of the six documents, dated A.D. 40, deals with money lent by our C. Sulpicius Faustus to a certain P. Annius Seleucus on the security of 13,000 modii of Alexandrian grain—almost double what Novius pledged and well above the 10,000 that, in Claudius' legislation, entitled dealers to apply for special privileges (Suetonius, *Claud.* 18).

The loans these men negotiated need not have been connected with the grain they put up as security; the money might have gone, say, for the purchase of a plot of land, a daughter's dowry, or what have you. On the other hand, the four-day lapse between the date of Novius' first loan and the time he turned over his security makes it very likely that there indeed was a connection, that the loan was to finance what was pledged.

If Novius needed funds for a purpose unrelated to the grain he gave as collateral, he would have turned over the collateral to his creditor and received the money. But here just the reverse took place: he gets the money on 28 June but does not surrender the collateral until four days later, 2 July. Why?

I suggest that, just like the borrower in a maritime loan, who gets his money in advance to purchase the shipment which will become his collateral, Novius needed the loan to buy a parcel of newly arrived grain; June, as we have said, is one of the two months in which most cargoes from Egypt arrived. And, just like

107

the creditor in a maritime loan, Evenus accommodatingly gave him the 10,000 sesterces before receiving the major part of the collateral, the 7,000 modii.[38] The money enabled Novius to get possession of the merchandise and begin transferring it from the dock to a warehouse.[39] When, four days later, this was accomplished, the grain was formally made over to the creditor.

We know definitely that Novius paid off one of his loans in installments. Very likely he paid off all of them that way, each time securing the release of some of the grain he had in pawn, which he then put on the market. By delaying selling until the summer was past, even though he had to add debt service to his costs, he presumably was able to make a better profit. The storage charges, normally an additional burden, in this particular case, as we have seen, were nominal.

P. Annius Seleucus took out his loan in February or March of 40; the 13,000 modii he pledged would have reached Puteoli, at the latest, by the end of the summer of 39. He would not have to fear the competition of newly arriving supplies until May at the earliest.

VI

A review of the evidence thus reveals that, during the first two centuries A.D., the state's interest in Rome's grain extended only to fulfilling the needs of the dole and of government personnel; the rest it left to private dealers. Under pressure it did on occasion turn its attention to them, but only to solicit, not command, their aid. There is no evidence of control through legislation or close supervision. There is no evidence of price fixing either directly by regulation or indirectly through large-scale selling or purchasing; the rare occasions when the emperors set prices are the exceptions proving the rule.[40] The new documents from Pompeii display these dealers in action, handling large stocks, operating on credit, gambling on the market.

Appendix

TP 15 *RAAN* 45 (1970) 213–15 = *AEpigr* 1972.86 28 June A.D. 37
Cn(aeo) Acceronio Proculo C(aio) Petronio Pontio co(n)s(ulibus), iv k(alendas) Iulias, C(aius) Novius Eunus scripssi me accepisse ob mutua

ab Eveno Ti(berii) Cessaris Augusti luberto Primiano apssente, per Hessucus ser(vus) eius et debere ei sesterta decem milia nummu(m) qua(a)e ei redam cum patiaerit, *etc.* iis sestertis decem milibus nummu(m) dedi pignoris ar(r)a(b)onis u[. . .] nomine tridici Al(e)xa(n)drini modium septe milia plus minus et ciceris, far(r)is monoc(o)pi, lentis in sac(c)is, ducentis modium quatuor milia plus minus qu(a)e om<i>nia possita habeo penes me in horeis Bassianis puplicis Putolanorum qu(a)e ab om<i>ni vi periculo meo est dico fateor. Actum Putiolis.

TP 7 *RAAN* 45 (1970) 229–30 = *AEpigr* 1973.143 2 July A.D. 37
C(aio) Caesare Germanico Augusto Ti(berio) Claudio Nerone Germanico co(n)s(ulibus) vi Non(as) Iulias, Diognetus C(aii) Novi Cypaeri ser(vus) scripsi iusu Cypaeri domini mei cora(m) ipsum me locasse Hesico Ti(berii) Iulii Augusti libert(i) P(rimiani) Eueni ser(vo) horreum xii horreis in Bassianis publicis Putolanorum medis in quo repositu(m) [e]st triticum Alexandrini quod pignori accepit hodie ab C(aio) Novio Euno, item in isdem horeis imis intercolumnia ube repositos habet saccos legumenum ducentos quos pignori accepit ab aeodem Eunum ex k(alendis) Iulis in menses singulos sestertis singulis nummis. Act(um) Putiolos.

TP 16 *RAAN* 45 (1970) 215–17 = *AEpigr* 1972.87 2 July A.D. 37
C(aio) Cessasare (*sic*) Germanico *etc.* C(aius) Novius Eunus scripssi me accepisse mutua ab Hess(i)co Eunni Ti(berii) Cessaris Augusti l(iberti) Primiani ser(vo) [mutua] et debere ei sestertia tr(i)a milia nummu(m) pre(ter) (sestertium) (decem) n(ummum) qu(a)e alio chirographo meo eidem debo *etc.* in qua om<i>nis sum(m)a dedi ei pignoris tridici Al(e)xandrini modium septe mil(i)a quot est possit(um) in horeis Bassianis puplicis Putola(norum) medis horesi quod [. . .] et sac(c)os ducen(t)os lentis, [ciceris], (far)ris monocopi et cados in quibus sunt modium quatuor milia qui sunt possiti in isdem horeis qu(a)e om<i>nia ab om<i>ni vi p(e)riculo meo est fat(e)or. Actum Put(i)olis.

TP 17 *RAAN* 45 (1970) 217–18 = *AEpigr* 1972.88 29 August A.D. 38
Ser(vio) Assinio Celere Sex(to) Nonio co(n)s(ulibus) iv k(alendas) Septeberes, C(aius) Novius E[u]nus scripssi me debere [Hes]uco C(aii) Cessaris Aug(usti) Ger(manici) [se]r(vo) Eveniano s[e]sterti(os) [mille] centum trigin(t)a numm(os) quos ab eo mutuo su[m]ssi qu[os reddam e]i ipssi aut C(aio) Sulpicio [Fausto] cum petiarit *etc.*

TP 18 *RAAN* 45 (1970) 218–20, 226–28 = 46 (1971) 196–97 = *AEpigr* 1973.138 15 September A.D. 39
Cn(aeo) Domitio A(fro) Aulo Didio Gallo co(n)s(ulibus) xvii K(alendas) Octobres C(aius) N(o)vius Eunus scripsi me (deb)ere Hesi(c)ho

109

C(aii) Caesaris Augusti Germanici s(er)v(o) (Eveniano) sestertios mille ducentos quinquaginta nummos reliquos ratione omni putata quos ab eo mutuos accepi quam summam iuratus promisi m(e) a(u)t ipsi Hesicho aut C(aio) Sulpicio Fausto redditurum p[ridie] k[alendis] Novembribus primis per Iovem Opt(u)mum Max[umum] et Numen Divi Aug[usti] et Genium C(aii) Caesaris Augusti quod si ea die non solvero me non solum peiurio teneri sed etiam poeneae nomine in dies sing(ulos) HS. XX nummos obligatum iri *etc.*

TP 44 *RAAN* 46 (1971) 195 = *AEpigr* 1973.167 = *RAAN* 51 (1976) 145–47 End of February or 1st half of March A.D. 40

C(aio) Laecanio Basso Q(uinto) Ter[en]tio Culleone co(n)s(ulibus) iii . . . Martias, Nardus P(ublii) Anni Sel[eu]ci servus sc[rip]si coram et iussu Se[leu]ci domini mei, quod is negaret se litteras sc[ire, me lo]casse C(aio) Sul[pi]cio Fausto horreum vicensimum et sextum, quod est in praedis Domitiae L[e]pidae B[ar]batianis superioribus, in quo repositum est tritici Alexandrini millia mod[i]um decem et tria, [. . .] mutuitur dominus meus cu[m u]suris q[*aa*]nt in mensibus singulis [sestert]is cen[tenis] nummis. Actum Puteolis.

Remains from previous face: in mensibus singulis sestertis centenis nummis Ac[tum Pu]tiol[is]

There is barely room for [quae] in the lacuna before *mutuitur,* and the restoration would make sense only if the verb can have the hitherto unparalleled meaning "hand over as security"; cf. Crook (below, n. 34) 236.

Notes

1. The following abbreviations have been used:

Cardinali = G. Cardinali, "Frumentatio" in E. de Ruggiero, *Dizionario epigrafico di antichità romane* iii 225–315

Marquardt = J. Marquardt, *Römische Staatsverwaltung* ii (Leipzig 1876)

Pavis d'Escurac = H. Pavis d'Escurac, *La préfecture de l'annone service administratif impérial d'Auguste à Constantin,* Bibliothèque des écoles françaises d'Athènes et de Rome, fasc. 226 (Rome 1976)

RAAN = *Rendiconti dell'Accademia di Archeologia . . . di Napoli*

Rickman = G. Rickman, *Roman Granaries and Store Buildings* (Cambridge 1971)

SEHRE = M. Rostovtzeff, *The Social and Economic History of the Roman Empire* (Oxford 1957[2])

van Berchem = D. van Berchem, *Les distributions de blé et d'argent à la plèbe romaine sous l'empire* (Geneva 1939).

For Athens, cf. H. Michell, *The Economics of Ancient Greece* (New York 1957²) 258–59; for Rome, Tacitus, *Hist.* 3.48 (Vespasian hastened to seize Alexandria and prepared to invade Africa in order to put pressure on Rome by cutting off the food supply).

2. Aristotle, *Ath.* 51.4 (⅔ of the grain entering the Peiraeus had to go to Athens); Dem. 34.37, 35.51 (no resident of Athens was permitted to ship grain elsewhere or to lend money for grain going elsewhere); Dem. 18.73, 50.17 (convoys).

3. For the literature on Aurelius Victor's sources, see Cardinali 306–307. On the reasonableness of the figure when compared with yields of the past century, cf. *ESAR* ii 481, iv 43–44. That 60,000,000 modii represents Rome's total consumption has met general acceptance. Beloch, to be sure, rejected it out of hand (*Die Bevölkerung der griechisch-roemischen Welt* [Leipzig 1886] 411) but that was because it did not at all accord with his calculations (a population of Rome of about 800,000 consuming an average of 36 modii per person per annum). Cardinali (307–308) seems to reject it but actually does not. At considerable length he insists that what Josephus is saying is that Egypt and Africa supplied not Rome's total consumption but only the needs of her dole for 4 and 8 months respectively, i.e., 4,000,000 and 8,000,000 modii respectively, since the dole required 12,000,000 (below, n. 6). However, he readily accepts Aurelius Victor's 20,000,000 as Egypt's total export. Thus, Egypt on his reckoning gave to the dole 20% of her total export. If we assume that Africa also gave 20%, then Africa's total export would have been 40,000,000, and that plus Egypt's 20,000,000 = 60,000,000. Pavis d'Escurac rejects (170) the 60,000,000 on the basis of an argument that is not only unconvincing but applies solely to the period from Augustus to Nero. Rickman, *The Corn Supply of Ancient Rome* (Oxford 1980) 10, considers 60,000,000 modii too high; he estimates the population of Rome at about 1,000,000 and calculates that that many people would need but 40,000,000 annually.

4. Beloch (above, n. 3, 411–12) and U. Kahrstedt (in L. Friedländer, *Darstellungen aus der Sittengeschichte Roms* iv [Leipzig 1921¹⁰] 18–19) take Spartianus' figure as referring to the city's total supply, Marquardt (123) and Rickman (309) as referring to tribute grain alone, Cardinali (308) as tribute grain plus state purchases, W. Oates (in *CP* 29 [1934] 113) as state purchased grain alone, Pavis d'Escurac (172) as tribute plus the yield from the imperial domains; *quot homines tot sententiae*. Beloch, Marquardt, and Kahrstedt cite the two passages together in support of each other. Yet the word *canon* as Spartianus uses it, whatever it may mean, cannot refer to Rome's total supply (see Oates' extended discussion 110–11, also van Berchem 106–108 and A. Berger, *Encyclopedic Dictionary of Roman Law*, Philadelphia 1953, s.v.), whereas the scholiast's *annona*, since he is talking of Pompey's day, can refer to nothing else but the city's total supply.

5. Suetonius, *Aug.* 40 (monthly distributions of the dole); *Nero* 10 (monthly distributions to the praetorians).

111

6. It is universally agreed that the dole was 5 modii per month, even though the figure rests on but a single citation, Sallust, *Hist.* 3.48(61)19, where he puts into the mouth of a tribune of the plebs a scornful reminder to Rome's citizens that the grain law reckons their freedom at 5 modii. The speech was supposedly delivered in 73 B.C., but there is no reason why the amount should ever have been changed. For the figure of 200,000 recipients, see *Res Gestae* 15; Dio 15.10.1. Earlier there were 320,000; at least this is the number who earlier received a handout of money from Augustus, and we assume they were identical with the recipients of grain (cf. van Berchem 26–27).

7. T. Frank (*ESAR* v 219) estimates 14,400,000 modii for the dole and government personnel together but does not tell how he arrived at the figure. Pavis d'Escurac (168) estimates 600,000 for the military personnel.

8. Cf. *SEHRE* 101–102.

9. One of Augustus' measures to alleviate a serious shortage in A.D. 6 was the doubling of the grain dole (Dio 55.26.2–3). It follows that the ordinary dole was at best half of a family's needs. On eligibility for the dole, see van Berchem 32–45.

10. J. Waltzing, *Les corporations professionelles chez les Romains* ii (Louvain 1896) 103–108, 401–403; R. Meiggs, *Roman Ostia* (Oxford 1973²) 277; Pavis d'Escurac 254.

11. *DarSag* i 276–77 (1873); Marquardt 123.

12. *Die kaiserlichen Verwaltungsbeamten* (Berlin 1905²) 235.

13. *RE* vii 137, 141 (1912).

14. *SEHRE* (1926) 137 = *SEHRE²* 145. Rostovtzeff states: "The problem of regulating the market was not tackled by the central government. On the contrary many serious obstacles were placed in the way of the free development of trade concerned with the necessities of life." The second sentence, if not a contradiction of the first, is at least a non sequitur.

15. A. Momigliano, *Claudius: The Emperor and his Achievement* (Oxford 1934) 49; H. Loane, *Industry and Commerce of the City of Rome* (Baltimore 1938) 121–23 (where she claims that the state regulated the price of grain, although on 154 she makes a somewhat contradictory statement); T. Frank, *ESAR* v 218–19; A. Piganiol, *Histoire de Rome* (Paris 1939) 256, 289.

16. *BIFAO* 47 (1948) 179–200 at 194–95.

17. Cardinali 303–11; Rickman 173 and 307–11; Rickman, *MAAR* 36 (1980) 261–77; Rickman, *Corn Supply* (above, note 3) 87–93 (where he overopti-

mistically concluded [88] that the argument for state control, "fashionable in the twenties and thirties, is now largely exploded").

18. F. Maier, "Römische Bevölkerungsgeschichte und Inschriftenstatistik," *Historia* 2 (1953–54) 318–51 at 321–22, gives a list of the various estimates. He doubts (327–28) the possibility of ever arriving at a convincing conclusion, as does G. Hermansen, "The Population of Imperial Rome: The Regionaries," *Historia* 27 (1978) 129–68 at 166–68.

19. Too high: Beloch (above, n. 3) 411–12; Rickman, *MAAR* 36 (1980) 263. Tribute only: A. Johnson in *ESAR* ii 481.

20. Hirschfeld's statement has been repeated without challenge: see Cardinali 307; Rostovtzeff, *RE* vii 137 and *SEHRE* 145, 700; van Berchem 83, n. 1; Schwartz (above, n. 16) 195; Pavis d'Escurac 263. The inscriptions cited in support are SIG^2 389 = SIG^3 839; *CIG* ii 2927, 2930; *AM* 8 (1883) 328–29; *Forschungen in Ephesos* iii, no. 16. SIG^3 839 expresses the Ephesians' thanks to Hadrian for donations to Artemis, for restoring their harbor, and for "furnishing supplies of grain from Egypt"; the grain, like the other items, must have been a gift from the emperor. *CIG* ii 2930, *AM* 8 (1883) 328–29, and *Forschungen in Ephesos* iii, no. 16 are inscriptions honoring citizens for the usual civic services, including the import of grain from Egypt. *CIG* ii 2927 adds the detail that the grain was "permitted." The emperor's reply to the grain dealers of Ephesus was first published by D. Knibbe in *ÖjhBeibl* 47 (1964–65) 6–10, improved text and interpretation in *AEpigr* 1968.478, and a still further improved text with extensive commentary by M. Wörrle in *Chiron* 1 (1971) 325–40. Wörrle, too, takes this and the other inscriptions as proof of state control of Egypt's exports (333–35), and he repeats approvingly Rostovtzeff's interpretation of the passage from Epictetus (337).

21. Thinning the population was also tried 300 years later but by then attitudes had changed: scholars were expelled and 3,000 chorus girls left to stay (Ammianus 14.6.19).

22. Cf. Waltzing 8 (above, n. 10) 402–403.

23. Humbert, *DarSag* i 277; Marquardt 123–24; Rostovtzeff, *RE* vii 142; van Berchem 80; Pavis d'Escurac 186–87. Marquardt imagined that the state, selling the grain at a minimal price, often took a loss and that consequently such sales were a form of *largitio*. Pavis d'Escurac, on the other hand, imagines that the state made so much profit out of them that from it the *praefectus annonae* was able to pay many of his recurring expenses (freight charges, stevedoring, warehousing) and perhaps even defray part of the costs of warehouse and port construction.

24. In A.D. 62 some state grain had been around so long it went bad (Tacitus, *Ann.* 15.18).

113

25. Cf. Tacitus, *Ann.* 3.54, where Tiberius reminds the Senate that "the life of the populace of Rome goes on every day amid the uncertainties of sea and weather"; *Ann.* 4.6 where Tacitus, in summing up Tiberius' reign to A.D. 23, talks of high grain prices caused by bad harvests and rough seas. In A.D. 70 fear ran through the city: the populace's one concern was food, and a rumor that Africa had revolted convinced everyone that supplies would be held back (*Hist.* 4.38). The news of the arrival of a ship from Alexandria carrying sand instead of the expected grain added to Nero's unpopularity in 68 (Suetonius, *Nero* 45). In 62 a storm destroyed 200 ships in Portus and a fire 100 others already up the Tiber, yet, notes Tacitus, the price of grain did not increase (Tacitus, *Ann.* 15.18); the clear implication is that normally interruption of the flow from overseas would send the price right up.

26. Cardinali 301, 305, 308; Oates (above, n. 4) 113 (who suggests that Spartianus' figure of ca. 28,000,000 refers to state-purchased grain); Pavis d'Escurac 176, 183, 185–86, 258, 269. Rostovtzeff's comparison (*SEHRE* 700) of the *sitos agorastos* mentioned in Egyptian papyri with the *frumentum emptum,* the grain purchased for Rome, mentioned in Cicero's Verrine orations, is the result of a misunderstanding of the Greek; see *P. Teb.* 369.6 note. Oates (113) and Pavis d'Escurac (186) suggest that the *pyros synagorastikos* mentioned in Egyptian papyri is state-purchased wheat for the international market, but this too is the result of a misunderstanding. We also find *krithê synagorastikos* (*BGU* 381), and barley, of course, was never shipped to Rome. The "purchased" wheat and barley were for the local garrisons; see *P. Teb* 396.6 note and *P. Oxy.* 2958 introd.

27. See Cardinali 293 for the inscriptions from North Africa. The exception is a decree honoring a certain T. Flavius Macer who under Trajan held the office of *curator frumenti comparandi in annona urbis* (*ILS* 1435 = H. Pflaum, *Les carrières procuratoriennes èquestres sous le haut-empire romain,* [Paris 1960–61] no. 98; cf. Cardinali 293; Pavis d'Escurac 125–27, 185). Pflaum characterizes the appointment as "une curatèle extraordinaire." Pavis d'Escurac (126) connects it with the drought in Egypt when Trajan, reversing the normal order of things, arranged to ship grain into that country (Pliny, *Panegyr.* 30–31). R. Longden (*CAH* xi 213, n. 2) prefers connecting it with the Jewish revolt of 116–17 which disrupted Egypt's ability to export and must have forced Rome to look to North Africa and elsewhere to make up the lack.

28. Pavis d'Escurac 259–60. Friedländer (above, n. 4) i (1919[9]) 27, posits agents buying up grain in the provinces to sell at Rome below cost.

29. Rostovtzeff, *RE* vii 142; Cardinali 305; Loane (above, n. 15) 13, 121; Schwartz (above, n. 16) 194; Pavis d'Escurac 169.

30. Tacitus, *Ann.* 2.87 (*saevitiam annonae*), 4.6 (*acri annona*), 6.13 (*gravitate annonae*); Suetonius, *Nero* 45 (*caritate annonae;* if the reading *lucranti* in this passage is correct, Nero, far from controlling high prices, was profiting from them).

THE ROLE OF THE STATE IN ROME'S GRAIN TRADE

31. L. Bove in *Labeo* 21 (1975) 329–31 provides a list with full bibliographical details up to TP 54. Others have been published in *RAAN* 51 (1976) 145–68, 53 (1978) 249–69; *Atti dell' Accademia Pontaniana* 29 (1980) 175–98. Cinnamus appears in twenty-five documents (TP 1, 2, 3, 9, 19, 20, 23–26, 30, 34, 35, 37–40, 43, 45, 48, 52, 53, 56, 64, 68), Faustus in nineteen (8, 14, 17, 18, 27, 28, 32, 36, 41, 44, 45, 50, 57–59, 62, 63, 66, 67) of the first fifty-four published. Joseph Georg Wolf, who has republished a number of the documents is preparing an up-to-date edition of the entire corpus.

32. On the intercolumnia space, see Rickman 52, 54, 197–98. Novius' 7,000 modii would be ca. 63 cubic meters in volume and that would fit easily into, e.g., the rooms of the Horrea of Hortensius at Ostia (see the dimensions in Rickman 67).

33. *SSAW* 297–99.

34. Cf. J. Crook in *Zeitschrift für Papyrologie und Epigraphik* 29 (1978) 235–36. According to *Dig.* 13.7.8, a debtor was responsible for the expenses connected with his *pignus*. E.g., if a slave given as security fell sick, the medical charges were to be paid by the debtor even if the slave ended up dead of the illness. If a house given as security was damaged by lightning, the debtor paid for the repairs even if it subsequently burned down. By analogy, then, storage charges for grain given as collateral should end up being paid by the debtor. In the Egyptian papyri we find, for example, cases in which rent paid in the form of grain is deposited in a warehouse in the lessor's name "free of all expense," which can only mean the warehouse charges; see N. Lewis (who kindly brought this parallel to my attention) in *Bulletin of the American Society of Papyrologists* 13 (1976) 167–69.

35. For legumes in jars, cf. *CIL* iv 5728, 5729 (amphorae marked *cicer*). Crook (see the previous note) mistakenly took the jars as signifying the presence of wine.

36. For second loans on the same security, see *Dig.* 20.4.18. For the relation between the value of the security and the size of a loan, see J. Macqueron, "Les tablettes de Pompéi et la vente des sûretés réelles," *Mélanges Roger Aubenas*, Université de Montpellier 1: Recueil de mémoires et travaux publiés par la société d'histoire du droit et des institutions des anciens pays de droit écrit, fasc. ix (Montpellier 1974) 517–26, esp. 519. On grain prices, cf. S. Mrozek's note, "Le prix des céréales à Puteoli en 37 de N.E.," *Eos* 61 (1978) 153–55.

37. Cf. *Dig.* 20.4.18 and Berger (above n. 4) s.v. "Prior tempore potior iure." J. Macqueron, "Un commerçant en difficulté au temps de Caligula," *Études offertes à Alfred Jauffret*, Publications de la faculté de droit et de science politique d'Aix-Marseille (Aix-en-Provence 1974) 497–508, argues (507–508) that Novius' financial troubles arose because the service of the annona requisitioned his grain, forcing him to take a price below the market for it. Mac-

115

ANCIENT TRADE AND SOCIETY

queron can cite in support of this idea only one presumed parallel, an instance of government requisition of some leather sacks held as security by a creditor (*Dig.* 13.7–43.1). The parallel is hardly cogent, since the requisition in question was done by the military, not the civil, authorities, and, what is more, when the creditor protested he got his goods back. Actually Macqueron's idea flies in the face of all we know about the relations between the state and the grain dealers.

38. On maritime loans, see W. Ashburner, *The Rhodian Sea-Law* (Oxford 1909) ccxvi-ccxix. For a summary of examples of Greek and Roman maritime loans, see G. de Ste. Croix, "Ancient Greek and Roman Maritime Loans" in H. Edey and B. Yamey, ed., *Debts, Credits, Finance and Profits. Essays in Honour of W. T. Baxter* (London 1974) 41–59.

39. I am interpreting the words *possita habeo penes me* of TP 15 as "what I am to have on deposit under my name."

40. See Rickman 310 for a thoughtful summary of the duties of the *praefectus annonae* and the service he headed.

5.
Unemployment, the Building Trade, and Suetonius *Vesp.* 18

In the present century, keeping people employed has become one of society's overriding concerns. Governments expend vast sums on public works whose prime purpose is to create jobs; private industry disregards available laborsaving machinery in order to protect the jobs that exist. Some historians are convinced that it is not just a phenomenon of our own day but can be found in the ancient past as well. A passage they universally quote as evidence is Suetonius, *Vesp.* 18. I propose to show that it need have nothing to do with creating or saving jobs; indeed, it may well involve the exact opposite, compulsory labor—the very aspect of ancient history to which N. Lewis has contributed so fruitfully.

Suetonius, after describing Vespasian's notorious closefisted-ness, redresses the balance by citing instances of his generosity. Among these is the case of an engineer who offered to transport heavy columns at minimal expense to the Capitolium; this would have been in A.D. 70, since the rebuilding of the temple was one of Vespasian's first acts.[1] The emperor rewarded the man handsomely, even though he did not accept the offer; he prefaced his refusal with the remark, "Let me feed the mob" (*mechanico quoque grandis columnas exigua impensa perducturum in Capitolium pollicenti praemium pro commento non mediocre optulit, operam remisit praefatus sineret se plebiculam pascere*).

117

For centuries this ancedote has been taken to mean that the engineer dangled before Vespasian some form of laborsaving device which Vespasian turned down in order to keep the workmen on the project from being fired and hence deprived of the chance to earn their daily bread. *Plebeculam,* commented Johann Schild in his edition of 1647, *intelligi voluit operarios viliores et victum ex opera quotidiana quaeritantes.*[2] Pieter Burman in his edition of 1736 added, *Omnes illi Mechanici, qui compendia laboris et sumtus inveniunt, plebi et operariis ex vulgo praeripiunt occasionem lucrandi ex quotidiana opera.* And a host of commentators, historians, and translators have perpetuated this view. Indeed, the translators, in order to make absolutely sure their readers will not miss the point, at times put far more or far different words in Vespasian's mouth than Suetonius did. All Vespasian said was, "Let me feed the mob." This has been transformed into "I must always ensure that the working classes earn enough money to buy themselves food," "saying that he should not be forced to take from the poor . . . the work that fed them," "lest the poor have no work," and the like.[3]

Not only have extra words been put into Vespasian's mouth but those Suetonius gave him have been distorted to accord with the universal preconception of what the passage is about. The diminutive *plebecula,* wherever else it appears, implies contempt. Cicero uses it in speaking of Rome's mass of wretched starvelings (*misera ac ieiuna plebecula, ad Att.* 1.16.11), Horace of Rome's low-minded clods who at recitals holler for the performing bears and the boxers (*Epist.* 2.1.186), Persius of a mob that a clever leader manipulates like sheep (4.6). It is only here, we are assured, that it needs must have a different sense, that it is "used by Vespasian in a merely pitying way";[4] hence the universal rendering of it as "the poor," "my poor commons," *aut sim.*[5]

That Vespasian's words have to be expanded and distorted this way has given scant pause to those who quote them as a classic instance of the suppressing of a laborsaving device to protect jobs. Some go even further. They use them as evidence that Rome's emperors, like governments today, may "have undertaken public works with a view to providing occupation for the needy."[6] To be sure, the emperors are not the only political leaders who have been credited with doing this: historians have attributed similar action to the Greek tyrants, Pericles, the Gracchi, and others.[7] A recent book has examined all these cases in detail, and the author, Gabriella Bodei Giglioni, demonstrates that there is no convincing evidence for any of them, that what chiefly sparked public works in antiquity was the availability of funds; concern for social welfare, if present at all, was secondary.[8] Yet even she believes that Vespasian must be considered the rare exception, that his retort to the engineer clearly indicated he had in mind public works as a way of combating unemployment.[9]

Only one writer, the social and economic historian M. I. Finley, has been aware that there are difficulties in casting Vespasian—or any Roman emperor for that matter—in the role of saver or creator of jobs. "I have never been able to understand this story," is his comment on our passage, "the emperors fed the populace at Rome with bread and circuses, not with jobs."[10] The fact of the matter is that the emperors had few jobs to offer, and certainly very few for the unskilled. The government's white-collar work, as we need no reminding, was in the hands of imperial slaves and ex-slaves. Its skilled blue-collar work was done in part by small independent artisans, but also in good part by slaves, while its unskilled was done totally by slaves.[11] The officials in charge of public works would let out contracts to a multitude of individual artisans and entrepreneurs. The stonecutting, bricklaying, carpentry, and the like, which required skilled labor, went either to artisans who perhaps worked alone but usually with slave assistants, or to entrepreneurs who would either subcontract what they undertook to free or slave craftsmen or use their own slave craftsmen.[12] Clearing, digging, hauling, and the like, which required no skill, went to entrepreneurs who operated with gangs of slaves. The slaves used by the artisans and entrepreneurs might be slaves they owned, or slaves they rented from professional suppliers, or a combination of both.[13]

Thus the transport of columns to the Capitolium would have been carried out by a work force of slaves either belonging to, or hired by, whoever had bid in the contract. Had Vespasian adopted some laborsaving device, it would not have affected the welfare of the plebs in the slightest but merely reduced the income of a number of entrepreneurs in the heavy transport business or in the business of renting out slaves. And Vespasian would hardly have referred to the likes of these as the *plebecula*—or worried about their starving.

Some who have dealt with our passage solve the puzzle by arguing that free workers were involved. We know that in agriculture, which at harvest time and other occasions had a seasonal need for extra hands, it was standard practice to hire casual free labor.[14] If the same were true of the building trade, then we would expect to find some free men at work on the Capitolium, and these would be the people whose welfare Vespasian had at heart. Those who adopt this argument cite as authority for the statement that casual free labor was common in the building trade the writings of P. Brunt.[15] What Brunt offers,[16] however, hardly deserves such confidence.

Brunt has but two ancient references to present as evidence. One is our passage—hence citing him to prove that Vespasian had free labor in mind simply produces a circular line of reasoning. The other is a passage from a letter of Cicero to Atticus (14.3.1) in which he mentions that the *structores* working on his villa at Tusculum went off *ad frumentum*. Brunt takes this to mean that Cicero's builders went off to collect their grain dole, and, if they were recipients of a grain dole, they must have been free. But Brunt is alone in taking *ad frumentum* in this sense: all others take it as meaning that the men went off to buy food or to pick up a few days' wages helping out as farm hands,[17] and this tells us nothing at all about their status.[18] And even if they were free, how do we know they were casual labor? They could well be the craftsmen who undertook the contracts for the work.

To buttress his scanty ancient evidence, Brunt tries to marshal support from other quarters. He cites the conjecture[19] that the distress Tiberius Gracchus sought to alleviate was exacerbated by unemployment consequent upon the completion of the Marcian aqueduct, unemployment of presumably free workers since Tiberius would hardly bother about slaves; however, that there was such unemployment is but a conjecture, and conjectures are not proof. He cites figures from Rome of the sixteenth century and Paris of the eighteenth to point up how large was the work force in the building trades at that time; this tells us absolutely nothing about Rome of the first century. The argument on which he places most emphasis is how wasteful, how uneconomic, it would have been for building contractors, whose work was sporadic, to use slaves: free labor could be hired and fired as needed, whereas slaves had to be maintained all year round, work or no work. He

120

overlooks the fact that slave labor did not have to be maintained all year round any more than free: as mentioned earlier, artisans and entrepreneurs did not necessarily own all the slaves they employed, they could rent any number they wanted for any length of time they wanted.

There is, then, no convincing evidence that Vespasian had free labor in mind.[20] Are we to admit with Finley that the point of the story eludes us? Or can we find a point which squares with what we know about labor in the ancient world?

The crux of the matter lies in the words *praemium pro commento*. This is without exception taken to mean that the emperor gave the *mechanicus* a reward for his "device" or "invention."[21] Some even specify "laborsaving device" *aut sim.*,[22] while R. Forbes, author of a shelfful of books on ancient technology, boldly assumes it was a "water-driven hoist," although there is no evidence whatsoever for that particular apparatus earlier than the sixteenth century.[23] But the word *mechanicus* in this period was used of an ordinary technical expert and not an inventor.[24] Even more important, *commentum* can mean "plan" or "project" just as well as "device" or "invention." Let us reexamine what Suetonius says with these two points in mind.

We happen to know that, when Vespasian started the rebuilding of the Capitolium, he tried to get the clearing of the ground, a job involving merely muscle, done for nothing: he shouldered the first load of soil himself by way of encouraging others to follow suit (Dio Cassius 65 [66].10.2); the attempt failed, and he willy-nilly had to pay for this part of the work, presumably by hiring a gang of slaves. The hauling of columns was another part that required muscle alone. If force of example could not get people to contribute their labor, were there not other, stronger, forms of pressure? Let us assume that one of the technicians employed on the project came to the emperor not with an invention but with a plan—the simple but revolutionary suggestion that he be allowed to recruit a work party from the plebs, using the dole as a *quid pro quo*. Behind such a plan would be the force of tradition, for the Capitolium had originally been built by the compulsory labor of the plebs (Livy 1.56.1) and people had not forgotten this (cf. Cicero, *Verr.* 5.19.48). The expense would truly be minimal, just the cost of equipment—blocks and tackles and rollers—and the salaries of the foremen to direct the work.

121

In the nature of the case, the recruits would come from the *plebecula,* the element of the population who lived from hand to mouth and would quickly feel the loss of their handouts. Vespasian's answer follows easily and naturally: "Let me feed them," he says, i.e., continue to give them their dole instead of making them earn it by the sweat of their brow.

We must remember that Suetonius tells us only that a technician offered an emperor who we know was eager to cut expenses a way of doing so, and that the emperor, though considering the way imaginative enough to merit a handsome reward, did not put it into execution.[25] What I have suggested fits both the facts of the story and the historical context far better than the assumption of a laborsaving device:[26] it makes Vespasian's refusal derive not from a concern, well-nigh unparalleled in ancient history,[27] for saving jobs but from the reluctance shown by all Roman political leaders to tamper with what was hallowed by custom. Even if I am wrong, as I well may be, I have at least demonstrated that there are other possible explanations for the anecdote than the one hitherto given. So, let us cease citing it as evidence for the suppression of laborsaving inventions, for the use of public works to alleviate unemployment, for the use of free labor in the building trade. It need have nothing to do with the first and second, and may well be evidence for just the opposite of the third.[28]

Addendum

P. A. Brunt devotes a long article, "Free Labour and Public Works at Rome," *JRS* 80 (1980) 81–100, to refuting the views concerning Suetonius, *Vesp.* 18 that I offered above.

I had argued that Brunt's evidence for the widespread use of free labor at Rome was slim, consisting merely of a passage of doubtful relevance from one of Cicero's letters, some conjecture about Tiberius Gracchus' motives, an analogy with the size of the building trades in Rome of the sixteenth century and Paris of the eighteenth, and the passage in question from Suetonius. His aim in this response is to reinforce his position, to demonstrate conclusively the use of free labor at Rome and, by thus invalidating the interpretation I suggested for the passage, retain it as evidence for free labor.

Brunt opens by acknowledging the justice of my doubts about the passage from Cicero; "I therefore withdraw it from the debate," he concedes (81). So far as the analogy with later ages is concerned, he considers my "scepticism about the relevance . . . simply astonishing" (92). I do not for a moment deny the usefulness of the analogy in throwing light on the number of those employed in the building trade. The question we are dealing with, however, is not the number of men employed but whether they were free or slave, and on that score I repeat: Rome of the sixteenth century and Paris of the eighteenth tell us nothing about Rome of the first.

Thus the crux of the matter is Suetonius, *Vesp.* 18.[29]

Brunt opens (82) his refutation—formally, as Point No. 1—by stating that if, as I suggested, the *mechanicus* had advised the conscripting of recipients of the dole to haul the columns up to the Capitolium, there would have to be some method of selection. Then—Point No. 2—this would have to be carried out by authorities with the power of coercion.

The answer to both points is: absolutely right.

Then—Point No. 3—forced labor, although certainly attested within Rome in early days and in areas outside in later, is never attested in Rome during the late Republic or Principate. Again the answer is: absolutely right—and this could well have been the reason why Vespasian rejected the idea.

Then, Point No. 4, "a *mechanicus* was not of rank and station to give the emperor advice of the type suggested by Casson," which point is followed (82–83) by a presentation of what was the professional and social standing of *mechanici*. As it happens, a little later (90) Brunt himself refers to a case in which an "*operarius* actually attained the ear of an emperor (Severus)." If an *operarius* was able to get the ear of a Severus, a *mechanicus* could get the ear of a Vespasian—even as some unnamed individual who chanced to have invented an unbreakable form of glass was able to get the ear of a Tiberius (Pliny, *N.H.* 36.195; Petronius 51; Dio Cassius 51.21.7). Why are we to think that the *mechanicus* proffered his suggestion through, as it were, the channels of standard operating procedure? Nothing in Suetonius' words makes this necessary—particularly if the anecdote is *ben trovato* rather than *vero*.

The heart of Brunt's article is given over to two sections on "The Administration of Public Works at Rome in the Principate" (84–88) and "The Hiring of Labour" (83–93). They are clear, detailed, and most useful treatments of the topics. But, as Brunt frankly confesses at the end (93): "All this does not indeed prove that casual labour was free labour."

Finally, in a series of sections titled "The Necessity for Employing Free Labour at Rome" (93–94), "The Availability of Free Labour" (94–96), and "Public Works and Social Policy" (96–98), Brunt comes to his basic argument: how else was Rome's free poor able to keep body and soul together save by hiring out as casual labor?

Actually he himself supplies a good part of the answer. He quotes (95) Keith Hopkins' suggestion of a "fantastic fragmentation of services and retail sales"—quotes it in order to insist upon its inapplicability because of "the size of slave holdings in the great urban households." What did such slave holdings have to do with retail sales? In Rome today every quarter has its open-air market with rows and rows of collapsible wooden stalls, each run by an individual or a family, often a husband and wife team, selling the same kinds of merchandise. A small market will have half a dozen, a large market dozens, of stalls cheek by jowl, all offering precisely the same fruits or precisely the same vegetables or precisely the same seafood, cheese, spiced meats, and so on—perfect examples of Hopkins' "fantastic fragmentation . . . of retail sales." And this is in contemporary Rome where, just around the corner, are supermarkets selling the identical fruits, vegetables, seafood, cheese, meats. Ancient Rome must have teemed with such markets; they must have provided a living for masses of her free poor, even as they do today.

And additional masses of the free poor must have made their living as humble artisans—not the artisans who worked on the temples, theatres, and other great monuments that the government put up but those who serviced the neighborhoods where they lived—the carpenter who built a new door for a house down the street or the mason who repaired one of its walls or the lime-burner who furnished the cement, etc.

Brunt conceives of there being a sizeable pool of unskilled labor made up of the peasants who had emigrated to Rome, men who "had no training in any urban craft" (96) and would contribute to forming "a great mass . . . in the city who were only fit for unskilled and casual labour." When peasants abandoned their farms they abandoned as well the villages where they lived (cf. K. White, *Roman Farming* [London 1970] 345); with no customers to serve, the local craftsmen—the harnessmaker, wheelwright, carpenter, miller, baker, and the like—must have gone along with them, must have joined the influx to Rome. These swelled the ranks, not of the unskilled, but of the humble artisans. Indeed, some of the peasants themselves must have joined these ranks too; we should not conclude that, just because a man spends most of his day tilling the soil, this is all he can do, that he is incapable of building his own fences, mending the straps of his harness when they snap, repairing parts of his ploughshare when they break, and so on.

As a matter of fact, much of Brunt's discussion of casual[30] free labor concerns only the skilled. In the section devoted to "Public Works and Social Policy" he argues that the building program at Rome must have had some social purpose, that the supplying of jobs must have been somewhat involved. I have pointed out how dubious such an argument is, but no matter.[31] In the examples he cites the labor involved is that of craftsmen, of *technitai* or *cheirotechnai* (see his n. 89 on p. 97). Yet in Suetonius, *Vesp.* 18 we are dealing with a task that calls not for craft but for brute force, the brute force needed to haul massive columns. I cannot prove beyond a shadow of doubt that the hauling was done by slaves but, in the context of what we know about such work in ancient times, this is certainly the most likely hypothesis.[32] And all of Brunt's twenty packed pages have not rendered that hypothesis a whit less likely.

Notes

1. Suetonius, *Vesp.* 8.

2. Suetonius' manuscripts read *plebiculam,* which, it is generally assumed, is just a writing for *plebeculam;* cf. C. *Suetoni Tranquilli de Vita Caesarum,* ed. G. Mooney (London 1930) note ad. loc.

3. R. Graves in the Penguin translation (1957), repeated by M. Grant in *The World of Rome* (London 1960) 75; M. Hadas, *Imperial Rome* (Time-Life 1965) 63; R. Forbes in C. Singer, *History of Technology* ii (Oxford 1956) 601. F. Bourne paraphrased it as "his remarks on the necessity of employing free labor on public works" (*The Public Works of the Julio-Claudians and Flavians* [Princeton 1946] 55).

4. Mooney (see above, n. 2).

5. "The poor commons" was used by Philemon Holland in 1606. J. Rolfe in the Loeb (1914) translates "my poor commons," R. Graves in the Penguin (1957) "the working classes." Similarly in other languages: "le pauvre peuple," H. Ailloud in the Budé (1932); "dem armen Volke," *Sueton, Die zwölf Cäsaren,* Adolf Stahr (Munich 1912), and the same in André Lambert's *Gaius Suetonius Tranquillus, Leben der Caesaren* (Zurich 1955); "alla minuta plebe," *Caio Suetonio Tranquillo, Le vite di dodici Cesari,* Guido Vitali (Bologna 1956).

6. T. Frank, *ESAR* v (Baltimore 1940) 54 and cf. 68, 236; H. Loane, *Industry and Commerce of the City of Rome* (Baltimore 1938) 85.

7. G. Glotz, *Histoire grecque i* (Paris 1938) 247 (tyrants); G. de Sanctis, *Pericle* (Milan 1944) 219; H. Wade-Gery in *JHS* 52 (1932) 207 (Pericles); H. Boren, *The Gracchi* (New York 1968) 101 (Gaius Gracchus); G. Ferrero, *The Greatness and Decline of Rome* iv (London 1908) 61 (Agrippa), 164 (Augustus).

8. Gabriella Bodei Giglioni, *Lavori pubblici e occupazione nell' antichità classica* (Bologna 1974), esp. 221–225.

9. Bodei Giglioni 180–84. Since she wrote, M. Robertson has come forth with yet another presumed instance of unemployment relief (*A History of Greek Art* [Cambridge 1975] 363–64), namely that around or shortly after 433 B.C.— this would mean Pericles was responsible—action was taken to help the stonecutters who must have been thrown out of work when the frieze and pedimental sculptures of the Parthenon were completed. The action, he suggests, was the repeal of a law controlling funeral expenditures, thereby permitting tombstones bearing reliefs. However, that such a law was ever on the books is pure inference and no more, inference from the disappearance of such tombstones at the end of the 6th c. B.C. and their reappearance at this time. They may have reappeared simply because the skilled labor to do them now was readily available.

10. M. Finley, "Technical Innovation and Economic Progress in the Ancient World," *Economic History Review,* 2nd ser. 18.1 (1965) 29–45 (reprinted in M. Finley, *Economy and Society in Ancient Greece,* ed. B. Shaw and R. Saller [London 1981] 176–95) at 43.

11. Gummerus, "Industrie und Handel," *RE* 1506–1507 (1916); M. Maxey, *Occupations of the Lower Classes in Roman Society* (Chicago 1938) 1–8, 87–89; M. Finley, *The Ancient Economy* (Berkeley 1973) 73–75; Loane (above, n. 6) 79–82.

12. Loane (above, n. 6) 83–84; Finley (above, n. 11) 74–75. Gangs of imperial slaves may have been used, but certainly not exclusively, as Loane (79–80) rightly reminds us. Vespasian tried to get volunteers to clear the ground for the rebuilding of the Capitolium (Dio Cassius 65 [66].10.2); the clear implication is that the government normally had to hire the labor for such work.

13. Gummerus (above, n. 11) 1506; Maxey (above, n. 11) 3. The evidence, as in the case of contracting for public works (cf. Finley [above, n. 11] 192), is richer from Greece, where we hear of men like Nicias, who had 1,000 slaves out on lease to concessionaires of Athen's silver mines, or Callias' son Hipponicus who had 600; cf. above, p. 41 and below, n. 15 ad fin.

14. Gummerus (above, n. 11) 1507; Finley (above, n. 11) 73; K. White, *Roman Farming* (London 1970) 335, 367–68.

15. H. Pleket, "Technology and Society in the Graeco-Roman World," *Acta Historiae Neerlandica* 2 (1967) 1–25 at 14, 25, and reaffirmed in *Talanta* 5 (1973) 24: S. Treggiari, *Roman Freedmen during the Late Republic* (Oxford 1969) 90; Bodei Giglioni (above, n. 8) 121. Finley subsequently changed his mind, for, in his *Ancient Economy,* published eight years later (cf. above, n. 11), he too takes it that Vespasian had casual free labor in mind. The only documentation he offers (191, n. 28) is a reference to the place in Athens where labor "shaped up," i.e., where day workers gathered to offer them-

selves for hire. But many, perhaps most, of these were slaves, owned by masters who derived an income from hiring them out; see above, p. 42.

16. "The Roman Mob," *Past and Present* 35 (1966) 3–27, at 9, 14–16, reaffirmed in *Italian Manpower 225 B.C.–A.D.* 14 (Oxford 1971) 381.

17. "My workmen . . . who went to purchase corn," W. Heberden in the Bohn translation (1870); similarly E. Shuckburgh (1909), D. Shackleton Bailey (1967), C. Wieland (1818: "unsere Werksleute, die, Getreide zu holen, . . . gegangen"), Nisard edition (1843: "les ouvriers qui étaient allés à Rome chercher du blé"). E. Winstedt in the Loeb (1918) translates, "who had gone off harvesting," and this is the sense J. Crook gives it (*Law and Life of Rome* [London 1967] 195), but the letter is dated 9 April and that is at least a month too early for the harvest (cf. White [above, n. 14] 483).

18. The contractor for work on one of Quintus Cicero's villas, for example, was a slave (*ad Quint. Frat.* 3.1.2).

19. H. Boren, "The Urban Side of the Gracchan Economic Crisis," *American Historical Review* 63 (1957–58) 890–902 at 895–98.

20. Other evidence that has been cited as proof of the use of free labor in public works are two inscriptions from the vicinity of ancient Ateste (Este today). One, found *in situ* on the banks of the Adige and published by F. Barnabei (*Notizie degli scavi* 1915 137–41 = *AEpigr* 1916.60), starts with the heading *decuria*, which here must mean work party (cf. Vitruvius 7.1.3), and under it lists the party's director, two *curatores*, one *pig(nerator?)*, the total (98) of men in the party, the number of feet (43) assigned to each, and the grand total (4214) of feet (*Decuria Q. Arrunti Surai, cur[atoribus] Q. Arruntio C. Sabello, pig[neratore?] T. Arrio, sum[ma] h[ominum] XCIIX, in sing[ulos] hom[ines] op[eris] p[edes] XLIII, s[umma] p[edum] ∞IƆƆ CCXIV*). The other, long known (*CIL* v.2603) but misunderstood, is identical in layout and wording (Barnabei 141–44). Barnabei plausibly concluded that they dealt with dike work along the river; he most implausibly concluded that "there cannot be the slightest doubt" (p. 140) that the party consisted of soldiers or veterans planted at Ateste by Augustus after Actium. Rostovtzeff not only accepted this but went even further (*Social and Economic History of the Roman Empire* [Oxford 1926] 498 = [1957²] 554–55): he took the inscriptions as proof of "a large use of free labor in public works." Barnabei's and Rostovtzeff's conclusions have been uncritically repeated: cf. G. Cozzo, *Ingegneria romana* (Rome 1928) 70; F. de Robertis, *La organizzazione e la tecnica produttiva* (Naples 1946) 140; Crook (above, n. 17) 195. There is evidence that Augustus settled a colony of veterans of Actium at Ateste (Mommsen in *CIL* v, p. 240) but none whatsoever to connect these bald, undated inscriptions with them. In fact, if the resolution *pig(nerator)* is correct, a forfeit for proper performance was involved, which is the sort of thing required of a private contractor, not of a work party of army personnel

127

operating under government orders. And, if private contractors did the work, the labor they employed could well have been slave.

21. "Device" was used by Philemon Holland in 1606. J. Rolfe (Loeb 1914) translates "his invention," R. Graves (Penguin 1957) "a simple mechanical contrivance." Similarly in other languages: "son invention," H. Ailloud (Budé 1932); "seine Erfindung," Stahr and Lambert; and "l'invenzione," Vitali (above, n. 5). Cf. Loane (above, n. 6) 85 and Frank (above, n. 6) 236 ("hoisting machine").

22. Grant (above, n. 3) 75; A Burford, *Craftsmen in Greek and Roman Society* (London 1972) 237; Brunt (above, n. 16) 16; cf. Pleket (above, n. 15) 10, 15.

23. Forbes (above, n. 3) 601; cf. L. White, Jr., *Mediaeval Technology and Social Change* (Oxford 1962) 160–61.

24. Cf. *DarSag* s.v. "Mechanicus" 1663 (1904).

25. Suetonius probably did not know what the plan was or he would have given at least some indication: the *argumentum ex silentio* in this instance I think has force. In any event, details were irrelevant; what was relevant was that the engineer suggested something highly useful, a way to save money.

26. Neither the Greeks nor the Romans ever showed the slightest interest in replacing muscle with some other form of power. They simply did not think in such terms: cf. Finley (above, n. 10) 29–32 and especially 35–36, his discussion of the water mill. The invention of the water mill was, in the words of a ranking historian of technology, "the first mechanical application of inanimate power, . . . an event of prime significance" (Lynn White, Jr., "Cultural Climates and Technological Advance," *Viator* 2 [1971] 171–201 at 178), yet, though certainly known to the Romans by the 1st c. B.C., and perhaps centuries earlier (cf. J. Ward-Perkins in *Papers of the British School at Rome* 29 [1961] 50–51), it saw no general use until the 5th or 6th c. A.D., if then. It came into its own only after the 10th, while the windmill was even later; cf. White (above, n. 23) 79–88, esp. 83. It was the Middle Ages that first saw "the invention of invention" (White, "Cultural Climates" 172). See chap. 6 for a full discussion of the subject.

27. I qualify with "well-nigh" since there is one indisputable case, Josephus, *A.J.* 20.219–22. Bodei Giglioni ([above, n. 8] 171–84) classifies it and our passage as exceptional instances, both reflecting, she claims, highly special circumstances, unemployment crises resulting from the sudden interruption of works in progress. Vespasian's case, as we have just seen, may well have nothing at all to do with unemployment. The passage from Josephus does indeed reflect exceptional circumstances, but Bodei Giglioni is unaware of how exceptional. In 20/19 B.C. Herod the Great had begun the rebuilding of the Second Temple at Jerusalem, and it reached completion sometime between A.D. 62

and 64. At this time, the *demos,* Josephus reports, "noting that over 18,000 craftsmen had been idled and would be without means of earning money, for they derived their living from working on the temple," urged Agrippa II, who had been entrusted by Claudius with the care of the temple (*A.J.* 20.222), to employ them for rebuilding a portico; he rejected that suggestion but put them to work paving the city's streets. The completion of the temple could hardly have been a "sudden interruption"; the end must have been in sight for years. What was exceptional, totally so, was the nature of the labor force. We need not accept Josephus' figure of 18,000. In an earlier passage (*A.J.* 15.390) he reveals that Herod, when he started the project, recruited only 11,000; as the work wound down, the number must have decreased rather than increased. More important, of Herod's 11,000, 1,000 were priests specially trained as craftsmen presumably for work in the consecrated areas where laymen were not allowed to enter. These men, or rather their descendents, must have been on the job to the end, putting the finishing touches on the interior. It is understandable that the Jewish community would feel a special responsibility towards them and that Agrippa would share it; cf. J. Jeremias, *Jerusalem in the Time of Jesus* (London 1969) 13, 22, 101.

28. My thanks go to my good friend Dr. Milton Scofield, a keen student of history, for the initial suggestion of the idea I have presented.

29. Brunt speaks (83) of Vespasian wishing "to maintain his *plebs.*" All we are told is that Vespasian wished "to be allowed to feed the mob," words I take to mean that part of the *plebs* which lived from hand to mouth.

30. That much of Rome's labor had to be casual—e.g., seasonal, as in the building trades—was one of Brunt's arguments for the widespread use of free labor: only free labor, he claimed, which could be hired and fired at will, was economically feasible. I pointed out that it was just as possible to hire and fire slave labor, by renting slaves from a dealer instead of owning them. Brunt's answer (94) is that such slave labor would have been prohibitively costly, since dealers would have had to add to the charges extra for the upkeep of the slaves during the slow season when there was presumably nothing for them to do. "What work," he asks, "are they engaged on, primarily in the winter months? I can think of none" (94). Yet one page earlier he had mentioned an apt form of work and a very important form to boot—the porterage of grain, which went on all year. And we can add the barging of grain as well, and very likely a certain amount of barging and porterage of wine and oil and building stone.

31. He includes as evidence (97) Cicero, *De Offic.* 2.52–60, in which "Cicero clearly implies" that great builders, though they talk of honoring the gods or embellishing the city, were in fact also assisting the needy. I see no such implication in the passage, certainly no clear implication.

32. It is clearly Rickman's view of such work; see Brunt 93.

6.
Energy and Technology in the Ancient World

Energy is the basis of modern civilization. It dominates the headlines, makes and breaks the economy of nations, determines their foreign policy. Yet it is a relative newcomer to history. It began to occupy men's minds only during the Middle Ages, not before. Egypt, Assyria, and Persia all fashioned their empires without it; Greece achieved her glory and Rome her splendor without it. Very possibly the glory and the splendor would have been still greater had Greeks and Romans turned their attention to utilizing sources of power other than the muscles of man or beast. For some reason they did not.

They did not, even though they were fully acquainted with a number of easily exploitable forms of energy. As far back as 3000 B.C., the Egyptians had learned to harness the force of the wind to drive their boats up and down the Nile. But neither they nor anyone else ever went further than boats: as we shall see shortly, the earliest windmills date from the seventh century A.D. or even later. By the first century B.C. the Greeks and Romans had learned to use the flow of water to turn mills, but all over the world grain continued to be ground slowly and laboriously by hand or animal. They were even aware of more sophisticated sources of power, such as compressed air, hot air, and steam. A Greek engineer named Ctesibius, who lived during the third century B.C. in the city of Alexandria—the center at the time of scholarly and scientific research—produced a hydraulic organ whose power was furnished by a column of water supported on a cushion of air. He designed a clock driven by water: flowing into a bowl at a fixed rate, it steadily raised a float topped by a figure whose hand pointed to lines representing hours engraved on a cylinder; the cylinder itself was made to rotate by the upward movement of the float. Another Greek engineer, named Hero, who also worked at Alexandria, though at a later time than Ctesibius, perhaps the first century A.D., describes certain inventions for use in temples which, by exploiting the expansive property of hot air, were able to arouse wonderment and awe among the congregations. One consisted of a pipe and some figures mounted on a disk; when the altar fire was lit, the hot air from it, passing through the pipe, caused the disk to revolve and the figures to appear to dance. In a second device, the hot air made the doors of a shrine open and shut. In a third, an altar flanked by two figures holding wine vessels and surmounted by a bronze serpent, the hot air produced a flow of wine from the vessels and a hiss from the serpent. Yet another is the earliest example on record of a steam engine: a hollow ball was mounted between two brackets made fast to the lid of a pot filled with boiling water; one of the brackets was also hollow, and the steam passing through it into the ball was vented in such a way that the ball was made to rotate (fig. 3). Hero even describes a windmill, a miniature version for providing the current of air required to power a small and simple type of organ. He includes any number of gadgets worked by means of levers and weights, among them the first known coin-operated machine: when a five-drachma piece was dropped through a slot in the cover of a sacrificial vessel filled with holy water, it triggered by means of a Rube Goldberg contraption a spurt from a spout on the side (fig. 4).[1]

All these devices were no more than ingenious gadgets. Neither Hero nor any other ancient technician ever took the crucial step of elevating them into machinery that could carry out a useful job. Admittedly there was a lot of ground to cover between a steam toy that spun a ball and an engine that could replace muscle in a significant way. The designer would have had to conceive of combining a boiler powerful enough to with-

131

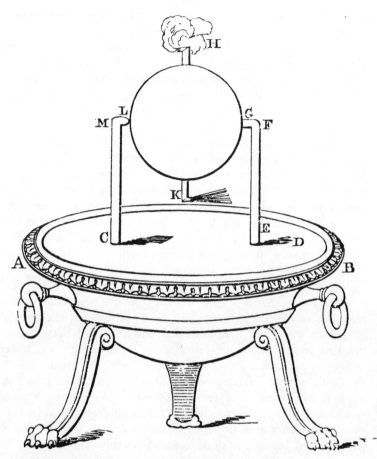

Fig. 3. Reconstruction of Hero's Steam Engine. When the water in the caldron (*A–B*) reaches the boiling point, steam passes from it through the pipe on the right (*E–F*) into the hollow ball mounted on pivots (*L, G*). The steam then passes out through the right-angled tubes (*K, H*) mounted opposite each other, thereby causing the ball to rotate. Reproduced from *Hero's Treatise on Pneumatics*, trans. B. Woodcroft (London 1851).

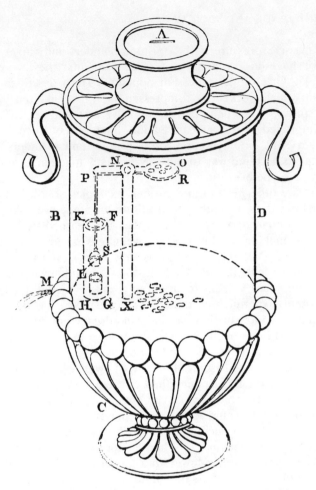

Fig. 4. Reconstruction of Hero's Coin-Operated Machine. A coin dropped into a slot (*A*) in the cover of a container (*B–D*) partly filled with water falls onto a plate (*R*) at one end of a short beam (*N*). The coin's weight causes the plate to sink, thereby tilting the beam and causing its other end (*P*) to rise. From that end there descends through a cylinder (*K–F* marks its top, *H–G* its bottom) a line whose end is tied to a lid (*S*). This lid caps a tube (*L*) which leads to a spout (*M*). The raising of the end marked *P* lifts the lid, thereby uncovering the mouth of the tube and allowing water to flow out through the spout. When the coin slips off the plate marked *R*, the beam resumes its horizontal position, and the end marked *P*, sinking back to its original place, allows the lid to stopper the tube and cut off the flow of water. Reproduced from Woodcroft.

133

stand massive pressure with a piston, cylinder, and valves. He did not have to invent any of these elements; they were all available. One of the pieces of apparatus Hero describes is a fountain which worked by compressed air, rather like our insecticide sprays; it was equipped with a valve that could easily have been improved to suit a steam engine. Examples of force pumps have survived employing powerful pistons and cylinders. All that had to be done was to put the elements together in proper fashion. No one ever did.[2]

There are other, even more curious, examples of how little the ancients cared about finding a substitute for manpower. As indicated a moment ago, by 3000 B.C. they had learned to fit boats with sails, making wind instead of sweating oarsmen provide the motive force. Yet this is as far as they went—even though by Hero's day at least the windmill must have been known, since he used a miniature version to drive an organ. Why did not he or some other experimenter think of simply increasing the size? Why did the introduction of the wind-driven grinding mill, a technological boon of the highest order, have to wait, as we shall see, for almost a thousand years more?

The most puzzling case of all is water power. By the end of the first century B.C., the Romans had efficient water mills. Of this there is no doubt whatsoever. The architect and engineer Vitruvius, who lived in Rome at that time, published a book on building design and construction in which he included a section on various types of machinery. When he comes to treating devices for raising water from a lower to a higher level, he describes a wheel fitted with an endless line of buckets that was driven by the flow of water—in other words, a waterwheel. He then adds that waterwheels are used for turning not only lines of buckets but also millstones—this offhand remark is all he has to say about what was to be one of man's most revolutionary labor-saving inventions! A poet who was Vitruvius' contemporary displayed at least an awareness of its promise. He wrote some lines of fancy verse about the lucky break slave girls assigned to grinding grain had gotten: from now on they can sleep late, since "water nymphs" will do their job for them by "leaping onto the top of the wheel and turning the axle."[3]

In short, the Romans had at their disposal a machine which in a later age was to serve people the length and breadth of Europe.

A water mill can do effortlessly in three minutes what would take
a man or beast an hour of hard labor; it should have swept over
the Roman world. It did nothing of the sort. Here and there
water mills certainly were to be found—after all, both Vitruvius
and the poet had seen them—but only here and there. The vast
majority of households, the vast majority of baking establish-
ments, went on grinding by hand or by man- or beast-turned mills
as they had for thousands of years, and they continued to do so
right up to the end of the Roman Empire. Eventually water mills
gained some recognition, but only in a limited way. Archaeologists have come upon the remains of a complex of water mills at
Arles in southern France dating somewhat after A.D. 300; it was
there to produce flour for the army, not the general public. The
general public had to wait yet another century or so and then
benefited only in a handful of important centers. Rome, for example, by the fifth century had a number of mills driven by the
flow in her great aqueducts. In A.D. 537 during one of the
struggles between Rome and the barbarian invaders, an army of
Goths surrounded the city and took the shrewd step of plugging
the aqueducts. This produced hunger as well as thirst, since it not
only cut the water supply but brought the mills to a halt. For
once in ancient times, necessity mothered an invention: the Romans responded to the crisis by creating floating mills, mills set
on boats anchored in the Tiber. The new type, obviously extremely useful wherever appropriate rivers existed, sparked no
more interest in the country at large than the old. A time would
come when floating mills lay at anchor up and down the Po River
and standard mills were turning up and down Italy, but that was
far in the future.[4]

It is strange how the ancients resisted any device that would
save them the sweat of their brows. In the first century A.D.,
someone designed a mechanical reaper. It was no complicated
affair, just an oversize comb-like set of blades mounted horizontally on a cart; shoved along by a donkey or mule, it would neatly
shear off the heads of grain, leaving the stalks. This was no
obscure invention born to blush unseen in some remote corner.
Pliny the Elder, the author of Rome's standard encyclopedia,
mentions it, and pictures of it were carved in relief on stone
monuments, a number of which have survived. To be sure, it
could only operate on level ground and appeal to farmers willing

135

to forgo the straw from the stalks. But there must have been any
number of these, and it certainly offered them a quicker and
easier way of reaping than trudging up and down slashing with a
sickle. No matter; it never saw use outside of a small section of
Gaul, roughly between where Reims and Trier are today, and
even there for no very long time.[5]

Rome declined and fell; there followed that gloomy period we
call the Dark Ages; and then, about A.D. 1000, the lights went on
again with the opening of the Middle Ages. And just about this
time, there was an abrupt about-face in men's attitude toward
using sources of energy other than muscle. By A.D. 1200 no community in Europe was without its water mill. Moreover, these
were doing far more than grinding grain: they were driving trip-
hammers and saws, operating the bellows of furnaces, turning
grindstones for finishing weapons and polishing armor, crushing
stones and other materials, reducing pigments for paint or pulp
for paper or mash for beer, performing some of the drudge-work
in tanning and fulling. Records reveal that as early as 1086 there
were no less than 5,624 mills in England alone, serving some
three thousand communities. By this time mills were to be found
not only along streams and afloat on rivers but along estuaries,
working through the action of the tides. Tide mills were not too
efficient, they had their drawbacks, but they multiplied neverthe-
less; obviously people, if they could not have what their luckier
riverside neighbors enjoyed, insisted on at least the next best
thing. The day of energy, in our sense, had dawned.[6]
  The rise of the windmill was even more dramatic than of the
water mill. The ancients, as we have seen, may have used water
power to a limited degree, but they totally scorned wind power
except for driving boats. Around the seventh century A.D. or so,
windmills are attested in Asia. By about 1150 they began to make
their appearance in northern Europe. By 1200 they dotted all of
Europe's great northern plains. They had one important advantage over water mills: in the north these stopped during the
winter when rivers froze over; windmills kept going all year
round. Eventually they made their way to the south of Europe as
well—although, for one reason or another, there were here and

there pockets of resistance to them, such as La Mancha in Spain; even at the end of the sixteenth century, they were still enough of a novelty there to astonish the likes of Don Quixote.

In short, so wide and effective was the technological surge that, to quote Lynn White, our ranking historian of technology, "by 1492 . . . Europe had developed an agricultural base, an industrial capacity, a superiority in arms, and a skill in voyaging the ocean which enabled it to explore, conquer, loot and colonize all the rest of the globe during the next four centuries."[7] Rome, restrained by her technological sloth, for all her might had been able to explore, conquer, loot, and colonize no further than the Mediterranean and the western end of Europe.

Why? Why was it that the Middle Ages brought a sudden interest among men in saving the sweat of their brows? Why did this never occur among the ancients? Let us take the second question first.

It is said that the Greeks never exploited steam, that they never converted Hero's toy into a useful engine, because they did not have the materials or technology for steamfitting, for fashioning and joining tubing to take the pressure. True enough, but beside the point: they simply did not think in terms of using steam power for utilitarian purposes. It is said that they never exploited the water mill because the Mediterranean does not have the rivers that would provide the flow required. This is not only beside the point but not even true. The rivers were perfectly adequate for driving the mills that were there during the Middle Ages. Moreover, the Romans—and the Etruscans long before them—were expert at providing a flow where there was none. What mills the Romans eventually did put into operation, as often as not, were run by water from aqueducts.[8]

These and other similar specific explanations that have been offered do not get us very far. What about the broad generalizations?

There is a school of thought, whose ranks have been swelled by the unswerving adherence of most Marxist historians, which holds that slavery was the culprit: the economy of the ancients was based on slavery and, the argument runs, with slaves to do

137

the work there was no incentive to develop technology. "Their slaves were their machines," asserts Benjamin Farrington, author of a series of widely used handbooks on ancient science and technology, "and so long as they were cheap there was no need to try to supersede them. The supply of slave labor seems to have outlasted the heyday of ancient science." There is no denying that the Greek and Roman economy was based on slave labor, although the most important segment, agriculture, depended upon it only at certain times and in certain places. But one can emphatically deny that slave labor was always plentiful and cheap. Except for those moments in history when the end of a successful war dumped a load of captives on the market, it was neither. Translating ancient money amounts into modern equivalents is tricky, but it is safe to say that under normal circumstances unskilled slaves, such as the poor devils who would spend their lives turning a millstone, would cost at least the equivalent of one thousand dollars, more likely two thousand. And, once an owner bought his slaves, he had to feed and house them three hundred and sixty-five days a year, through sickness and through health, whether there was work for them or not. And, if they died, he had to write the cost off as a total loss (there was no such thing as insurance in ancient times). The argument that the ancients scorned water or wind power because slaves were so much cheaper will simply not stand up.[9]

Another school of thought lays the blame on the cheapness and plentifulness of labor in general, whether slave or free. "Labour was too cheap for much thought to be given to machinery," declares W. W. Tarn, one of the foremost historians of the Greek and Roman world. "Labour . . . was plentiful and cheap until the end of the third century [A.D.], precisely the period when the donkey-mills or slave-driven mills of Rome were gradually ousted by the water-mill," declares R. Forbes, author of the standard works in English on ancient technology. Both men are wrong. There rarely was a surplus of labor; as a matter of fact, all the signs, as we shall see in a moment, indicate just the opposite. And donkey- or slave-driven mills never were "gradually ousted by the water-mill," as Forbes asserts. The water mill, as pointed out above, made its appearance only in a handful of big cities and army supply centers; everywhere else people went on grinding their flour just the way their ancestors had.[10]

138

There is an anecdote that the adherents of this school often cite. Rome's Emperor Vespasian, who ruled from A.D. 69 to 79, was once approached, we are told, by an engineer who offered to haul big stone columns to the top of the Capitoline Hill for a very small charge; Vespasian gave him a handsome reward but refused his services on the grounds that he wanted "to be allowed to feed the mob." They assume that the story indicates an excess on the Roman labor market, a mass of unemployed whom the government supported by work projects. But "unemployment" and "work projects" are twentieth-century concepts; antiquity knew nothing of them. Ancient governments did not go about creating work to provide jobs. Certainly the emperors of Rome did not, even though they were faced with the chronic problem of maintaining the "mob," i.e., the thousands of poor Roman citizens who centuries earlier had drifted to the city and ever since led an idle existence. The emperors took care of them by means of the proverbial "bread and circuses," feeding them through public handouts of grain and keeping them content by entertaining them with free gladiatorial combats and horse races. In any case, these people were in no way part of the labor force. Manual labor, such as the handling of columns, was normally done by slaves, so the only ones who would have profited from Vespasian's rejection of the engineer's offer were not any theoretical unemployed but the owners of the teams of slaves who held the contracts for the hauling. Commentators on the story imagine that the engineer had in mind some power-lifting machinery, but this is pure fantasy. A more likely explanation is that he suggested to Vespasian something no emperor had ever thought of doing before—to entice some of the handout-receivers to put in a few days or a few weeks of work for pay. This would no doubt have cost Vespasian much less than the hire of teams of slaves; their owners, after all, had to charge enough to cover the cost of maintaining them all year round, work or no work, and of writing off the loss whenever any died or was injured. Vespasian, however, said no; he wanted to "be allowed to feed the mob," i.e., carry on the traditional policy of giving them handouts, not try any newfangled ideas of putting them to work.[11]

Another argument against those who blame the technological laggardness on a surplus of labor is that what clues we can gather point just the other way. A number of treatises on farming in

Italy, written between the second century B.C. and the first A.D., have survived. They make allusion to the difficulties farmers had because of the scarcity of hands. There were times when Egypt, one of the breadbaskets of the ancient world, suffered from countrywide shortages of labor. Indeed, it has been argued that a key factor inhibiting the internal growth of the empires that were established in the wake of Alexander the Great's conquests was the limited agricultural manpower available: it was never possible to increase the number of peasants beyond a certain figure, and, because of this, food production was never able to rise to levels that could support more or larger urban centers. Obviously the solution would have been the development of mechanical aids to relieve the peasant's backbreaking toil and increase his output. It was never done. Even when a mechanical aid existed, such as the reaper described above, it was not exploited.[12]

Michael Rostovtzeff, author of the definitive studies on the social and economic history of the ancient world, was well aware of the shortcomings of slavery or cheap free labor as an explanation of the Greeks' "slow technical progress and . . . restricted range of output." He argues that "the causes of these limitations are chiefly to be found, on the one hand in local production of manufactured goods and the arrest of the development of large industrial centres, and on the other in the low buying capacity and restricted number of customers."[13] This explanation simply puts us in a circle. Industrial centers could not develop because they could not be fed without increasing the production of food, and, as we have just seen, the fixed or even declining number of peasants prevented this. And without such industrial centers, the number of potential customers would inevitably be restricted and buying power low. Men did not break out of the circle until the Middle Ages. Why not in ancient times?

We cannot call upon mountains of statistics to help us with the answer, for there are no such from the ancient world. All we can do is go through whatever writings have survived, from agricultural treatises to lyric poetry, in search of anything that will throw light, no matter how feeble, on the problem. There is an anecdote told by Lucian, a satirist and lecturer of the second century A.D., that it is a good deal more to the point than the story about

Vespasian and the engineer. In an essay which purports to be autobiographical, Lucian recounts how he embarked upon his career. He had a dream, he informs us, in which two women struggled for possession of him, one mannish and dirty and unkempt and covered with stone dust, the other lovely and poised and well dressed. The first sought to entice him to become a sculptor, to achieve the greatness of Pheidias and Praxiteles, the other to turn to education and follow an intellectual career. If you become a sculptor, the lovely women warned him, "hunched over your work, your eyes and mind on the ground, low as low can be, you will never lift your head to think the thoughts of a true man or a free spirit." Lucian did not hesitate: he joyously embraced the life of the mind.

The prejudice against working with one's hands that we see in this story runs all through Greek history. Among the Greek gods, Apollo, god of music, or Ares, god of war, or Hermes, messenger of Zeus, are all gloriously handsome; Hephaestus, god of the forge, is ugly and lame, and when he hobbles about Olympus he makes the rest of the divine family break out into "unquenchable laughter," to quote Homer's phrase. The Greeks admired and respected the artisan's work; they neither admired nor respected the artisan. Socrates, who happened to be a stonemason by trade, was often to be found lounging around the workshops of his fellow craftsmen—but not his blue-blooded pupil Plato, scion of one of Athens' best families. In the Utopias he conjures up, Plato relegates craftsmen to the lowest rung of the social ladder. Xenophon, a fellow aristocrat, points out that in those Greek cities which pride themselves on their military reputation, citizens are not allowed to practice a craft. Aristotle, tutor to Alexander the Great, sniffily remarks that "the finest type of city will not make an artisan a citizen." One reason for the prejudice was that, from the very beginning, many artisans were slaves; one effect of the prejudice was to ensure that more and more of them would be. Throughout Greek history, the free and slave craftsman shared work, often laboring side by side. Records of the building of Greek temples and other structures have been preserved, and from them we can see that the stone blocks, the column drums, the sculptures, the scaffoldings, and all else were fashioned by free and slave masons and carpenters working together and being paid exactly the same wage; the only difference

141

was that the free man kept his, while the slave turned his over to a master. Work of the hands, no matter of what quality, whether the rough hacking of stone in a quarry or the delicate carving of a sculpture, was something that could be done by slaves, and in the eyes of the upper-class—the class to which without exception all ancient writers and intellectuals belonged—was not for them. Cicero, categorizing the pursuits that men follow, declares without qualification that "all craftsmen are engaged in a lowly art, for no workshop can have anything about it appropriate to a free man." They were all, as it were, sicklied o'er with the pale cast of slavery.[14]

A passage in one of Plutarch's lives makes it crystal clear why Ctesibius, Hero, and the other scientists of antiquity stopped at toys and gadgets and never went on to machines—except in that one field which all through history has had a special claim on men's faculties, the art of war. In his *Life of Marcellus,* the famed general who led the Roman forces during much of the Second Punic War, he describes the trouble Marcellus had in besieging the strongly fortified town of Syracuse. Before the invention of cannon, laying siege to any walled city was no easy job, but Marcellus was having particularly rough going because the king of Syracuse had entrusted the defense to antiquity's most renowned engineer, Archimedes. Archimedes devised fiendish catapults which hurled monstrous stones upon attacking troops, fiendish cranes with huge claws that fastened upon attacking ships and lifted them right out of the water, even a brobdingnagian burning glass that could set them on fire from a distance. After describing the formidable array, Plutarch remarks that Archimedes, though he had won universal acclaim for his military inventions,

> never wanted to leave behind a book on the subject but viewed the work of the engineer and every single art connected with everyday need as ignoble and fit only for an artisan. He devoted his ambition only to those studies in which beauty and subtlety are present uncontaminated by necessity.[15]

In a word, the intellectuals would have nothing to do with anything that had practical value, and the aristocrats, the members of the ruling classes, would have nothing to do with the grimy, sweaty folk who built their houses, made their shoes,

142

fashioned their armor, ground their grain, and so on. But what of the businessman? In spite of his prejudices, should he not have been interested in something that would save him the cost and maintenance of slaves or the wages of workers—or even the need to go out and look for workers? He should have been, but he was not. He had rather a different attitude toward profit from what we are familiar with. The ancients, to be sure, were just as fond of money as we are; upper class or lower, they were perfectly aware that it was a good thing, that enjoying life was not possible without it. But they had their own ideas on how to make it and what to do with it after making it.

Throughout the whole of ancient times, men were convinced that wealth should properly come out of land. All great fortunes were landed fortunes: if they did not start out that way, they ended that way. Take the case of Trimalchio, the hero of the best-preserved scene in Petronius' *Satyricon,* a brilliant and devastating satire about Rome's *nouveaux riches* in the first century A.D. Trimalchio, an ex-slave who became a multimillionaire, got his start by taking a flyer in the import of wine. When his ship came in, he made a killing—and promptly switched to real estate, the buying of farm properties. He has acquired so much that, as Petronius has him boast, though there are vast tracts of his holdings he has never even seen, he won't be content until he buys up all Sicily, so that he can travel from Naples right to a port of departure for north Africa without once having to leave his own property. Trimalchio would have applauded enthusiastically Cicero's statement that "of all things from which income is derived, none is better than agriculture, none more fruitful, none sweeter, none more fitting for a free man." Cicero exaggerates; there were any number of pursuits more fruitful, but that was of secondary importance compared with agriculture's preeminent respectability, its fittingness for a free man.

Next to owning land came commerce, the sort of venture in which Trimalchio had gotten his start. But it was a good cut below. Hear Cicero on the subject: "Commerce, if it is on a small scale, is to be considered lowly; but if it is on a large scale and extensive, importing much from all over and distributing to many without misrepresentation, it is not to be too much disparaged"— in other words, at its very best, barely respectable.

Lower even than commerce was industry—industry, the form

143

of endeavor in which results depend squarely upon productivity, which has most to gain from technology. Ancient industry, it so happens, never progressed beyond the large workshop stage. You will read in the writings of archaeologists descriptions of centers of ceramic production that sound like operations employing a labor force of thousands, but that is only because the archaeologist's stock in trade is potsherds, and he tends to be overawed by the quantities he finds. The biggest pottery manufactories we know of were all owned by single individuals and never employed many more than fifty men. The very biggest privately owned (as against government owned) industrial operation we know of was a shield-making establishment that employed something in the neighborhood of one hundred. Back in the eighteenth century David Hume had written: "I do not remember a passage in any ancient author, where the growth of a city is ascribed to the establishment of a manufacture." Despite a century of archaeological discovery, his words need no qualification. There were no Manchesters or Birminghams in the ancient world, no equivalent of our New England mill towns.[16]

Let us grant that Greeks and Romans did not exploit the potential of industry for making money and that we cannot therefore expect technological advance in that area. What about agriculture? We saw earlier that urban growth was restricted by the farmers' inability to feed more city mouths. Sometimes they could not even feed their own mouths; famines were not at all uncommon in ancient times. In the days of the Roman Empire there was plenty of land, with rich landowners holding the lion's share of it; why did they not seek to make better use of their resources? Pliny, who was himself an owner of large estates, actually asserts that, for a landowner, "nothing pays less than cultivating your land to the fullest extent."[17] Why?

The answer lies in another of the fundamental differences in attitude between then and now: the ancients simply did not think in terms of maximum profits; the prevailing mentality of the age was acquisitive, not productive. One strove, like Trimalchio, to acquire as much land as possible but not to wring it to produce as much profit as possible. Take, for example, old Cato, who lived in the second century B.C. and wrote one of the treatises on farming that have survived. He is the classic example of the shrewd, frugal, hardworking Roman landowner. He has endless

144

advice to give on how to run a farm economically: precise pre-scriptions for the amount of rations of clothing and food to be issued to the help, how many hours to work them, what jobs to give them on rainy days; he cautions that they must be made to work on holidays, and that old and worn-out animals and slaves must be discarded just like worn-out tools. But if you were to ask his advice on what crops sold the best or netted the most profit, about quickness of turnover, capital investment, and other stan-dard bits of today's economic wisdom, he would not know what you were talking about. Such matters were totally beyond the ken of the ancient farmer, peasant, or owner of vast estates. One of Cato's hard and fast rules was that a farmer "should be a seller, not a buyer." The same rule is expressed in different lan-guage by Columella, another expert on agriculture, who wrote in the first century A.D. Some landowners, he tells us, "avoid annual expenses and consider it the best and most certain form of in-come not to make any investments." In other words, money not spent is money earned. If it costs more to install a water mill than a donkey-mill, then a donkey-mill it shall be.[18]

As a matter of fact, profitability of operation was so far from the ancient farmer's mind that he did not even have the book-keeping which would make it possible. We happen to have some of the records—they were a lucky find in an archaeological exca-vation—from a big Egyptian estate of the third century B.C. They reveal that the system of accounting in use was fine for the con-trol of stock and staff but could not possibly yield the information required for efficient exploitation. The owner had not the slight-est idea of which of his numerous crops was the most profitable, what his cost per crop was, and so on.[19]

We see, therefore, that it was not lack of knowledge which lay behind the poor technological record of the ancients but their lack of interest. The attitude of mind that made the artisan a human being of a lesser order, that glorified landowning as against land-use, and that left industry at a relatively primitive level rendered technological advance of scant moment. And so we need not be surprised that the water mill and the windmill, though known, were, in the one case, far from fully exploited, and, in the other, not exploited at all. But what was it that

145

changed matters so dramatically in the tenth century? Why was it that, from then on, men grasped eagerly at all ways to ease their labor, to increase their productive capacity? Why was it that a man of the Middle Ages, Hugh of St. Victor, coined the phrase *Propter necessitatem inventa est mechanica,* "Necessity is the mother of technology," a phrase that would never have come to the lips of a Greek or Roman? By Hugh's time technology had been integrated into men's thinking habits. They had learned to turn to it automatically as the way of solving certain problems; they had, in short, invented invention. To a Greek or Roman, invention was merely the result of happy accident. Among their heroes are no James Watts, no Thomas Edisons, no men who devoted a lifetime to studying, experimenting, perfecting a device. Their classic story is of Archimedes' sudden discovery of the principle of specific gravity while in his bath pondering how to test the honesty of a goldsmith. What was it that made people from the tenth century A.D. on aware of the usefulness of labor-saving devices, aware of technology, eager to invent?[20]

Lewis Mumford thinks that the answer is to be found in that quintessentially mediaeval institution, the monastery. "The monastery," he writes, "through its very other-worldliness, had a special incentive to develop mechanization. The monks sought . . . to avoid unnecessary labor in order to have more time and energy available for meditation and prayer; and possibly their willing immersion in ritual predisposed them to mechanical (repetitious and standardized) solutions. Though they themselves were disciplined to regular work, they readily turned over to machinery those operations that could be performed without benefit of mind. Rewarding work they kept for themselves: manuscript copying, illumination, carving. Unrewarding work they turned over to the machine: grinding, pounding, sawing."[21]

It is an intriguing theory but hard to prove. The earliest mills did arise in monasteries, but that could very well be nothing more than a reflection of the key position enjoyed by monasteries in the life of the times. At any rate, in short order mills were saving labor everywhere, not merely in the monasteries. The earliest mediaeval mill we know of dates from 983; as we mentioned above, within a century there were at least 5,624 in England alone.

146

Yet Mumford was on the right track in seeking an explanation in that feature which most of all divides the mediaeval world from the ancient: religion. Unlike the deities of paganism, the Christian god was a Creator God, architect of the cosmos, the divine potter who shaped men from clay in his own image. In the Christian conception, all history moves toward a spiritual goal, and there is no time to lose; thus work of all sorts is essential, becomes in a way a form of worship. Such ideas created a mental climate highly favorable for the growth of technology.[22]

But this alone cannot explain what happened in mediaeval Europe. There were, after all, two forms of Christianity, that practised in the Greek East as well as the Latin West, both equally ardent in embracing the fundamentals of Christian teaching; yet technology got no further in the East than it did in ancient Greece and Rome. Progress was limited to the Latin West. Why?

This is a problem that has particularly engaged the attention of Lynn White, whose name we have had occasion to mention earlier. He looks for the explanation in a basic difference in spiritual direction between the two churches. The Eastern generally held that sin is ignorance and that salvation comes by illumination, the Western that sin is vice and that rebirth comes by disciplining the will to do good works. The Greek saint is usually a contemplative figure, the Latin an activist.

The effect of the Western view was to restore respectability not only to the artisan but to manual labor, to remove the disrepute under which it had suffered during all of ancient times. And in this monasticism played a significant role. From the beginning, the monks had been mindful of the Hebrew tradition that work was in accordance with God's commandment. Here, too, there was a division between East and West. The East had not undergone invasion and pillage as had the West. Its level of culture had not descended as low, its intellectual and literary life continued much as before, and in this climate the Greek monks tended to concentrate on sacred studies. But in the West civilization had fallen so devastatingly low that the monks had to assume responsibility for all aspects of culture, profane as well as sacred, the life of the body as well as of the mind. Out of this grew an interest in practical affairs in general and, in particular, in the physical aspects of worship, a line of interest that led to the embellishment

147

ANCIENT TRADE AND SOCIETY

of the church and the service through technology. Whereas Eastern churches forbade music, holding that only the unaccompanied voice can worthily worship God, we find the cathedral at Winchester as early as the tenth century boasting a huge organ of four hundred pipes fed by twenty-eight bellows that required seventy men to pump them. By the middle of the twelfth century organs were given a part in the supreme moment of the service, the Mass itself. The East never permitted clocks in or on their churches; in the West, as soon as mechanical clocks were introduced they appeared both on towers outside and walls inside. The writings of Western monks express their delight not only at the mechanical devices that enhanced their religious life but at those that made their secular activities so much easier, the water-powered machines that did the milling, fulling, tanning, blacksmithing, and other such tasks. As one of them puts it: "How many horses' backs would have been broken, how many men's arms wearied, by the labor from which a river, with no labor, graciously frees us?" Technology was hailed as a Christian virtue. In a psalter that was illuminated near Reims about A.D. 830, an illustration of one of the psalms shows David leading a small body of the righteous against a formidable host of the ungodly. "In each camp," writes White, "a sword is being sharpened conspicuously. The Evildoers are content to use an old-fashioned whetstone (fig. 5). The godly, however, are employing the first crank recorded outside China to rotate the first grindstone known anywhere. Obviously the artist is telling us that technological advance is God's will."[23]

The Western attitude toward work and toward technology, as an expression of Christian faith, thus stands in contrast equally to the ancient Greco-Roman attitude and to that of the mediaeval Eastern Church. It is dramatically symbolized in an illustration in a manuscript of the Gospels that was produced at Winchester shortly after the year 1000.[24] Here God is portrayed as he would never be in the Eastern church, as a craftsman holding scales, a carpenter's square, and a pair of compasses (cf. fig. 6). In the minds of men of the age, He is conceived of as the master craftsman of the cosmos. We are a full swing of the pendulum away from Homer's Zeus, who used to join his fellow deities in laughing unquenchably at the ugly, limping Hephaestus.[25]

148

Fig. 5. The Armies of David and the Evildoers Prepare for Battle. Utrecht Psalter, folio 35v. Photo courtesy Bibliotheek der Rijksuniversiteit, Utrecht.

Fig. 6. God, Architect of the Universe. Österreichische Nationalbibliothek Codex 2554, folio 1v. Twelfth century. Photo courtesy Österreichische Nationalbibliothek, Vienna.

Notes

1. Ctesibius' organ and clock, B. Farrington, *Greek Science* (Pelican 1949) 201–204. Hero's hot air devices, J. Greenwood, *The Pneumatics of Hero of Alexandria* (1851, reprint ed. London 1971) 95 (revolving disk), 57 (shrine), 83–84 (figures and serpent). Hero's steam engine, J. Landels, *Engineering in the Ancient World* (Berkeley 1978) 28–29; windmill, 26–27; holy water dispenser, 203.

2. Fountain valve, Landels (above, n. 1) 30; force pumps, 75–83.

3. Earliest sails, *SSAW* 12. Vitruvius' water mill, Landels (above, n. 1) 17. Vitruvius' offhand remark, 10.5. The poet, *Anth. Pal.* 9.418; cf. Landels (above, n. 1) 17.

4. Efficiency of water-driven mills, C. Singer, *A History of Technology* ii (New York 1956) 598; complex at Arles, 598–99; Rome's mills, 601; floating mills, 607.

5. The mechanical reaper, K. White, *Roman Farming* (Ithaca 1970) 182–83, 453.

6. Water mills in the Middle Ages, L. White, *Medieval Technology and Social Change* (Oxford 1962) 83–85; "Cultural Climates and Technological Advance," *Viator* 2 (1971) 171–201.

7. Windmills, L. White, *Medieval Tech.* (above, n. 6) 85–88; M. Finley, *Ancient Slavery and Modern Technology* (London 1980) 138, 182 (bibliography). "By 1492," L. White, "Cultural Climates" (above, n. 6) 172.

8. Ancients lacked steamfitting technology, A. Drachman, *The Mechanical Technology of Greek and Roman Antiquity* (Copenhagen 1963) 206. Rivers lacked flow, cf. M. Finley, "Technological Innovation and Economic Progress in the Ancient World," *Economic History Review* 18 (1965) 29–45 (reprinted in M. Finley, *Economy and Society in Ancient Greece*, ed. B. Shaw and R. Saller [London 1981] 176–95) at 36. Etruscans provide a flow of water, J. Ward-Perkins in *Papers of the British School at Rome* 29 (1961) 50–52.

9. "Their slaves," *Science in Antiquity* (London 1962²) 113. Cost of slaves, above, chap. 2, nn. 25, 30, where the purchasing power of the drachma is reckoned at about 10 dollars, which is conservative.

10. "Labour was too cheap," W. Tarn, *Hellenistic Civilization* (London 1952³) 301. "Labour . . . was plentiful," Singer (above, n. 4) 602. Cf. F. Braudel, *The Structures of Everyday Life: Civilization and Capitalism 15th–18th Century* i (New York 1981) 339: "in the ancient world . . . mechanization was

ultimately blocked by cheap labour." Watermill had scant effect, Finley (above, n. 8) 29.

11. See chap. 5.

12. Scarcity of hands on farms, K. White (above, n. 5) 375, 450, 452. Shortages of labor in Egypt, Rostovtzeff, *SEHHW* 714, 718, 720, 726, 732. Empires' internal growth limited by peasantry, C. Préaux in *Third International Conference of Economic History, Munich 1965* (Paris 1970), section viii 61.

13. *SEHHW* 1230.

14. Lucian's dream, Lucian, *Somnium.* "Hunched over your work," *Somnium* 13. "Unquenchable laughter," *Iliad* 1.599. Citizens not allowed to practice a craft, Xenophon, *Oec.* 4.3. "The finest type," Aristotle, *Pol.* 3.3.2 (1278a). Free and slave side by side, M. Finley, *The Ancient Economy* (Berkeley 1973) 79. "All craftsmen are engaged," Cicero, *De Offic.*1.150–51.

15. Plutarch, *Marc.* 17.3–4.

16. Ancients fond of money, Finley (above, n. 14) 35–36. Wealth should come from land, Finley (above, n. 8) 39. Trimalchio wants to buy all Sicily, *Satyricon* 48. "Of all things from which," Cicero, *De Offic.* 1.150–51. "Commerce, if it is," ibid. Centers of ceramic production, cf. Finley (above, n. 8) 41–42; (above, n. 14) 136–37. Potteries employ not many more than fifty, Finley (above, n. 14) 74; shield-making shop with one hundred, 72. "I do not remember," see "Of the Populousness of Ancient Nations," in his *Essays* (World Classics ed. [1903] 415).

17. *N.H.* 18.36.

18. Prevailing mentality, cf. Finley (above, n. 14) 122. Cato's rules, K. White (above, n. 5) 360, 364–65. "Should be a seller," Cato, *De Agri Cultura* 2.7. "Avoid annual expenses," Columella, *De Re Rustica* 4.3.3.

19. Big Egyptian estate, K. White (above, n. 5) 454.

20. *Proper necessitatem,* cf. L. White, "Cultural Climates" (above, n. 6) 175; invented invention, 172. Invention among ancients a happy accident, Finley (above, n. 8) 35.

21. *The Myth of the Machine* (London 1967) 269.

22. L. White, "Cultural Climates" (above, n. 6) 187.

23. Eastern vs. Western church, L. White, "Cultural Climates" (above, n. 6) 189; Hebrew tradition, 191; Greek east suffered less, 193; technology and the

church service, 197–98. "How many horses' backs," from a twelfth-century description of the Abbey of Clairvaux cited by L. White, *Medieval Tech.* (above, n. 6) 195, n. 108; "in each camp," 198.

24. L. White, "Cultural Climates" (above, n. 6) 189.

25. The ancient world was not alone in its distaste for replacing muscle with machines. In a recent study of society from the 15th century to the 18th, Fernand Braudel points out how reluctant men were during this whole period to exploit inventions, how stubbornly they resisted technological progress. His conclusion is that

> as long as daily life proceeded without too much difficulty in its appointed pathway, within the framework of its inherited structures, as long as society was content with its material surroundings and felt at ease, there was no economic motive for change. . . . It was only when things went wrong, when society came up against the ceiling of the possible that people turned of necessity to technology (*The Structures of Everyday Life* [New York 1981] 435).

His words fit equally well the development presented above. Under the impact of relentless barbarian invasians, things in the western Roman Empire went very wrong indeed. And, under the impact of Christianity and the irresistible attractions of monasticism, daily life there strayed from its hitherto appointed pathway, abandoned the framework of its inherited structures. The stage was set for the Middle Ages' ubiquitous exploitation of windmills and water mills.

7.
The Scrap Paper of Egypt

In 1778 an Italian merchant while traveling near Cairo bought from a group of Arabs a document written on—to him—an unusual form of paper, a kind made from the fibres of the papyrus plant. Perhaps he had heard about the spectacular find just twenty-five years earlier of eight hundred scrolls of such material in a lava-covered building at Herculaneum, the victim, like nearby Pompeii, of Vesuvius' eruption in A.D. 79. His purchase was a roll three and a half feet long covered with indecipherable writing. The Arabs had forty to fifty others; they were using them for fuel, since the stuff gave off a rather pleasant smell, in any event an improvement over such alternatives as camel dung. On his return to Italy he presented his acquisition to Cardinal Stefano Borgia. The language was identified as Greek, written, however, not in the careful printed fashion familiar from mediaeval manuscripts, but in a cursive handwriting such as people use for letters. The cardinal entrusted his new possession to a professor of Greek from the University of Copenhagen, Niels Iversen Schow, who happened to be in Rome at the time. To everybody's disappointment it turned out to be no great piece of literature, no lost play of Sophocles or the like, but merely a list, drawn up in A.D. 192, of names of men from a little village in what is today the Fayum who were being called up for compulsory labor on the local dikes.

Today we know that this was not the first example of Greek writing on papyrus paper to come out of Egypt. One, for instance, had somehow fallen into the hands of the erudite sixteenth-century scholar Giovanni Giacomo Grineo; unacquainted with the cursive script, he concluded, for some reason known only to himself, that the language was Turkish. A few others had turned up as well, but all, because of the unfamiliar writing, had gone unrecognized. The Charta Borgiana, to use the title with which scholars subsequently dignified this list of lowly workmen, was the first to be properly identified and formally published.

In 1798 Napoleon launched his bravura invasion of the valley of the Nile. It swiftly aroused in Europe not only an interest in the hoary land but an appetite for collecting its hoary antiquities. During the next half century a stream of objects, enthusiastically carried off by resident diplomats, merchants, and casual visitors, flowed from Egypt to Europe. The big game were the statues, jewelry, stones inscribed with hieroglyphics, and the like, but every now and then specimens of papyrus paper were included in the booty, some with Egyptian writing on them but more with Greek. One lucky collector got himself a copy of the *Iliad,* but most of the pieces were, like the list of dike workers, humdrum documents—bills of sale, accounts, letters, etc.[1]

Then, in 1877, just a century after Cardinal Borgia had received his gift, there suddenly appeared on the antiquities market in Cairo a huge quantity of papyrus documents written in a number of ancient languages: Syriac, Hebrew, Arabic, Latin, but especially Greek. The various European counsuls and others jumped in to buy for their countries. Austria, thanks to funds supplied by its Archduke Rainer, went off with almost the lion's share, no fewer than seventy thousand in Greek and thirty thousand in Arabic. It later developed that the dealers had gotten them all from the peasants of the Fayum who had come upon them while rummaging through ancient piles of refuse, the source of a kind of rich earth they favored as fertilizer.

By now the world of scholarship was becoming aware of the unique historical value of these pieces. They were far too precious to leave their collecting to the random activity of peasants and their distribution to the greed of antiquities dealers. Archaeologists at work in Egypt were alerted to keep their eyes open for them. The first to make a strike was the renowned Flinders Petrie. What is more, he was able to add yet another source besides rubbish heaps where papyrus documents were to be found. The ancients, he discovered, had at least one way of recycling their waste paper: digging at a site in the north of the Fayum during the years 1889 and 1890, he came upon mummies that had been laid to rest in papier-mâché cases, cases made out of discarded papyri glued together to form a kind of cardboard. Unsticking them without destroying the writing presented a problem, but the technicians managed to solve it.

Then a pair of English excavators hit an archaeological gusher. Bernard Grenfell and Arthur Hunt, while excavating Oxyrhynchus, south of the Fayum, the site of what had once been a flourishing provincial Roman capital, unearthed a staggering number of pieces: the pair spent thirty years publishing seventeen volumes of transliterations and translations; their successors have pushed the number of volumes almost to fifty, and there is still a way to go. Grenfell and Hunt were successful as well at the ruins of a village in the Fayum called Tebtunis. This had been in ancient times a center for the worship of the sacred crocodiles, and in it was a cemetery full of their mummified remains; a gratifying number, it turned out, had been packed in cases of recycled papyri. Other archaeologists from all over—France, Germany, Italy, America—joined the search for this new kind of archaeological treasure. Philologists interested themselves in the writing and language of the documents, historians in the contents. Centers and institutes sprang up in various universities and museums. A new scholarly discipline had come into being—papyrology, the study of ancient Egypt's waste paper.[2]

Papyrus paper was made from the reeds that grow in profusion along the Nile. Today they have retreated to Upper Egypt, but in ancient times they were everywhere, being especially dense along the manifold streams of the Delta area. They are the reeds that we see in Egyptian tomb pictures, with Egyptian nobles gliding through them in their canoes on the hunt for marsh birds; they are the bulrushes of which Moses' cradle was made. The first step in turning them into paper was to take the stems and slice them along their length, cutting off long razor-thin strips. The strips were laid horizontally side by side, one above the other to the width the sheet was to be, usually between four and ten inches. Then a second layer was put over the first, this time with short strips running vertically, i.e., at right angles to the other layer. The long and narrow sheet that resulted, now two-ply as it were, was next put in a press and squeezed till the juices of the plant, which has some gum in its make-up, permeated the whole evenly, and then taken out and put in the sun to dry. The finished sheets were pasted end to end and rolled up, twenty to a roll. Authors of books might buy whole rolls, but anyone who just wanted some stationery had a piece the desired length snipped off. Papyrus paper is heavier and thicker than the paper of today but, if of good quality, not a bit inferior. It is certainly tough. Its mortal enemy is damp; saved from that, it can lie in the sand or in a tomb for thousands of years and emerge in fine shape, able to be handled with no more than ordinary care. Wilhelm Schubart, one of the great papyrologists, used to confound audiences by rolling and unrolling a document of pharaonic times that was over three thousand years old.

The writing was done by reed pen with split point dipped in an ink made of lampblack and gum and water. The ink is as tough as the paper: excavators have dug up many a piece with the writing as shiny and black as the day it was set down.[3]

Until late in the last century, students of the ancient world had little more to go on than the works of its historians, of Herodotus, Thucydides, Livy, Tacitus, and so on. These men were not interested in anything other than the large-scale, the grandly important: the fate of nations, the doings of kings and statesmen, widespread natural disasters. Occasionally they would mention ordinary people but only in generalized terms: how these had been affected en masse by the overthrow of a government that ruled them, by the arrival of a new leader among them, by the tide of a war that swept over them, by a plague that hit them. In the nineteenth century two new scholarly disciplines arose that considerably expanded our stock of information, archaeology and epigraphy. But they too tended to concentrate on the high and the mighty. Excavators kept laying bare the remains of grandiose temples and palaces, only occasionally of private dwellings, and practically never of slums. Epigraphy, the study of inscriptions on stones, was somewhat more helpful. Although the fullest and most important usually detailed the doings of governments, kings, magistrates, etc., many came from tombstones, those over graves of the humble as well as the haughty. Such inscriptions often give the deceased's métier and occasionally some details about it; the stone itself, by its size and material and workmanship, provides some indication of financial status. Scant information, to be sure, but better than none at all.

Then came the discovery of Egypt's papyrological riches. Here were pieces of writing which, since they were found in the nation's waste dumps, were totally haphazard and ran the gamut from outdated files of lofty government officials to scribbled lovers' notes, from pages with formal columns of figures ripped out of discarded tax registers to scraps with the scrawled incoherent curses irate Egyptians hurled against their enemies, from elegant missives beautifully written by professional secretaries to the ungainly copy sheets of schoolboys. All of this suddenly opened up to us a world that had been totally lost, the world of the ordinary folk of the past. Suddenly we were able to follow, from birth to death, the vicissitudes of the Toms, Dicks, and Harrys of Egypt, particularly in the days from ca. 300 B.C. to A.D. 500, when first the Greeks and then the Romans ruled the valley of the Nile.

Our information is limited to Egypt. This is solely because of its climate. Though Egypt was the home of the manufacture of papyrus paper, she shipped it all over. It was everywhere in demand, since it was the most economic form of writing material, far cheaper than parchment or vellum. People from Spain to Syria wrote on it, and there must have been as much of it going into their wastebaskets as in Egypt. But none has survived. Damp, as we mentioned earlier, is fatal to papyri, and only in perennially dry Middle and Upper Egypt can they last through the centuries. Some pieces have been recovered from Palestine and Irak and a few other places, but very few and preserved only through lucky accident.

We grumble today about how the government keeps track of our every move, how we do nothing but fill out forms, how we will all end up buried in paper. If it is any consolation, things

157

were much the same two thousand years ago. The documents found in Egypt show, in discouraging abundance, that the files of the Roman Empire's bureaucracy bulged with papyrus scrolls recording the doings of all, high and low, from cradle to grave.

To begin with, births were registered every bit as carefully then as now. If you were a Roman subject but not a citizen, as most living in Egypt were, you made a formal declaration to the authorities of the local district headquarters. "To Socrates and Didymus, . . . clerks of the metropolis, from Ischyras . . . and his wife Thaisarion," a typical example begins. The couple identify themselves by father's name and mother's name and paternal grandfather's name, by age, and by distinguishing features—and here alone does their practice differ from ours: they prefer to use scars and birthmarks instead of color of eyes and hair. After identification comes the meat of the document: "We hereby register the son, Ischyras, born to us and being one year of age in the present 14th year of Emperor Antoninus Caesar (A.D. 150 or 151)." Ischyras, Jr. kept this precious piece of papyrus all his life; it was proof, among other things, that he was freeborn, not a slave.

Ischyras' birth declaration was written in Greek, as were the vast majority of the documents from Egypt. Alexander the Great had conquered the land in 332 B.C., and in his wake waves of Greeks flooded in, gradually becoming the country's social upper crust. In 30 B.C., after Mark Antony had fallen on his sword and Cleopatra had put an asp to her bosom, the Romans made Egypt into one of the provinces of their empire, and soon thereafter a new, uppermost, crust was formed of Roman citizens, not only Romans who settled down there but local Greeks who managed to achieve naturalization. Parents who were Roman citizens followed a loftier procedure in registering their children, consonant with their more elevated status. Instead of a mere declaration to local headquarters, the father reported a birth to Alexandria, capital of the province, where it was entered in an official register maintained there. Then he was given a certified copy of the entry, written in Latin and on waxed tablets rather than papyrus. Thus, when Caius Herennius Geminianus and Diogenis Thermutharion had a daughter born to them in A.D. 128, they secured such a tablet that read in this wise:

158

In the Registry of Births posted at the Forum of Augustus [the Forum of Augustus, a main square in Alexandria, was the address of the *Atrium Magnum,* "Great Hall," the building that housed the birth records office] . . . , in tablet no. 8 . . . , page 9, under date of the 6th day before the Kalends of April [27 March]: "C. Herennius Geminianus . . . registered as Roman citizen a daughter, Herennia Gemella, born of Diogenis Thermutharion . . . on the 5th day before the Ides of March [11 March]."

This ancient style of certified copy was little Herennia Gemella's proof of Roman citizenship, just as certified copies of birth certificates on file with the Board of Health prove American citizenship.

Even illegitimate children were registered—not, however, by entry in the official archive but just by a carefully witnessed affidavit. "Sempronia Gemella," reads a document written in A.D. 145, "who is under the guardianship of Gaius Julius Saturninus, has called upon the witnesses signing below [the document ends with signatures of seven such witnesses] to testify that, on the 12th day before the Kalends of April [21 March], she gave birth, from father unknown, to twin sons and that she has named these Marcus Sempronius Sarapio and Marcus Sempronius Socratio." She then adds that she drew up such an affidavit since "the law forbids the entering of illegitimate sons or daughters in the Registry of Births." Having no father's name to give the boys, she willy-nilly gave them her own family name, Sempronius.

Had Sempronia been raped? Or had she had a passionate moment with some passing fancy? Or was that Roman guardian of hers the father? All we know is that the twins were wanted, that the mother took legal steps to establish their identity. They were lucky. Unwanted children were ruthlessly gotten rid of. There is an oft-quoted letter written, sometime in the first century B.C., by a husband off in Alexandria to his wife up the Nile at Oxyrhynchus. He was a loving husband who closes his missive with the words, "You told me not to forget you. How can I ever forget you?" In the very sentence before this he writes: "Do, please, take care of the little one. As soon as we receive our pay, I'll send it up to you. If, as could well happen, you give birth, if it's a male, let it be; if it's a female, cast it out."[4]

It would have been cast out on the town dump, where it could be picked up by those who were seeking for slaves and, instead of buying them fully grown, were willing to pay for raising them from birth and to accept the risk of their dying before reaching a usable age. Such slaves crop up often in the documents; "foundlings from the dunghill" they are called. The mistress of a house that took in one of these infant rejects could hardly be expected to suckle it; the usual practice was to turn it over to a wet nurse, as we know from finding examples of the contracts that were drawn up on such occasions. Here, for instance, are the key passages of an agreement drawn up in A.D. 26 between a wet nurse named Taseus and a man named Paapis. She goes on record that

> she has received from him a female infant which he picked up from the dunghill for service as a slave, and to which he has given the name Thermutharion; that she will raise and suckle it with her own milk; that she will, furthermore, nurse it for a period of two years commencing with the present 17th of Pachon [12 May], on the understanding that Paapis shall give her 60 drachmas yearly for food, clothing, and all other expenses on behalf of the infant, and she hereby acknowledges . . . receipt from Paapis of 60 drachmas, cash, as payment in full for the first year. . . . She binds herself to provide total protection and care for it, as is proper, not to have sexual intercourse in order to avoid spoiling her milk, not to get pregnant, not to take on the suckling of a second infant . . . and to restore the infant to Paapis duly cared for, as is proper. If some human misfortune should happen which is manifestly such [i.e., the infant should die of natural causes], she shall not be held liable, and, if Paapis should choose to entrust to her another infant, she shall take over its care for the remaining period of time under the conditions set forth above.

Despite all legal precautions, the death of these foundlings could cause infinite trouble, as we learn from a document found in the ruins of Oxyrhynchus, one of the first published by that pioneering team of papyrologists, Grenfell and Hunt. It is a stenographic record of a trial held in A.D. 49 before a local magistrate named Tiberius Claudius Pasion:

Pesouris versus Saraeus.

> Aristocles, lawyer for Pesouris: "My client Pesouris, in the 7th year of the reign of the Emperor Claudius [A.D. 49], picked up from the dunghill a male infant named Heraclas. He entrusted it to the defendant. . . . She received her wages for the first year. When the due date for the second year arrived, she again re-

ceived her wages. . . . However, since the infant was being
starved, Pesouris took it away from her. Then she, finding just
the right moment, managed to enter our house and carried the
infant off. . . ."

Saraeus: I had weaned my own child, and these people's infant
was entrusted to me. I received from them my total wage. . . .
After that the foundling died, while a balance of the money was
still in my hands. Now they want to take my own child from
me."

The situation called for a Judgement of Solomon: the Roman
magistrate was in exactly the same predicament. There had been
two children in Saraeus' house when she was serving as wet
nurse, her own and Pesouris' foundling. One died. Pesouris carried the survivor off, claiming it was the foundling, but Saraeus
managed to get it back, claiming it was her own son. The document concludes with Pasion's verdict:

The magistrate: "Inasmuch as the child, from its features, seems
to be Saraeus', if she and her husband will attest in writing that
the foundling entrusted to her by Pesouris died, my judgement
following the decisions of His Honor, the Governor [i.e., of
Egypt], is that she shall keep the child as her own but return the
money she received."

Not a dramatic Solomonic resolution but an attempt at compro-
mise: Saraeus gets the child after putting down in black and white
under oath that it was hers, and Pesouris is to be soothed by
recovering all his money, even the part for the period, more than
a year, when the foundling was still alive and being suckled.

But Pesouris refused to be soothed, as we learn from a second
papyrus found in the same place, the copy of a complaint that
Saraeus' husband lodged with the governor shortly thereafter. In
it, after reviewing the facts, he states:

My son was returned to me in compliance with your orders . . . ,
as recorded in Pasion's stenographic record. But Pesouris does not
wish to comply with the judgement, and he is interfering with me
in the practice of my trade [the husband was a weaver]. I therefore
am appealing to you, my savior, to obtain justice.

Did he eventually get Pesouris off his back? We will never
know; the documents from Egypt, haphazard pickings that they

161

are, yield mostly disconnected fragments, rarely a story from beginning to end.

Female foundlings were raised mostly to be household slaves. Males could also be apprenticed out to learn a trade or profession. "I have placed with you," goes an agreement drawn up in A.D. 155 with a specialist in shorthand, "my slave Chaerammon to learn the writing signs that your son Dionysius knows . . . for the fee agreed upon between us, 120 drachmas of silver, holidays excluded." Young Chaerammon, though a slave, was infinitely better off than the children of the free poor. The valley of the Nile was largely given over to agriculture, so most of these were condemned from birth to the peasant's grinding routine, and, of course, to illiteracy. We catch glimpses of them in those documents—for the bureaucracy's all-pervading network caught up even the lowly in its toils—that end with the formula, "Since he does not know letters, I have written for him," followed by the signature of the writer, usually a professional scribe.[5]

Any family that could afford it taught the children to read and write, girls as well as boys. A common practice was to have a tutor live in—hardly in the lap of luxury, to judge by a letter from the head of a household who instructs the recipient to "send to my daughter's teacher . . . whatever I didn't eat, so he'll be keen on working with her." Boys might be sent off to take their lessons with a schoolmaster, either in town, if the place was big enough to support one, or out of town if not.

The system of teaching was, like ours of a century ago, by rote. This we know from multitudinous examples of written exercises that have turned up, papyri on which appear, in childish hands, *ba be bi bo bu* or *bab, gag, dad, thath,* etc. One hardworking pupil learned his conjugations and declensions by being made to copy out the sentence, "The philosopher Pythagoras, having departed, while teaching letters advised his students to keep away from meat," in all possible grammatical permutations: "To the philosopher Pythagoras, having departed, while teaching letters it seemed right to advise"; "O Philosopher Pythagoras, depart and teach letters and advise"; and so on, even in the plural: "The Pythagorases, having departed, while teaching letters, advised, etc." And, again as in our schools of the last century, there was much copying out of wise or moral sayings: "It is Zeus who sends us our daily nourishment"; "He who does no wrong needs no law"; "Letters are the greatest beginnings in life"; in this last one we can surely detect the hand of the schoolmaster who set the assignment. Sometimes the sayings were put in question-and-answer form: "What is pleasing to the gods? Justice"; "What in life is evil? Envy"; "What in life is fresh and wonderful? Man"; "What in life is sweet and must be shunned? Woman."[6]

In well-to-do households, where the parents were often away from home, the children had a chance to put in practice what they had learned through letters to them. Often we find references to these in the parents' correspondence. "My little Heraidous, when she writes her father, doesn't send me any greetings, and I don't know why," complains an aggrieved mother. Sometimes we find the letters themselves. There is a by now famous one, in an ungainly script and with hair-raising grammar and spelling, of the kind that makes parents wish the children had never learned to write. Theon, Sr. had promised to take Theon, Jr. along on his next trip and then had, as it were, sneaked out by the back door. Junior writes:

> You did a fine thing! You didn't take me with you to the city! If you don't want to take me to Alexandria, I won't write you a letter, I won't talk to you, I won't wish for your good health. What's more, if you go to Alexandria, I won't shake your hand or say hello to you ever again. So, if you don't want to take me with you, that's what will happen. Mother said to Archelaus [probably a slave attendant], "Take him away! He upsets me!" You did a fine thing: you sent me presents. Big presents! Chicken feed! They pulled a trick on the 12th, when you sailed. Send for me, please! If you don't send, I won't eat, I won't drink! That's what will happen!

Junior then closes with the Greek equivalent of "Your loving son."

Once having learned their letters, boys were sent to a schoolmaster, often out of town, for the next stage in their education. The prime subject was literature, first and foremost Homer. "I took care," writes a mother to a son studying away from home, "to send [to your schoolmaster] and find out how you were and to learn what you were reading. He said six." In the context, the number needed no qualification; it meant the sixth book of the *Iliad*. After Homer came Euripides and Aesop. Mathematics was also an important discipline: addition, subtraction, multiplication, fractions, weights, measures, and some simple geometry. Students were set such problems as: How many people can fit as spectators in a hall of such and such shape and size? How many measures of grain can fit in a receptacle of such and such shape and size? Those interested in getting ahead, in preparing themselves, say, for a government job, went on to study Latin. We have examples of the trots they used, copies of Vergil with word-for-word translation in Greek.

Judging from what they wrote home, boys who went away to school took their studies seriously and worked hard. "Don't worry, Father, about my studies," one reports, "I'm keen about my work. I also take time off." "Look here," writes another to his father, "this is my fifth letter to you, and you haven't written to me except just once . . . and haven't come here. After assuring me, 'I'm coming,' you didn't come to find out whether my teacher was paying attention to me or not. And he asks about you practically every day: 'Isn't he coming yet?' And I just say, 'Yes.' Do your best to come to me quickly, so he'll teach me, as he's eager to do. If you had come up here with me, I would have been taught long ago." One gathers that the father was to bring not only himself but the tuition as well. Publicly financed education lay centuries and centuries in the future; all these teachers, from the humble tutor in the house fed on scraps to the professor who taught Latin, charged for their services.[7]

When children reached adulthood, they, like their parents before them, were caught in the net of paperwork that the government cast over the land. Every fourteen years there was a "house-to-house census," as it was called. The landlord of each dwelling reported all persons living there, as well as the house property any of them owned. Here is a sample, from an apartment or boarding house in the town of Arsinoë. To judge from what the tenants did for a living and their almost total lack of property, the building must have stood in a poorer section of town. The landlord states:

> I own in the Moeris quarter a share of a house . . . for which
> I . . . report for the house-to-house census of the past 28th year of
> Emperor Aurelius Commodus Antoninus Caesar [A.D. 189] the
> following occupants . . .

164

Pasigenes, son of Theon, grandson of Eutychus, subject to poll tax, donkey driver, age 61

Eutychus, his son by Apollonous who is daughter of Herodes, age 30

Heracleia, wife of Pasigenes, daughter of Cronion and ex-slave of Didymus who is son of Heron, age 40

Thasis, daughter of both [i.e., Pasigenes and his second wife Heracleia], age 5

Sabinus, son of Heracleia and Sabinus, grandson of Cronion, subject to poll tax, wool carder, age 18

Sarapias, son of Heracleia, age 22, . . .

Tapesouris, wife of Eutychus, his sister on the father's side, daughter of Isadora, age 18. . . . Tapesouris owns in the Moeris quarter a sixth share of a house inherited from her mother.

Whoever purchased or inherited property had to file a declaration with the appropriate authorities. Whoever took up a trade, or wanted to apprentice someone to learn a trade, had to file with the appropriate authorities. To enter the Egyptian priesthood, a man underwent circumcision; even that act required approval from the authorities. When a certain Eudaimon, son of Psois and Tiathres, decided that hereafter he would sign himself "son of Heron and Didyme," i.e., the Greek translation of his parents' Egyptian names, presumably to enhance his social tone, he had to get permission, in this case from a top treasury official. He submitted his request to the local clerk, who passed it on to the local magistrate; since the local magistrate at the moment happened to be the local clerk acting as such, in perfect Pooh-bah fashion the clerk in his capacity as clerk wrote a letter to himself in his capacity as magistrate.[8]

The key purpose behind all this bureaucratic paperwork was, as today, the payment of taxes. The dwellers in Egypt paid taxes on land both in cash and kind, taxes on house property, taxes on sheep, pigs, camels, beer, tax on working a trade, tax on certain manufactures. Thousands of receipts for these multifarious levies have been found. All, of course, were made out by hand; the clerks, monotonously repeating the same phrases over and over again, rendered them in an almost indecipherable scrawl on scraps of papyrus or just on fragments of broken pots, the cheapest form of writing material available. The higher social classes enjoyed exemption from some of these burdens, and excavators, rummaging about the ruins of houses, often find the precious papers that proved the right to such exemption; the holders were careful to put them away in a safe place.

The most privileged group in the land were the Roman citizens. The documents show that this age, in contrast to so many others in man's past, boasted an open society; people were not locked into their social and economic level but could work their way up into money and position. Indeed, not a few of the Greek-speaking subjects of Rome managed to enter the charmed circle of Roman citizens. One path was via the navy; it was slow, but it had the great advantage of being open to all, even to boys with native Egyptian blood in their veins. A hitch in the navy was twenty-six years, and citizenship came only at the end, along with discharge, but that did not discourage able-bodied eager lads. It helped, as always, to come from a family already a few notches up the ladder—as in the case of young Apion who, having signed up sometime in the second century A.D., was shipped from Egypt to the naval base at Misenum near Naples, and on arrival wrote the folks back home:

> Apion to Epimachus, his father . . . , many greetings. First of all, I hope you are well and will always be well, and my sister and her daughter and my brother. I thank our god Sarapis that, when I was in danger at sea, he quickly came to the rescue. When I arrived at Misenum I received from the government three gold pieces for traveling expenses. I am fine. Please write me, Father, first, to tell me that you are well, second that my brother and sister are well, and third so that I can kiss your hand because you gave me a good education and because of it I hope to get quick promotion, if the gods so will. . . . I have sent you by Euctemon a picture of myself. My name is Antonius Maximus, my ship the *Athenonice*.

The letter closes with regards to various friends and relatives. Like any young recruit in any age, Apion hungers for news from home and sends the family a portrait of himself, very likely showing him resplendent in his new uniform. In these pre-camera days it had to be a miniature, and in these pre-postal service days he must find someone heading for the family's neighborhood to deliver it. Now that he is in the Roman navy he drops his outré Egyptian name for a good Roman one.

In 1926, when archaeologists from the University of Michigan were excavating the little village of Caranis, in one of the houses they came upon two letters that had obviously been carefully preserved by the mother to whom they had been addressed. Like Apion's, they were written by a young naval recruit; they date sometime around the beginning of the second century A.D. In the first he reports that he is "now writing to you from Portus [the harbor of Rome], for I have not yet gone up to Rome and been assigned." The second has the final word:

> I want you to know, Mother, that I arrived safely at Rome on the 25th day of Pachon [20 May], and that I was assigned to Misenum. I don't know my ship yet, for I haven't gone to Misenum at the time of writing this letter. Please, Mother, take good care of yourself. And don't worry about me—I've come to a good place!

Quite possibly the mother never saw her son again. Most of these recruits, during their twenty-six years in Italy, took up with local girls, started a family, and established so many bonds there that on discharge they preferred to stay where they were. Apion certainly never went back: we have a letter from him to his sister, written years after he had enlisted. He now uses only his Roman name; he had married, and he has three children, a son and two daughters.[9]

Those who came from the higher social strata had it infinitely easier than these enlistees in the navy. The pride of the Roman army, the legions, were by law open to Roman citizens only. Since this source could not always be counted on to furnish the numbers needed, the sons of upper-class Greek families settled in Egypt were permitted to enlist and, to satisfy the admissions requirement, were given the citizenship upon signing up. Not only that but, once in, family connections could smooth the path for them. Take the case of a certain young Pausanias, who was a soldier in the legion stationed at Alexandria at the mouth of the Nile. That was not good enough for him; he wanted to be in a cavalry unit. Pausanias, Sr. was able to wangle a transfer to one at Coptos in upper Egypt, much nearer to home, as he explains in a letter to his brother:

> I have written to you before about my boy Pausanias taking service in a legion. However, since he no longer wanted to serve in a legion but in a squadron, on hearing about this I had to go and see him, even though I didn't want to. So, after much pleading on the part of his mother and sister . . . , I went to Alexandria and used ways and means till he was transferred to the squadron at Coptos.

167

It sounds so familiar, the adored son expressing a wish and mother and sister badgering the poor father till he does something about it.

Here is a letter from another mother's darling, also attached to the legion at Alexandria. Roman servicemen had to provide their own uniforms and equipment; this was obviously much on his mind:

> On receiving this letter it would be very nice of you if you sent me 200 drachmas. . . . I had only 20 staters left, but now not one because I bought a mule carriage and spent all my change on it. I'm writing you this to let you know. Send me a heavy cape, a rain cape with a hood, a pair of leggings, a pair of leather wraps, oil, and the wash-basin, as you promised, . . . and a pair of pillows. . . . For the rest, then, Mother, send me my monthly allowance right away. What you said when I came to you was, "Before you reach your camp, I will send one of your brothers to you." And you sent me nothing, . . . you left me this way without a thing. You didn't say, "I don't have an obol, I have nothing," you just left me this way, like a dog. And when my father came to me, he didn't give me an obol, not a rain cape, not anything. They all make fun of me: "His father is a soldier, and he's given him nothing." He said he'll send me everything when he gets home. But you have sent me nothing! Why? Valerius' mother sent him a pair of belts, a jar of oil, a basket of meat, a double-sized garment, and 200 drachmas. . . . So, please, Mother, send me, don't neglect me this way. I've gone and borrowed some change from a buddy and from my sergeant. My brother Gemellus sent me a letter and breeches. I'm sorry I haven't gone anywhere near my brother, and he's sorry I haven't gone anywhere near him. He wrote me a letter scolding me because I went to another camp. I'm writing you this to let you know. It would be very nice of you if, on receiving this letter, you sent right away.

Not all the upper-class boys who entered the service found the going that easy. We have a batch of letters that, in the early years of the second century A.D., a certain Terentianus wrote to his father, Claudius Tiberianus. Both parent and son bear good Roman names, and the correspondence is in fluent Latin as well as Greek, but the son is only a sailor serving on the ancient equivalent of a destroyer in the flotilla based at Alexandria and is trying as hard as he can to get transferred to a cohort in a legion;

apparently at that particular time there were no openings. One letter of his, for example, runs as follows:

> I have sent you . . . two mantles, two capes, two linen towels, two sacks, a wooden bed. I had bought the last together with a mattress and a pillow, and while I was lying sick on the destroyer they were stolen from me. . . . Please, Father, if it seems all right to you, send me from where you are some low-cut boots and a pair of felt socks. Fancy boots are worthless. . . . And I beg you, send me a pickax. The adjutant took from me the one you sent me. . . . God willing, I hope to live thriftily and to be transferred to a cohort, but here nothing gets done without money. Letters of recommendation are useless, unless a man helps himself [with money].

Either luck finally smiled on Terentianus or he somewhere found the money to grease palms because, in a later letter, he signs as "soldier of the legion."[10]

In 1899 the indefatigable Grenfell and Hunt, while excavating a tiny village, came upon a group of papyri that concerned the doings of someone with the good Roman name of Lucius Bellienus Gemellus. Most were from his hand, in a careless colloquial Greek spelled in hit-or-miss fashion; it is written Greek at about the level of Huck Finn's written English. A contract in which he identifies himself as "veteran of the legion" may provide a clue: he perhaps got what education he had while in the service. How he managed to enlist in the first place, we have no idea; for all we know, he may have been a Roman citizen to begin with, though a nearly illiterate one.

Bellienus was born about A.D. 32, enlisted about A.D. 52, and emerged at the end of his hitch with enough money saved up to buy himself farmland. The papers we have date from A.D. 94 to 110, when he had already made his mark, owning no less than nine pieces of property, including grain land, vineyards, olive orchards, and vegetable gardens. Two he ran by himself and most of the others through a trusted slave bailiff, Epagathus. He also had the help of a grown son, Sabinus. We have quite a few letters he wrote to these two. Despite the hair-raising spelling and syntax, they were perfectly clear, mostly a volley of staccato commands closed by his favored coda, the phrase "Now you do as I say!" Sabinus' responses are in eminently correct Greek; as so often happens in the families of self-made men, the children get a proper education. The light of Bellienus' life was his grandson, the "little one," as he always calls him. Sabinus, for example, is ordered to send into town for twelve drachmas worth of fish to celebrate some occasion for "the little one." Another time Epagathus is ordered to keep his eyes open for a chance to buy thirty fish to send into town where Bellienus has gone "on account of the little one."

Right up to the very end, Bellienus was on top of everything and held the reins firmly in his hands. Epagathus gets called down because instead of transporting a herd of pigs, he drove them on foot and "lost two little pigs because the journey was so hard, even though you had in the village ten animals fit for work. . . . I expressly ordered you to stay at Dionysias for two days until you bought 20 bushels of lotus seed. They say lotus seed is 18 drachmas at Dionysias. Whatever you find the price to be, buy the 20 bushels because we need it. Hurry the irrigating of all the olive orchards, . . . and water the rows of trees. . . . Now you do as I say." To Sabinus he complains bitterly about the hay one of his donkey-drivers bought, "a rotten bundle at 12 drachmas, a little bundle and rotten hay, completely spoiled—no better than dung!" There was more to Bellienus' success than hard work, care, and a sharp eye for saving a drachma. He was adept in that ancient Near Eastern art, the handling of bakshish. "I want to let you know," he writes his son, "that Ailouras, the royal clerk, has become deputy for the magistrate Erasus, in accordance with a letter from His Honor, the Governor [of Egypt]. Would you please send him a bushel of olives and some fish, for we need him." And in the last letter we have from him, written when he was seventy-seven in a hand so shaky it is barely legible, he instructs Epagathus to "buy some Isis Day gifts for the ones we usually send to, especially the magistrates."[11]

We hear nothing about Bellienus' wife, but this is accidental. The women of Greco-Roman Egypt were by no means mere household appurtenances, as they were in so many other epochs of man's past. They could come and go as they wanted, handle their own property, pass it on by will to whomever they wished, run their own businesses, even, on occasion, serve as magistrates. When they entered into marriage their interests and rights were protected by written agreement. This was particularly true of middle-class women or higher, who generally brought a substantial dowry to their husbands. Here, for example, are the terms under which Philiskos and Apollonia became man and wife in 92 B.C.:

> Philiskos . . . acknowledges to Apollonia . . . that he has received from her in copper money 2 talents and 4,000 drachmas [16,000 in all], the dowry agreed upon by him for her, Apollonia. Apollonia shall remain with Philiskos, obeying him as a wife should obey her husband, owning their property jointly with him. Philiskos, whether he is at home or away from home, shall furnish Apollonia with everything necessary and clothing and whatsoever is proper for a wedded wife, in proportion to their means. It shall not be lawful for Philiskos to bring home another wife in addition to Apollonia, nor to have a concubine or boy-lover, nor to beget children by another woman while Apollonia is alive, nor to maintain another house of which Apollonia is not mistress, nor to eject or insult or ill-treat her, nor to alienate any of their property with injustice to Apollonia. If he is shown to be doing any of these things or does not furnish her with what is necessary or clothing or the rest as stipulated, Philiskos shall immediately pay back to Apollonia the dowry of 2 talents and 4,000 drachmas of copper. Similarly, it shall not be lawful for Apollonia to spend night or day away from the house of Philiskos without Philiskos' knowledge, or to have intercourse with another man, or to ruin the common household, or to bring shame upon Philiskos in whatever may cause a husband shame. If Apollonia voluntarily wishes to separate from Philiskos, Philiskos shall pay back to her the bare dowry within ten days from the day it is demanded. If he does not pay it back as stipulated, he shall immediately forfeit the dowry he has received plus one-half.

Further down the social scale, things became much more casual. When Tryphon, a weaver from Oxyrhynchus, married Saraeus in A.D. 36, he merely issued her a receipt for the dowry:

> I acknowledge receipt from you at the Serapeum in the city of Oxyrhynchus through the bank of Sarapion, son of Cleandrus, of 40 silver drachmas . . . , one pair of gold earrings worth 20 silver drachmas, one pure white tunic worth 12 silver drachmas, so that the sum total is 72 silver drachmas, . . . in consideration of which I have given my consent. . . . If we separate from each other, you shall have the right to keep the pair of earrings.

Tryphon clearly drove a hard bargain. But there was a reason for it: he had been badly burned in an earlier marriage, and he was

171

taking no chances with this second one. His first wife had walked out on him, and not empty-handed, as we learn from a complaint he lodged with the authorities:

> I lived in marriage with Demetrous, daughter of Heraclides, and I indeed made provision for her even beyond my means. But she, having other thoughts about our union, finally went off and carried away my possessions, of which an itemized list is given below. Wherefore, I ask that she be made to come before you in order to meet her just deserts and to restore my possessions to me. This petition is without prejudice to all other claims I have or shall have against her.

We do not know if he ever got satisfaction from Demetrous, but he apparently did from Saraeus. From other documents that survived, we see that their marriage lasted at least twenty-three years.[12]

The Roman bureaucracy, with its apparatus for registering all of Egypt's inhabitants, keeping track of their property and ways of earning a living, collecting myriads of taxes from them, naturally had an apparatus for taking care of disturbances in the established order of things, for handling crime. That crime exists in all ages is a generalization which hardly needs to be demonstrated. But in Greco-Roman Egypt we meet it not as an impersonal historical abstraction but, as it were, from the jottings on the police blotter, the verbatim statements that victims drew up for the authorities, or the reports of the authorities themselves.

"After being away, upon returning to the village," writes a certain Ptolemaeus to the district magistrate, "I found my house pillaged and everything that had been stored in it carried off. Wherefore . . . I apply to you and request this petition be entered on the register so that, if anyone is proved guilty, he be held accountable to me." The last sentence is the standard legal formula for swearing out a complaint; we find it in more or less the same form in document upon document. "Certain parties," runs a statement dating A.D. 176, "with intent to rob came to my house in the village during the night before the 22nd of the present month Hathyr [18 November], taking the opportunity

172

afforded by my absence owing to mourning for my daughter's husband. Removing the nails from the doors, they carried off everything stored in my house, of which I will present an itemized list at the stated time. Wherefore I apply to you and request etc." Occasionally we learn exactly how the robbery was carried out: "a door that opened onto the street and had been bricked up they broke down, probably using a log to batter it, and, entering the house this way, carried off from what was in the house ten bushels of barley and nothing else; I suspect that these were removed piecemeal through the same door because of marks of the dragging of a rope on it. . . . Wherefore, making application etc." In this case, the housebreakers, like those of today who go only for cameras or television sets, took the one item that was assured of quick and easy sale.

At times the culprits were known to the victims and made no effort to hide their identities; they may have been pursuing some vendetta or perhaps were merely drunk and disorderly. A complaint lodged in A.D. 131 reads: "On the first day of the present month of Thoth [29 August], Orsenouphis and Poueris, both sons of Mieus, and Theon and Sarapas, both sons of Chaeras, and [three more names] . . . brazenly attacked the house I own in the village. . . . While I was parleying with them, they beat me on every limb of my body, and they carried off a white tunic and cloak, a cape, . . . a pair of scissors, beer, a quantity of salt, and other items which at present I do not know."

Outside of the villages and towns the danger was even greater. A husband advises in a letter to his wife, who was to sail up the Nile to join him, to "bring your gold jewelry, but don't wear it on the boat." On the open road there was murder to fear, not merely robbery. "Just as we were rejoicing at being about to arrive home," writes a certain Psois in the latter part of the third century A.D., "we fell into an attack by bandits . . . and some of us were killed. . . . Thank god, I escaped with just being stripped clean." Wealthy travelers took along a coterie of armed slaves as protection; poorer moved in groups or waited around till they found some government official headed in the desired direction and attached themselves to his cortège.

Hunters, whose profession required the spending of time alone or nearly alone in desolate places, were particularly vulnerable. "My father," reports Aurelia Tisais on the twenty-sixth of

173

Choiak (22 December) to the chief of police of her village, "who is a hunter, left home with my brother Nilus as long ago as the 3rd of the present month to hunt hares; to date they have not returned. I suspect, therefore, that they have suffered a fatal end. I apply to you . . . so that . . . there be held accountable to me those who may prove guilty." And here is the text of a laconic report from a policeman:

> On the 5th of the present month, while patrolling the fields near the village, I found a pool of blood but no body. I learned from the villagers that Theodotus, son of Dositheus, having set out in that direction, has not yet returned. This is my report.

For some reason he canceled out the words "but no body." His last sentence shows that he felt there was a connection between the blood and the man who had disappeared; did he omit those words because including them would seem to lessen the implication of murder?

We have a letter from a son to his father, who apparently was being forced to remain at large out of reach of his foreman; the latter, the son informs him, "is looking for you and I suspect has something new against you." So fearful is the son of his father's safety that he observes, "Often, in view of the unsettled state of things, I wished to tell you that I wanted to engrave a mark on you"—in other words, brand him, like an animal, so that, in the event of death, he might be able to identify the body and give it proper burial.

The streets of town offered yet another danger. In all ages before the introduction of house plumbing, a common fashion of getting rid of waste was to empty the chamber pots out the window. In 219 B.C. Heracleides lodged an irate complaint with the authorities because

> on 21 Phamenoth [16 March], on my going into Psy on private business . . . an Egyptian woman, whose name is said to be Psenobastis, leaned out from an upper story and emptied urine into the street so that it slopped over me. When I got angry and scolded her . . . with her right hand she pulled my clothes so that my breast was left bare and she spit in my face, with bystanders present who can testify to my being victim of unjust treatment. When some of the bystanders scolded her, she climbed up to the upper story from where she had poured urine on me.[13]

174

Egypt, since time immemorial, was saturated with religion, fertile in the proliferation of deities. During the thousands of years in which the pharaohs ruled the land, the priests had formed a well-organized, powerful group. When the Greeks and Romans took over, they extended their authority to include the religious bodies and the priesthood, just as they had everything and everybody else, as we can tell from the documents that deal with such matters. On the one hand, the government astutely subsidized religious institutions: "In accordance with the king's instructions," write the priests of the goddess Hathor, worshipped in the form of a sacred cow, to the minister of finance, "to provide one hundred talents of myrrh for the burial of the Hesir [the sacred cow], will you please order this to be done." On the other hand, the government recouped some of its outlay by auctioning off posts in the priesthood; since these, over and above the dignity they conferred, entitled the holder to a cut of the offerings in cash and kind that the faithful made to the temple, there was usually no lack of candidates. Thus, a certain Pakebkis, already a priest in the temple of the crocodile god, in A.D. 146 writes to a top treasury officer that he wishes

> to purchase the office of prophet in the aforesaid temple . . . on the understanding that I shall . . . carry the palm branches and perform the other functions of the office of prophet and receive . . . one-fifth of the total revenues taken in by the temple . . . at a price . . . of 2,000 drachmas, which I will pay, upon ratification of my appointment, to the local public bank on the customary dates; furthermore, that my descendants and successors shall have ownership and possession of this office forever with all the same privileges and rights upon payment (by each) of 200 drachmas admission fee.

The businesslike, hard-boiled fashion in which Egypt's religious offices were run did not diminish one whit the power of her gods. The chief deity was Sarapis, a combination of Zeus and the Egyptian bull deity Apis; he had been deliberately created by the first Greek ruler of Egypt, Ptolemy I, around 300 B.C., but his worshippers gave no thought whatsoever to his synthetic origin. Letter after letter includes the phrase, "I thank the god Sarapis" for this or that, even as the young naval recruit Apion whom we mentioned earlier thanked him for being saved from a storm at sea. Sarapis had famous sanctuaries at Alexandria and Memphis, as well as lesser ones elsewhere. That at Memphis included not only a temple but also elaborate living quarters to accommodate worshippers who felt themselves possessed by the god; they would move in and remain until a divine sign signified their release. When a man responded to Sarapis' call, it could not help but work hardship on the family. Here, for example, is a wife's reaction, mostly packed into one long exasperated sentence:

> When I received your letter . . . in which you announce that you have become a recluse in the Sarapeum at Memphis, I immediately thanked the gods at hearing you were well, but your not coming home when all the other recluses have come home, I do not like one bit because, after having piloted myself and your child through such a bad time and gone to every extremity because of the price of food, I thought that now, at least, with you home, I would get some respite, but you haven't even thought of coming home, haven't given any regard to our circumstances, how I was without everything even while you were here, to say nothing of so long a period passing and such bad times and your not having sent us anything. What's more, Horus, who delivered your letter, reports that you've gotten your release, so I really don't like it at all!

Sarapis offered salvation—hence the strength of his attraction. He could also cure illness, but this was a secondary aspect of his power. The healer god of Egypt par excellence was Imouthes-Asclepius, a combination of Imhotep, or Imouthes, as the Greeks called him, the Egyptian god of medicine, and Asclepius, his Greek counterpart. The fusing of deities was a common practice in paganism; worshippers felt that this way they were able to appeal to two gods with one prayer.

Imouthes-Asclepius' most important sanctuary was at Memphis, and here flocked the sick and the halt, as they do today to Fatima or Lourdes, seeking the god's help. The priests in charge made them follow a fixed procedure: first they purified themselves with a ritual bath, then, at nightfall, entered the temple proper and lay down. As they slept, in a dream they learned what solution the god had for them. In a few, notable, cases it was a miracle: they arose the next morning hale and hearty. More often it was a prescription, usually spelled out plainly, occasionally enigmatically. The prescriptions were rarely exotic or outré. Most of the time they involved the taking—or not taking—of certain

176

baths, exercises, or foods, or the application of specified unguents or salves, or the downing of doses of specified drugs.

We have an eyewitness account of one of Imouthes-Asclepius' more dramatic cures, thanks to a unique papyrus discovered in 1903 by Grenfell and Hunt at Oxyrhynchus. On one side of the page is a long screed proclaiming the glory of yet another ranking Egyptian deity, the goddess Isis; it lists the manifold names she bore and the varied powers she exercised. On the other side is what purports to be a Greek translation of an ancient Egyptian book about Asclepius, with prefatory statement by the translator on what impelled him to undertake the job. He had long had such a work in mind, he informs us, but he really buckled down to it when it became an act of pious gratitude in thanks for a miracle worked on his own behalf:

> When . . . for three years my mother was distracted by an ungodly quartan ague which had seized her, . . . we came as suppliants before the god, entreating him to grant my mother recovery from the disease. He, having shown himself favorable, as he is to all, in dreams cured her by simple remedies; and we rendered due thanks to our preserver by sacrifices. When I too afterwards was suddenly seized with a pain in my right side, I quickly hastened to the helper of the human race; and he, being again disposed to pity, listened to me and displayed still more effectively his peculiar clemency, which, as I am intending to recount his terrible powers, I will substantiate.

> It was night, when every living creature was asleep except those in pain, the moment when the divinity used to manifest itself in its more active state. I was burning with fever and convulsed with loss of breath and coughing because of the pain in my side. My head was heavy from my suffering, and I was dropping off half-conscious into sleep. My mother . . . was sitting without enjoying even a brief moment of sleep, distraught at my torment. Suddenly she spied—it was no dream or sleep, for her eyes, though not seeing clearly, were fixed wide open—a divine apparition. It came in, terrifying her and easily preventing her from seeing the god himself or his servants, whichever it was. All she could say was that there was someone of more than human height, clothed in shining garments and holding in his left hand a book; he merely eyed me two or three times from head to foot and then disappeared. When she had recovered herself she tried, still all atremble, to wake me. Finding me drenched with sweat but with my fever completely gone, she knelt down in worship

177

to the divine manifestation. . . . When I spoke with her, she wanted to tell me about the god's unique ability, but I, anticipating her, told her all myself. For everything she had witnessed with her own eyes had appeared to me in my dreams. After these pains in my side had ceased, and the god had given me one more healing treatment, I proclaimed his benefactions to all.

This account was written toward the end of the first century A.D. or the beginning of the second. Asclepius, Sarapis, Isis, and all the other immortal gods of Egypt had but a few hundred years of life ahead of them. In A.D. 385 the sanctuary of Sarapis at Alexandria, his most celebrated and most richly endowed, was destroyed; that act more or less tolled the death knell of the pagan gods.

But Christianity had to fight for its victory. For long its adherents were under constant suspicion which at times flared up into empire-wide pogroms. The phrase "persecution of the Christians" conjures up in our mind's eye a picture of martyrs thrown to the lions. That did happen, but it was only the tail end of a long bureaucratic process. We have found in Egypt documents that reveal the humdrum administrative paperwork that lay behind martyrdom. A pagan was free to worship any god, to partake of burnt offerings or pour libations for deities of all kinds, Egyptian or Greek or Syrian or the state gods of the Roman Empire. Christians were not. And so, when the Emperor Decius in A.D. 250 decided to launch a government-sponsored persecution, he issued an order that all his citizens and subjects were to take, as it were, a loyalty test, were to give public proof of their religious devotion. The orders went out to the provincial governors, they passed them on to the district heads, and they in turn to all communities, great and small. In each of these a commission administered the test to everyone without exception, even priests and priestesses of the pagan cults. We know this, for we have recovered at least fifty of the certificates of proper performance that the commissioners issued. Here is a sample (Fig. 7):

> To the officials in charge of the sacrifices, from Aurelius Sakis of the village Theoxenis, together with his children Aion and Heras, temporarily residents of the Village Theadelphia. We have always been constant in sacrificing to the gods, and now, in your presence, in accordance with the regulations, we have sacrificed and

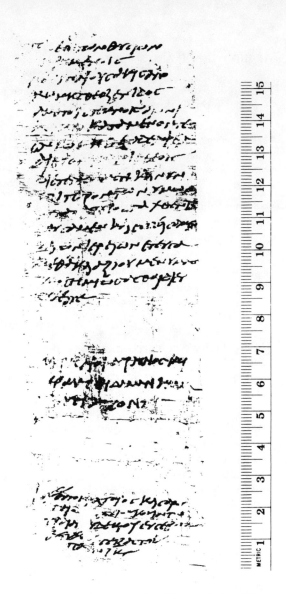

Fig. 7. Attestation of Performance of Pagan Sacrifice. Aurelius Sakis'
attestation that he had duly performed sacrifice to the Roman emperor.
The first paragraph, written by some government clerk, contains the
body of the attestation. The second, written by another clerk, records
that the government officials, Aurelius Serenus and Aurelius Hermas,
formally witnessed the act. The third, in the first clerk's handwriting,
gives the date. P. Mich. iii.157. A.D. 250. Photo courtesy University of
Michigan Library.

179

poured libations and tasted of the sacred offerings, and we request
that you certify this for us below. Farewell.

(Second hand) We, Aurelius Serenus and Aurelius Hermas,
saw you sacrificing.

(First hand) The first year of the Emperor Caesar Gaius Mes-
sius Quintus Traianus Decius Pius Felix Augustus, Pauni 23 [17
June A.D. 250].

Some followers of Christ took their loyalty test with mental
reservations. Others managed to obtain certificates through influence or bribery. Those who drew the line at such compromises
were executed, a certain number by being sold to impresarios of
gladiatorial games who used them for the midday event, the letting loose of famished wild beasts upon condemned criminals tied
to stakes.[14]

Christianity conquered the valley of the Nile as it did all other
parts of the Roman Empire. From the fourth century on,
dwellers there prayed to God instead of the gods, the Church
replaced the multitudinous pagan sanctuaries, and titles such as
presbyter, deacon, bishop, etc., made their appearance. We
know this thanks to the papyri which continue, as before, to
throw their unique light on the day-to-day doings of this corner of
the ancient world. And they do so for almost two centuries after
the coming of Islam to the land, up to the moment when, once
and for all, Roman Egypt became Arab Egypt.

Notes

1. The Italian merchant, O. Montevecchi, *La Papirologia* (Turin 1973) 30.
Grineo, ibid.; copy of the *Iliad*, 31.

2. Austrian purchases in 1877, E. Turner, *Greek Papyri* (Princeton 1968) 21–22;
Petrie's find, 24; Grenfell and Hunt, 26–31.

3. Manufacture of papyrus paper, Turner (above, n. 2) 3–5. Schubart confounds
audiences, N. Lewis, *Papyrus in Classical Antiquity* (Oxford 1974) 58. Ink,
Turner 2.

4. "To Socrates and Didymus," *Sel. Pap.* no. 309. "In the Registry of Births,"
P. Mich. iii.166; "Sempronia Gemella," 169. "You told me not," *Sel. Pap.*
105.

5. "She has received from him," *P. Reinach* ii.103. "Pesouris *versus* Saraeus," *P. Oxy.* 37. "My son was returned," *P. Oxy.* 38; "I have placed with you," 724.

6. "Send to my daughter's teacher," *Sel. Pap.* 116. *Ba, be, bi,* P. Collart, "A l'école avec les petits grecs d'Égypte," *Chronique d'Égypte* 11 (1936) 489–507 at 497. "The philosopher Pythagoras," F. Kenyon, *JHS* 29 (1909) 29–40. "It is Zeus who sends," Collart 499. "What is pleasing to the gods," Kenyon 36–37.

7. "My little Heraidous," *P. Giss.* i.78. "You did a fine thing," *P. Oxy.* 119. "I took care," *Sel. Pap.* 130. Study of Euripides, Aesop, mathematics, Collart (above, n. 6) 502; mathematics problems, 505. Trots of Vergil, Montevecchi (above, n. 1) 397. "Don't worry, father," *Sel. Pap.* 137; "Look here, this is my fifth," 133.

8. "I own in the Moeris quarter," *Sel. Pap.* 313; approval of circumcision, 338; Eudaimon, son of Psois, 301.

9. "Apion to Epimachus," *Sel. Pap.* 112. "Now writing to you" and "I want you to know," *P. Mich.* viii.490, 491. Apion's later letter, *BGU* ii.632.

10. "I have written to you before," *Sel. Pap.* 149. "On receiving this letter," *BGU* iii.814. "I have sent you . . . two mantles," *P. Mich.* viii.468. "Soldier of the legion," 476.

11. Bellienus, *P. Fayum* 110–23; N. Hohlwein, "Le vétéran Lucius Bellienus Gemellus, gentleman-farmer au Fayum," *Études de Papyrologie* 8 (1957) 69–71. Purchases of fish for "the little one," *P. Fayum* 113, 116; "lost two pigs," 111; "a rotten bundle," 119; "I want to let you know that Ailouras," 117; "buy some Isis day gifts," 118.

12. Philiskos acknowledges to Apollonia," *Sel. Pap.* 2. "I acknowledge receipt from you at the Serapeum," *P. Oxy.* 267; "I lived in marriage with Demetrous," 282.

13. "After being away," *P. Teb.* 330; "certain parties with intent to rob," 332. "A door that opened," *P. Oxy.* 69. "On the first day of the present," *P. Teb.* 331. "Bring your gold jewelry," *P. Mich.* iii.214. "Just as we were rejoicing," *P. Strass.* 233 and *Chronique d'Égypte* 39 (1964) 150–56. "My father who is a hunter," *Sel. Pap.* 336; "on the fifth of the present month," 335; "is looking for you and I suspect," 153. "On Phamenoth 21," *P. Lille* ii.24.

14. "In accordance with the King's instructions," *Sel. Pap.* 411; "to purchase the office of prophet," 353; "When I received your letter . . . in which," 97. "When . . . for three years," *P. Oxy.* 1381. "To the officials in charge," *P. Mich.* iii.157.

181

8.
Rome's Trade with the East: The Sea Voyage to Africa and India

Introduction

P reviously not twenty ships dared . . . peep outside the Straits [of Bab el Mandeb], but now great fleets are sent as far as India and the extremities of Ethiopia." So runs Strabo's oft-quoted comment (17.1.13 [798]) on Rome's twin lines of trade in the east, with India and with the east coast of Africa. Strabo wrote at the time of Augustus. Half a century or so later, Pliny the Elder delivered his equally oft-quoted remark (6.101) about the fifty million sesterces that purchases from India annually drained from the Empire. This far-flung commerce was, no question about it, of substantial economic importance. East Africa, together with Arabia, supplied the incense that smoked on the altars, and the myrrh that perfumed the rich, the length and breadth of Rome's extensive dominions. India supplied their spices, ivory, silk (importing it from China), and other luxuries.[1] The purpose of this paper is to examine more closely than has been done before the precise sailing conditions that governed voyages to these two areas and thereby reveal certain significant aspects that up to now have either escaped notice or not received the consideration they merit.

The sole way to East Africa, and the best to India, was by sea.

182

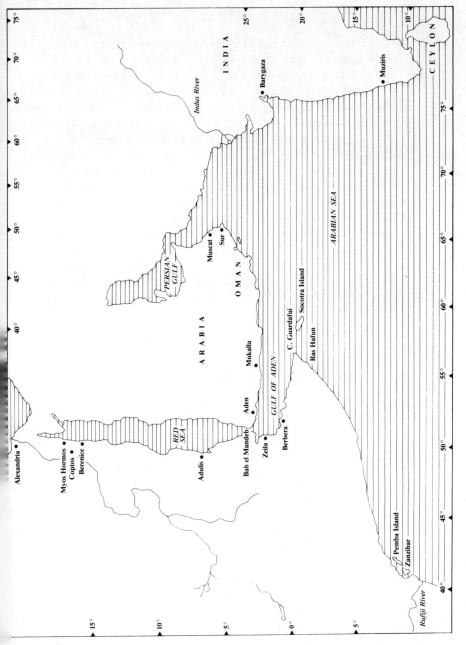

Fig. 8. Sea Trade with Africa and India.

183

The trading ventures to both were managed by the merchants of Alexandria. At their direction, the meager exports the Greco-Roman world sent to the East—they were of scant value compared with what was imported—were collected and put aboard Nile boats, brought upriver to Coptos, transferred there to donkeys and camels, and carried across Egypt's eastern desert to either Myos Hormos or Berenice, the major ports on the Egyptian side of the Red Sea. Conversely, at these two ports were discharged the cargoes that arrived from East Africa and India; reversing the path of the exports, they were taken overland to Coptos, ferried down the Nile to Alexandria, and from there distributed all over the Mediterranean world.[2]

From Myos Hormos or Berenice movement eastward was solely by water, and it involved long voyaging. The African trade route reached down to Zanzibar, more than three thousand nautical miles away, while the Indian went either to the Indus River delta or other points on the northwest coast or to the Malabar coast, a journey of well over twenty-five hundred miles in the one case and three thousand in the other.

This exotic aspect of Rome's commerce has received its share of attention in the scholarly literature. And all who have treated it have recognized that what made voyages over such distances feasible was the monsoons, the winds of the Arabian Sea and western Indian Ocean that blow from the northeast during the winter months and then conveniently switch to the southwest during the summer.[3] We have two witnesses, both writing about the middle of the first century A.D. or slightly later, to the use of the monsoons by the ancients. The first and most reliable is the anonymous author of the *Periplus Maris Erythraei.*[4] This work, the single example of its kind to have survived, is a combination of coast pilot and merchant's guide for two trade routes: one along the western shore of the Red Sea, the southern of the Gulf of Aden, and the eastern of Africa to Zanzibar or a little further, the other down the Red Sea and along the southern coast of Arabia and across the Arabian Sea to India. The author (57) notes that skippers on the India run had for long cautiously hugged the shore but then learned to sail directly over open water by exploiting the southwest wind. He says nothing about the return, but our second witness, Pliny the Elder (6.106), supplies the lack, informing us that ships left India in December-January, i.e., when the northeast monsoon was well established.

Presumably the vessels that made these monsoon passages were the same types that plied the Mediterranean. This certainly must have been true for the passage to India since, as we shall see, it involved rough winds and waters, and the Mediterranean seagoing freighters of the age were particularly well suited for such work. Not only were they big—the largest were well over one thousand tons burden—but they boasted massively strong hulls whose planking was held together by thousands of close-set mortise and tenon joints, a method of construction unique to Greek and Roman shipwrights. Their rig, too, made for safety, its major component being a vast broad square sail on a relatively short mainmast; it was, however, slow and only effective with a following wind.[5] The Arab dhows that sail to India today and have for centuries are less limited; with their lateen sails they can travel against the wind—although, being much feebler in construction than ancient craft, only against a light one.[6]

The Monsoons

To say that the monsoons blow from the northeast in winter and southwest in summer is only partly true and can be misleading. In the first place, there are transition periods in spring and autumn as one monsoon comes to a close and the other begins; at such times the wind ceases to be fixed and turns variable until the new monsoon takes hold. Even more important, the two monsoons differ greatly in their nature. The southwest is boisterous and stormy; to quote Alan Villiers, who wrote from extensive personal experience, "Rain falls heavily during its continuance, and the weather is usually so bad that the exposed ports on the Indian coast are closed and the smaller trading vessels take shelter. . . . The other monsoon—the northeast—is as gracious, as clear, and as balmy as a permanent trade, and it is this wind which wafts the great dhows—the argosies of Araby—on their long voyages from the Persian Gulf to Zanzibar and beyond, and which blows the Indian dhows from the Malabar coast to Mombasa and the Madagascar coast."[7] Lastly, the Red Sea, which had

185

Chart of Prevailing Winds from the Red Sea to East Africa and India

	A June to August	B September	C October	D November to December	E December to March	F April	G May
1 Red Sea south of 20° N	N, NW	N, NW shifting to variable	S, SE	S, SE			S,SE shifting to N, NE
2 Gulf of Aden	S, SW, W		variable, shifting to E, ENE	E, ENE			E, ENE also variables
3 East African Coast to Zanzibar	S, SW	S, SW shifting to NE with variables and calms		N, NE		NE shifting to S, SW	
4 Northwestern Coast of India	SW	W, SW with variables and calms	S, SW shifting to NE	N, NE		NW to SW	S, SW
5 Southwestern Coast of India	SW	W, SW shifting to W, NW	light northerlies	N, NE		NW to SW	S, SW

to be traversed going and coming, has its own wind pattern which does not totally coincide with the monsoons. The accompanying chart shows what the winds in general are, month by month, in the areas under consideration.[8]

All who have written on the subject of Rome's Indian Ocean trade make no distinction between voyages to India and Africa but treat them together. And it is easy to see why: after all, they were both about the same length, some three thousand nautical miles, and took place in roughly the same waters and under the same monsoon winds. The point of what follows is to reveal that these similarities are superficial, that the two trading ventures were not at all alike. To India and back could be done within a year but involved considerable danger. To Africa took twice as long but was a sailor's dream.

The Voyage to Zanzibar

The *Periplus* (1–18) provides a detailed account of the route to East Africa. At Myos Hormos or Berenice vessels loaded up with the sort of goods that has figured in trade with primitive peoples right up to this century: cheap clothing and cookware and dinnerware, metals for making into ornaments or utensils or weapons, and, for the tribal chieftains, luxury garments and objects of gold and silver. They proceeded along the western shore of the Red Sea, where their first important stop was at Adulis (Massawa), Ethiopia's only good seaport; here they took on ivory and tortoise shell. Then they coasted along the south shore of the Gulf of Aden, putting in at points all along the way to trade for the myrrh and incense for which the region was famous. Rounding Cape Guardafui, they sailed down to Ras Hafun, still picking up myrrh and incense, and then continued south along the eastern shore of Africa to Menouthias Island, which is either Pemba or Zanzibar, and finally, Rhapta, which is either Dar es Salaam or at the mouth of the Rufiji River, depending upon the identification of Menouthias.[9] Here, as at Ethiopia, the usual cheap trade goods were exchanged for ivory and tortoise shell.

Ships heading for Africa, the *Periplus* informs us (14), left Egypt in July. This is what we would expect. It enabled a skipper to travel:

> from Egypt to the Gulf of Aden with the favorable northerlies (Chart 1A), and
> through the Gulf of Aden with the favorable southwest monsoon (Chart 2A).

In the Red Sea, because of its dangerous shoals, all vessels sail only during the day, putting in toward nightfall at the nearest available anchorage.[10] Consequently, even if they traveled steadily, getting quickly in and out of the ports they stopped at, they still would have required at least thirty to forty days to reach Cape Guardafui.[11] In any event, there was no sense in arriving there before the onset of the northeast monsoon in October; a better time yet was mid-October or the beginning of November when it had definitely settled in (Chart 3 C/D).[12] Until then the southwest monsoon was still blowing, and even more efficient sailing craft than the ancients' square-riggers could not have beat down the coast of East Africa against it.[13] The *Periplus* (14) specifically

187

mentions that some ships tramped, selling and buying cargo at every point along the way, while others made directly for the incense ports of the African horn. They all must have traveled leisurely, taking from seventy-five days (say 15 July to 1 October) to over one hundred (15 July to 1 November) to reach Cape Guardafui. Once there, as we shall see in a moment, there was no need whatsoever to hurry.

The next stage, from Guardafui southward, was not only smooth sailing but quick, with the northeast monsoon at a vessel's heels (Chart 3D). The distance is some fourteen hundred nautical miles and current is favorable as well as wind.[14] The voyage, during which vessels could sail day and night (cf. *Periplus* 15), might have lasted but two weeks, but we must, of course, allow for stops en route.

Thus arrival in the vicinity of Zanzibar would have taken place in November or December. Now, once there, a skipper was committed to spending no less than eight months in the area. The earliest he could possibly leave, and then only if he intended to dawdle on his way up the African coast, was August. For he had to time his voyage so that he

> would sail from Zanzibar to Guardafui no later than September–October in order to catch the end of the southwest monsoon (Chart 3B/C),
>
> reach Guardafui not before October in order to catch the early northeast monsoon which would provide favorable winds for traversing the Gulf of Aden (Chart 2C), and
>
> catch favorable winter southerlies in the Red Sea (Chart 1C/D).[15]

If we allow for the sail from Guardafui back to Egypt the same amount of time as on the outbound voyage, thirty to forty days, he would arrive home in November or December, a year and a half after his departure. This left six months or so to collect a cargo for another venture to the area the next July. In effect, two years were required for a round trip.

It was the dogleg into the Gulf of Aden that caused the trouble, the need, after sailing north to Cape Guardafui, to make an abrupt left turn and head west. Ships returning from Zanzibar to the Persian Gulf or to India had a straight run and hence could depart with the oncoming of the monsoon in April, after a layover that might be as short as three months.[16] Today dhows bound for the Red Sea may leave with it, taking advantage of the fact that in May the winds of the Gulf of Aden are not yet firmly locked into the southwesterly direction they will have in June but offer some variation.[17] This option was not open to a skipper of an ancient craft with its square rig, slower and less flexible than a dhow's. He could not leave until mid-April or so,[18] and, if the variables in the Gulf held him up,[19] he might not reach the Straits of Bab el Mandeb until the end of May—just when the wind would turn against him in the Red Sea (Chart 1G). Besides, even if he was lucky enough to have a fair passage all the way, he would arrive no earlier than June, and this would hardly leave time to unload, refit, and take on a new cargo for departure in July. By lingering in Zanzibar until the closing days of the southwest monsoon, he would be assured of fair and moderate winds all the way and plenty of time to prepare for a new round trip.

Is it not possible that vessels which started from Egypt went only as far as Africa's horn, leaving the long leg to Zanzibar and back to others for whom the voyage would involve far less waiting for the turn of the monsoons? The *Periplus* (16) distinctly mentions that Rhapta—either Dar es Salaam or on the Rufiji River south of it—was a port of call for Arab craft; could they not have handled its trade? That would leave for Greco-Roman vessels only the trip from Egypt to the horn and back, which could easily be done within half a year, outbound in July-September (Chart 1A/B, 2A/B) and the return in October-December (2C/D, 1C/D).[20] Very possibly some did it this way—but the author of the *Periplus* nowhere speaks of them. What is more, in a handbook written in Greek and therefore addressed to Greek-speaking merchants and skippers, he carries on his description without a break as far as Rhapta; the clear implication is that it was regularly part of the trade route.

Though the voyage was long for these Greek traders, it was easy, since all of it took place under ideal sailing conditions. Outward bound, the leg through the Gulf of Aden was done during the closing days of the southwest monsoon when it had lost much of its bite, and the leg down the coast of East Africa under the mild northeast monsoon. Homeward bound, the leg back up the coast took place during the closing days of the southwest monsoon and the traversing of the Gulf of Aden during the opening days of the northeast monsoon. Indeed, the voyage is so

189

undemanding that currently merchants entrust their goods, and passengers their lives, to dhows of such modest size and in such wretched condition and so hopelessly overcrowded that they could not possibly survive even the slightest storm at sea.[21]

The Voyage to India

Ships left Egypt for India, as for Africa, in July, the *Periplus* (39, 49, 56) informs us. They did so for the same reasons, to take advantage of the summer northerlies in the Red Sea (Chart 1A) in order to get down to its exit at Bab el Mandeb, and of the southwest monsoon (Chart 2A) in order to get out of the Gulf of Aden. And, again as the *Periplus* (57) specifically informs us, carried by the southwest monsoon they sailed over open water either to the mouth of the Indus River or Barygaza (on the Gulf of Cambay) on India's northwest coast or to Muziris on the southwest coast.

How long did the voyage take? Pliny the Elder offers some data (6.104). He agrees with the author of the *Periplus* that vessels made their departure in mid-summer. He then states that "Ocelis in Arabia [on the Straits of Bab el Mandeb] or Cane in the incense country [probably Husn al Ghurab in the Hadhramaut west of Mukalla][22] was reached in about thirty days. . . . From Ocelis . . . one sails with the southwest wind to Muziris . . . in forty." These figures are cited by everyone who has written on the subject, almost always without question.[23] Yet the first is most curiously expressed and the second must be a mistake. Why give the same traveling time to Ocelis and Cane, when Cane is over two hundred miles further? It is like giving the same time for the voyage, say from Marseilles to both Messina and Naples. The second figure, forty days from Bab el Mandeb to Muziris (just north of Cochin), since the distance in round numbers is two thousand nautical miles, works out to an average speed of two knots. Yet if a ship left Egypt in mid-July, and then thirty days later Ocelis in mid-August, it would have on its heels the southwest monsoon just when that strong wind was blowing its hardest, averaging more than twenty to thirty knots in the waters between the horn of Africa and the southwest coast of India.[24] Ancient sailing craft were capable of doing between four and six knots with favorable winds in the Mediterranean, as we glean from voyages Pliny himself describes;

surely they would have done at least as well on the run to India
under the southwest monsoon, in other words made the crossing in
twenty days, half the time Pliny allots.[25] Somehow there is a tendency to gloss over Pliny's errors or forgive them. "Ships sail back
from India," he says (6.106), "at the beginning . . . of December
or at any rate . . . before January 15," which is precisely what we
would expect, since by that time the northeast monsoon had set in.
"Moreover," he adds, "they sail from India with the southeast
wind." "By a slip," explains E. H. Warmington, author of the
definitive study of Rome's India trade, "Pliny calls [the northeast
monsoon] Volturnus [southeast]."[26] With the same forbearance,
let us say that by a slip he wrote forty instead of twenty.

The return was no problem: departure in December-January
meant that it took place during the benign northeast monsoon
(Chart 4D/E, 5D/E). And, since this lasted from November to
April, one could shove off even earlier or later.[27] But there was
no leeway for the outbound voyage; that had to be timed as
carefully as the homebound from Zanzibar which we discussed a
moment ago. So far as winds were concerned, leaving the Red
Sea ports in June might seem as good as July (Chart 1A, 2A, 4A,
5A). But there was more to be considered than the direction of
the wind. Departure in June would bring a vessel to India's
shores in August—and that was to be avoided at all cost. During
most of the summer, sailing conditions on India's west coast are
so dangerous that practically all maritime activity ceases. This is
particularly true of the southwestern coast, where Muziris, the
end of Pliny's "forty-day" voyage lay. At present in this area the
marine insurance rates, which vary between 1 and 1.75 percent
during the northeast monsoon, rise to 20 percent by the end of
May when the southwest monsoon has set in, and during June,
July, and August, marine insurance is simply not available at any
price. By September it is again offered at the fairly reasonable
rate of 2.5 percent.[28] It follows that ancient vessels must have left
their Red Sea ports in July and not before in order to reach the
coast of India no earlier than September, when the southwest
monsoon was approaching its end and beginning to quiet down.
Arrival anytime later, in October, was inadvisable since it would
have exposed ships to the contrary winds of the northeast monsoon (Chart 4C, 5C).

Thus the skippers who plied between Roman Egypt and India

were not foolhardy: by delaying their departure until July, they avoided India's coast when it was most dangerous. But they still had to carry out a good part of their ocean crossing during the time when the southwest monsoon was blowing its hardest, often stirring up violent storms. From the writings of Arab navigators of the late fifteenth and early sixteenth centuries we know that in that age Arab skippers also used the southwest monsoon, but delayed departure until the end of August and the beginning of September when it was beginning to slacken. They were able to do so since their ships were either fast enough to reach India before the coming of the northeast monsoon, or, failing that, with their lateen rigs could sail against the feeble breezes of its early stages.[29] The ancients did not have this alternative. As the author of the *Periplus* (39) puts it in his matter-of-fact way, "The crossing with these [southwest winds] is risky but absolutely fair and shorter."

Conclusion

Thus, two areas of trade, which traditionally have been treated together, turn out upon examination to be totally different in the demands they made on both shipowners and merchants. A venture to Africa was safe, cheap, and involved only short coastal hauls. Consequently it was open to owners of craft of no great size, on which they had expended no great amount of money for upkeep (like the "incredibly small and decrepit" dhows Alan Villiers saw making the voyage[30]), and whose scant cargo space they might charter to a handful of small-time traders. And neither owners nor traders were much concerned about storms at sea. However, though their stakes were modest and relatively safe, two long years had to pass before there were any profits to pocket.

On the other hand, ventures to India—at least the ones our sources consider the most important, those that exploited the direct crossing over open water—were just the reverse. It took only a year for the capital invested to yield a return. But the amount of capital required was formidable, and there was a definite element of risk. Such trading ventures were open only to the owners of powerful vessels able to endure the force of the southwest monsoon and to the merchants with the money to purchase enough of the costly merchandise India exported—spices, silks, and the like—to fill the capacious holds. The India trade was for large-scale operators, whether shipowners or traders.

Notes

1. For a masterly study of the India trade, see E. H. Warmington, *The Commerce between the Roman Empire and India* (Cambridge 1928). Archaeology has added some information since Warmington wrote: see M. Wheeler, *Rome Beyond the Imperial Frontiers* (London 1954), chaps. xii–xiii. On trade with Africa, see chap. viii. In East Africa archaeology has so far undertaken only surveys, and these have yielded discouragingly little; see H. N. Chittick, "An Archaeological Reconnaissance of the Southern Somali Coast," *Azania* 4 (1969) 115–30, and "An Archaeological Reconnaissance in the Horn: The British-Somali Expedition, 1975," *Azania* 11 (1976) 117–33, as well as his brief but useful summary, "Early Ports in the Horn of Africa," *International Journal of Nautical Archaeology* 8 (1979) 273–77.

2. Pliny *N.H.*, 6.102–103, gives in detail the route to Berenice. For Myos Hormos, see Strabo 2.5.12 (118). It seems to have been—or become—less important; cf. R. Bagnall, *The Florida Ostraka*, Greek, Roman, and Byzantine Monographs 7 (Durham 1976) 34–39. Berenice was well over 200 miles south of Myos Hormos, which meant, for returning vessels, that much less beating against the northerlies which prevail in the Red Sea above latitude 20° north.

3. E.g., M. Charlesworth, *Trade-Routes and Commerce of the Roman Empire* (Cambridge 1926²) 60; Warmington (above, n. 1) 43–51; G. Hourani, *Arab Seafaring* (Princeton 1951) 24–28; Wheeler (above, n. 1) chap. x; R. Böker, *RE* Suppl. 9 (1962) s.v. "Monsunschiffahrt nach Indien"; M. Cary and E. Warmington, *The Ancient Explorers* (Penguin 1963²) 95–96.

4. The date of the *Periplus*, after a recent flurry of heated argument to lower it to the 3rd c. A.D., is back to its previous favored place, the second half of the 1st c. A.D. For a judicious review of the problem, see W. Raunig, "Die Versuche einer Datierung des Periplus maris Erythraei," *Mitteilungen der anthropologischen Gesellschaft in Wien* 100 (1970) 231–42, esp. 240, and, for a listing of the bulky bibliography on the question, M. Raschke in *ANRW* ii.9.2 (Berlin 1978) 979–80, nn. 1342–43. The working out of a solid chronology for the kings of Nabataea establishes a terminus ante quem of A.D. 70; see G. Bowersock, "A Report on Arabia Provincia," *JRS* 61 (1971) 219–42 at 223–25 and *Roman Arabia* (Cambridge, Mass. 1983) 70.

5. See *SSAW* 183–90 (size of Mediterranean freighters), 201–208 (hull structure), 239–43 (rig).

6. Thus Ibn Mājid, author of a treatise on navigation published toward the end of the 15th c., cautions that, in certain crossings from the south coast of

Arabia to the island of Socotra, "they do not travel . . . unless the wind is light because they are traveling contrary to the Kaws [southwest wind]" (G. Tibbets, *Arab Navigation in the Indian Ocean before the Coming of the Portuguese,* Oriental Translation Fund, n.s. xlii [London 1971] 229). A few lines later he speaks of a " 'wind of two sails' also needing a light wind"; a "wind of two sails" was a course not even involving a head wind but just a wind on the beam, its name deriving from the fact that one would sail with it on one side and then, returning, on the other (Tibbetts 369). Alan Villiers describes a voyage in a dhow during which they beat for 500 miles along the south coast of Arabia; it was against breezes so mild that the ship often merely ghosted along and was frequently becalmed (*Sons of Sinbad* [New York 1949] 26, 30, 48–49).

7. *Monsoon Seas* (New York 1952) 7.

8. For the monsoons, see U.S. Defense Mapping Agency, Hydrographic Center Pub. 61, *Sailing Directions for the Red Sea and Gulf of Aden* (1965^5, rev. ed. 1976) section 1–26 to 28 (Red Sea), 1–29 to 31 (Gulf of Aden); Pub. 60, *Sailing Directions for the Southeast Coast of Africa* (1968^5, rev. ed. 1975) section 1–23; Pub. 63, *Sailing Directions for the West Coast of India* (1967^5, rev. ed. 1976) section 1–26 to 27.

9. The identification has long been a source of controversy; for the bibliography, see Raschke (above, n. 4) 933, n. 1139. Over a century ago Charles Guillain, a seaman who had traveled the waters in the days of sail, set forth the nearly equal claims of Pemba and Zanzibar to be identified with Menouthias and decided in favor of Zanzibar; see his *Documents sur l'histoire, la géographie, et le commerce de l'afrique orientale* (Paris [1856]) 1.110–15. The latest to take up the question, B. Datoo ("Rhapta: The Location and Importance of East Africa's First Port," *Azania* 5 [1970] 65–75) leaves it open.

10. Cf. Carsten Niebuhr's experience in 1762 (see T. Hansen, *Arabia Felix: The Danish Expedition of 1761–1767* [New York 1962] 209) and Alan Villiers in 1938 (above, nn. 6, 7).

11. Ancient ships could make between 4 and 6 knots with a fair wind (*SSAW* 288) and thus log roughly 50 nautical miles during a day's run. Gullain (above, n. 9) 1.96–97 estimated 48 for the first part of the journey down the east coast of Africa and 60 for the second, the difference caused by variation in the strength of the current (cf. below, n. 14). The distance from Myos Hormos to Cape Guardafui is ca. 1700 nautical miles.

12. As Ibn Mājid puts it (above, n. 6, 234), "Those who travel from Aden and Yemen to Zanj [the African coast off Zanzibar] should start on the 320th or the 330th day [8 or 18 October]." Cf. Guillain (above, n. 9) 1.95: "La mousson de l'est se fait sentir [in the Gulf of Aden] dans la première quinzaine d'octobre, et les bateaux qui vont à l'est de ce cap [Guardafui] doivent avoir dépassé son meridien avant le 1er novembre."

194

13. Cf. the rueful words of a British naval commander who in 1799 tried to sail a full-rigged ship against the even milder northeast monsoon: "Thus terminated one of the most perplexing and tedious Voyages ever made by any Ships. It is, I believe, the first Attempt ever made to beat up the *Coast of Africa* against the *Easterly Monsoon,* and it is to be hoped Nobody would ever attempt it again" (A. Bissell, *A Voyage from England to the Red-Sea and along the East Coast of Arabia to Bombay . . . 1798 and 1799* [London 1806] 47).

14. Cf. Guillain (above, n. 9) 1.96: 1.3 knots of current as far as some 60 miles south of Ras Asswad (4° 34′N), 2–3 from there on.

15. This is the way the ship that carried Henry Salt from Zanzibar to Aden in 1809 did it; see his *Voyage to Abyssinia* (1814, reprint ed. 1967) 94–99. The southwest monsoon carried them north to Cape Guadafui by 27 September, then a light wind typical of the transition period and adverse current prevented progress all of the 28th, after which the northeast monsoon wafted them to Aden by the 3rd of October. Zanzibar was by no means the only place where the alternation of the monsoons could cause long layovers. "Because of the Azyab [northeast monsoon] . . . he who is forced to moor in Yemen," states Ibn Mājid (Tibbetts [above, n. 6] 227), "must stay there a whole year when bound for India" (from October, when the northeast monsoon sets in, until September of the following year, when the southwest monsoon has quieted down sufficiently to allow a safe passage and arrival [cf. below, n. 27]).

16. Alan Villiers traveled on a dhow from the Persian Gulf that arrived at Zanzibar in February, which was late since others had arrived in January, and left on 15 April (above, n. 6, 206, 269). Arrival in January and departure in April is standard practice; cf. A. Prins, "The Persian Gulf Dhows," *Persica* 2 (1965–66) 1–18 at 5–6. Cf. Bissell (above, n. 13) 35: "The small *Trading Vessels* from Muscat, and the Red Sea, after discharging their Cargoes, which is chiefly *Dates,* always *dismantle,* and *move* into an *Inner Harbour,* at the *back* of the *town,* and wait the *return* of the [southwest] *Monsoon.*"

17. Cf. Datoo (above, n. 9) 67.

18. Vessels could not leave Zanzibar until the southwest monsoon had established itself, and this might be well into April; cf. Bissell (above, n. 13) 37: "They [the locals of Zanzibar] ridiculed the *Idea* of our going away, before the SW Monsoon set in, and said we should be plagued with *Calms* and *Variable Winds,* with *Southerly Currents* till the *Middle* of *April.*"

19. Dhows generally shun the Gulf of Aden during May precisely because the winds then cannot be trusted; cf. Ibn Mājid's statement quoted above, n. 15, and the observations of a naval officer who visited Berbera in 1848: "From April to the early part of October, the place was utterly deserted . . . ; but no sooner did the season change, than . . . small craft from the ports of Ye-

men . . . hastened across, followed, about a fortnight to three weeks later, by their larger brethren from Muscat, Soor, and Ras el Khyma. . . . By the end of March . . . , craft of all kinds . . . commence their homeward journey. By the first week of April the place is again deserted." (*Journal of the Royal Geographical Society* 19 [1849] 54–55; also quoted by Richard Burton in his *First Footsteps in East Africa* [London 1856, reprint ed. 1966] 225–26).

20. In a papyrus document of the 2nd c. B.C. that contains an agreement for a loan to finance a trading voyage to Punt—the Somali coast—the length of the loan was set at one year. The editor suggests that that was the time required for the round-trip voyage; see U. Wilcken, "Punt-Fahrten in der Ptolemäerzeit," *Zeitschrift für ägyptische Sprache und Altertumskunde* 60 (1925) 86–102 at 94 and cf. R. Bogaert in *Chronique d'Égypte* 40 (1965) 149. It was the time required plus a good deal to spare, as we would expect in view of the uncertainties of travel by sailing ship.

21. Cf. Villiers (above, n. 6) 141, 154–55, 282.

22. For the identification, see Schoff 116, and G. Mathew in H. N. Chittick and R. Rotberg, eds., *East Africa and the Orient* (New York 1975) 159–60.

23. W. Kroll, *RE* s.v. "Schiffahrt" 419 (1923); Warmington (above, n. 1) 46, 48, and 342, n. 48; Wheeler (above, n. 1) 126; Cary and Warmington (above, n. 3) 97; G. Van Beek in *Journal of the American Oriental Society* 80 (1960) 139. Schoff (233) renders Pliny's words without comment. Hourani (above, n. 3) 26 is aware that 40 days is hardly fast but does not question the figure. Warmington does see an error in Pliny's numbers—but in the wrong place. In 6.84 Pliny tells of a traveler, the freedman of a certain Annius Plocamus, who was caught by strong northerlies off Arabia and blown helplessly until, 15 days later, he landed on Ceylon. Warmington (341, n. 30) suggests altering Pliny's *xv* to *xl* to bring it in line with the figure of 40 days we are discussing. The distance from Arabia to Ceylon is some 1,500 to 1,600 nautical miles, and this, traversed in 15 days, would work out to an average speed of something over 4 knots—which, as I show below, is more or less what we would expect with winds of presumably gale force or near it. I would reverse Warmington's suggestion and read *xv* instead of *xl* in 6.104!

E. Ascher in two articles in the *Journal of Tropical Geography* (a publication of the universities of Singapore and Malaya) entitled "Graeco-Roman Nautical Technology and Modern Sailing Information" (30 [1970] 10–26) and "The Timetables of the Periplus Maris Erythraei and of Pliny's Voyage to India" (34 [1974] 1–7) questions Pliny's figure—but he questions practically all Pliny's data and the *Periplus* to boot. This is because Ascher is convinced—it must be by intuition, for he cites no sources, either primary or secondary, and indeed there are none to cite—that the Roman merchantman was "undoubtedly inferior to her Greek and Phoenician forebears," was of such a "clumsy nature . . . [that] in a strong wind [she] was liable to be swamped" ([1970] 13); manifestly such a wretched type of ship could not

196

make the voyages Pliny and the *Periplus* attribute to it, so Ascher then proceeds to tell us what Pliny and the *Periplus* should have said. We have nothing but the vaguest notion of what Phoenician craft were like (and no one has ever suggested that they were the forebears of "Roman" merchantmen), but we do know for certain that the ships plying the seas in the days of the *Periplus* were vastly bigger, sturdier, and better rigged than Ascher's "superior" Greek forebears (cf., e.g., Lucian, *Navigium* 5). Those vessels "liable to be swamped"? Ascher has not even read the account of St. Paul's shipwreck!

24. *Sailing Directions for the . . . Gulf of Aden* (above, n. 8) section 1–31.

25. For speed of ancient craft, cf. *SSAW* 282–88. Dhows frequently make the voyage in 20 days (Van Beek [above n. 22]); though faster than ancient ships they sail, as we shall see in a moment, when the winds are more moderate.

26. Above, n. 1, 48.

27. Since the winter was precisely the time for returning from India to the Red Sea, one is puzzled by the way commentators have consistently interpreted a passage in *Periplus* 32. The author there describes Moscha, one of the ports for the export of frankincense located on the Dhofar plain just west of Oman (cf. Schoff 140–142). Among the vessels that loaded up here were "those that sailed by [*parapleonta*] out of Limyrike [the southwestern coast of India] or Barygaza [Broach] and passed the winter [*paracheimasanta, sc.* at Moscha], the time of year being late." Schoff's translation reveals that he takes these to be Arab craft returning from India (he even renders *parapleonta* "returning"), and he has been followed by Warmington (above, n. 1) 342, n. 34; Wheeler (above, n. 1) 117; Van Beek (*Biblical Archaeologist* 23 [1960] 79); W. Müller (s.v. "Weihrauch," *RE* Suppl. 15.727 [1978]). But there is no reason for Arab craft to stop and winter at Moscha; winter was precisely the time to return from India not only to Arabia but anywhere west of it. C. Müller, in his commentary to the passage (*Geographi Graeci Minores* [Paris 1855] 1.282), suggested they were vessels which *serius enavigaverant quam ut secundo etesiarum flatu in Africae oram deferri possent*—which makes no sense either; winter was precisely the season for sailing from Arabia to Africa (cf. the observations of a naval officer quoted above, n. 19). The ships must have been Indian, not Arab; having lingered in Arabia too long to catch the end of the southwest monsoon in August-September, they had to wait through the winter until it returned the following spring; cf. Ibn Mājid's statement quoted above, n. 15.

28. The 15th- and 16th-c. Arab writers on navigation took it for granted that most of the ports on India's west coast were closed from May to July and practically all of them in June and July (Tibbetts [above, n. 6] 367–68). For the insurance rates, see R. Bowen, "The Dhow Sailor," *The American Neptune* 11 (1951) 5–46 at 12.

29. The Arab navigators recommend departing for India as follows (Tibbetts [above, n. 6] 365): from Zeila and Berbera on 24 or 25 August, from Aden between 24 and 29 August (although Ibn Mājid will allow up to 18 September), from Shihr or Mishqās or Zafar (on the south coast of Arabia roughly 300, 400, and 600 miles respectively east of Aden) on 3 September or 14 September or (Ibn Mājid again) 8 October. These are consistently later than the ancients' departure date. This is understandable. The later one left, the weaker were the winds of the southwest monsoon that were encountered and the safer the crossing, a crucial consideration for Arab craft, whose mode of construction was far feebler than the Greco-Roman (cf. J. Hornell, *Water Transport* [Cambridge 1946] 234–35). The same departure dates prevail today; see Van Beek (above, n. 22) 139 (*pace* Raschke [above, n. 4, 937] who accuses him of not saying exactly what he does say). Van Beek, by accepting Pliny's figures, wrongly concludes that the ancients also left this late in the season.

30. Above, n. 6, 141.

9.
The Location of Adulis
(*Periplus Maris Erythraei* 4)

The port of Adulis was the most important on the western shore of the Red Sea. Through it passed the major part of Ethiopia's trade,[1] and as Ethiopia's Axumite kingdom grew politically and economically, particularly from the fourth through the sixth century A.D., so did Adulis.[2] From it were exported such native products as ivory, rhinoceros horn, and tortoise shell; into it came a variety of imports from near and far, from Egypt, Arabia and India—even, some argue, from China.[3] Adulis must have been, in consequence, a large and bustling entrepôt. Yet precisely where its harbor lay, where the ships put in to load and unload their cargoes, is a puzzle.

We are fortunate in having an eyewitness description provided by the author of the *Periplus Maris Erythraei*, who wrote sometime in the second half of the first century A.D.[4] At that time Adulis was

an officially recognized trading post located on a deep bay, extending due south, in front of which is an island called Oreinê ["Rocky"] lying about two hundred stades from the innermost point of the bay towards the open sea, and with both its shores parallel to the mainland. . . . Formerly they used to anchor at this outermost[5] point of the bay on what is called Didorus Island right by the mainland. But there is a ford to it that is able to be crossed by foot, and by means of this the natives dwelling in the area used

199

to raid the island. Adulis, a village of moderate size, stands on the mainland opposite Oreinê, twenty stades inland. From it to Coloe,[6] a city in the hinterland that is the chief trading post for ivory, is a journey of three days, and from there to the metropolis itself, called Axum, another five. . . . In front of the trading post in the open sea to the right lie numerous other small sandy islands called Alalaiou which furnish the tortoise shell brought to the post by the Fish-Eaters.

Thus, in seeking to identify the location of Adulis and its harbor, we should look for a site that a) is on or near the mouth of a deep bay extending southwards; b) has in front a rocky island (Oreinê), usable as an anchorage, which is toward the open sea, is two hundred stades (about twenty miles) from the innermost point of the bay, and is so oriented that its shores are parallel with the mainland; c) has somewhere in the general vicinity another island (Didorus) so near the mainland that one can cross to it by foot; d) has several sandy islets in the open sea to the right of where the village (as against its harbor) lies.

The obvious candidate for the "deep bay extending due south" is Annesley Bay—or the Gulf of Zula, as it is also called—which lies between 15°3′ and 15°32′ north latitude (fig. 9). It is deep, is oriented north-south, and is in the area where, according to the line of travel and distances given in the *Periplus,* Adulis should be: the strip of coast that has served and still serves as starting point for the routes which mount to the uplands where Axum lies.

This part of the world was for long almost *terra incognita.* Annesley Bay was not properly located and charted until the beginning of the nineteenth century.[7] The first European to visit its shores and render an account of what he saw was Henry Salt, whose *Voyage to Abyssinia* appeared in 1814. In it he reported the discovery of ancient ruins about halfway down the western shore of the bay. They were by the bank of a river some three-quarters of a mile northwest of the modern village of Zula and some four miles in from the coast. The natives called them "Azoole," and, indeed, it was a reasonable conjecture that the name Zula itself was ultimately derived from the same source.[8] Salt concluded that this was the site of Adulis, a conclusion that has never been called into question.[9]

Archaeological investigation of the site did not come until well-

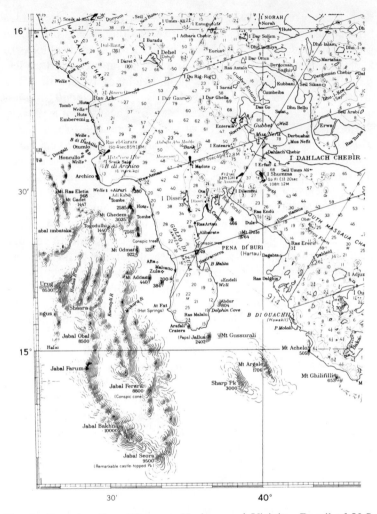

Fig. 9. Annesley Bay, Massawa Harbor, and Vicinity. Detail of U.S. Hydrographic Center Chart no. 62008.

201

nigh a century later, when R. Sundström in 1907 carried out a brief investigation.[10] He was able to trace the ground plan of an important building that had been constructed of ashlar blocks of a black porous stone; rectangular in shape, it measured no less than 38 by 22.5 meters, rose to a height of two stories, was approached by a monumental staircase, and included columns and marble veneering in its decoration. The following year R. Paribeni published the results of a more extended exploration.[11] This brought to light both the scanty but unmistakable remains of a native village that long predated Classical times and the abundant and impressive remains, many of them Christian, of a flourishing town of the fourth to sixth century A.D., the age to which Sundström's discovery belonged.[12] Paribeni unearthed quite a few coins, issues of Axum, of which forty-two were of gold; these ranged chronologically from the beginning of the fourth century, or a bit earlier, up to the ninth and tenth.[13] Despite the late date of some of the coins, the excavation revealed clearly that, at the time when the power of Islam spread over this part of the world, the town suffered first destruction and then decay.[14]

The excavation seemed to put the identification beyond any doubt. Here were the ruins of buildings; here was evidence of activity and civilization consonant with what we knew about Adulis in its heyday, the fourth through the sixth century A.D. What is more, the location agreed nicely not only with the words of the author of the *Periplus* but also with those of Procopius and Cosmas Indicopleustes, for all three state that Adulis was a short distance inland. Yet there is one insuperable difficulty that almost every one of those who so confidently made the identification simply glossed over: the site of these ruins, aside from being inland, does not in any way fit the indications given in the *Periplus*.[15]

There is no harbor proper anywhere near the ruins, but just a stretch of beach that descends into the water at so gentle an angle that one must go out hundreds of yards to find sufficient depth to float a seagoing vessel.[16] To be sure, as we shall see later, this does not preclude use as an anchorage. What is decisive is the fact that there are no islands whatsoever along this shore, nothing to answer to the Didorus Island, which, the *Periplus* informs us, stood close to the mainland and for long served as Adulis's harbor.

It so happens that on the coast just twenty-five or so miles north[17] of where the ruins lie, there is just such an island. Moreover, it forms part of a superb natural harbor, the only one in the region—Massawa. Massawa in fact fits so very well with what we read in the *Periplus* that knowledgeable commentators who wrote before Salt's discovery did not hesitate to identify it as the site of Adulis.[18] Didorus Island would be what is today called Taulud; the modern causeway bearing water pipes and telephone lines that connects it with the mainland runs over shallows that could well have been the ford used by the raiders referred to in the *Periplus* (fig. 10). And the harbor, just as now, would have been the deep and well-protected inlet bounded on the south by Taulud and Massawa islands and on the north by the peninsula that juts out from the mainland.

If Taulud was Didorus Island, then surely Oreinê, which became the anchorage when marauding made the Taulud-Massawa harbor too dangerous, must be Dissei Island. It faces the open sea at the mouth of Annesley Bay; it is just about twenty miles from the innermost point of the bay; it is so oriented that both its shores lie parallel to the mainland; and it can aptly be called "Rocky," being "volcanic with a series of conical peaks, the summit of which is Monte Dissei, 335 feet high."[19] In fact, it is the sole island in the area that merits such a name. Off its southeastern shore, as it happens, there is a good anchorage. Finally, the sandy islets that were a source of tortoise shell, "in front of the trading post in the open sea to the right," would certainly include Sheik Said, which on older maps is actually called "Isle de la Tortue," and perhaps the islets between it and Dahlac Chebir. Some commentators see a connection between the ancient name Alalaiou and the modern Dahlac.[20]

Massawa then suits nicely the description in the *Periplus* of Adulis's original anchorage. The *Periplus* locates the village and trading post (*kômê; emporion*), as against its harbor, twenty stades—some two miles—inland opposite Oreinê. Inasmuch as Oreinê is said to be "toward the open sea" and the sandy islets to be "in front of the trading post (*emporion*) in the open sea," it follows that Adulis more or less faced open water. And from this it follows that we cannot possibly place the Adulis of the *Periplus* on the ruins found by Salt, since these do not face open water but are halfway down the bay from its mouth.

From about A.D. 750, when Islam began its hegemony over the Red Sea, to the present day, Massawa has been the port par

203

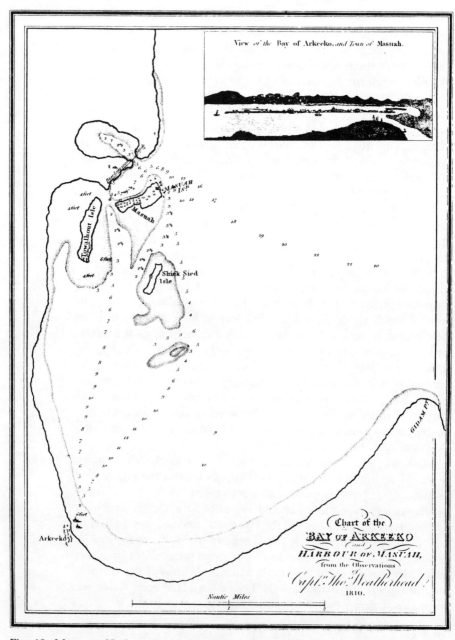

Fig. 10. Massawa Harbor. Reproduced from H. Salt, *Voyage to Abyssinia* (London 1814).

204

excellence for the area.[21] But Massawa has one serious drawback: it lacks drinking water.[22] As a consequence, it long served only as a harbor, while the town proper grew up on a shore point five or so miles to the south, at Arkiko. Here were the residences, business offices, and warehouses; here goods arriving from the harbor on small boats were transferred to porters or camels for the rugged climb upland, and goods arriving from there were transferred to small boats to be ferried to the harbor for loading aboard seagoing craft.[23]

Arkiko itself cannot be identified with the Adulis of the *Periplus,* for that, we are told, was two miles from the coast. It might well have been inland from Arkiko; if it were so located, Sheik Said would lie to the right toward the open sea, and Dissei would be roughly opposite. No ancient remains have been found there, but that can be explained. The *Periplus* describes Adulis as a "village of moderate size" (*kômê symmetros*); in other words, it was merely a large native settlement, no doubt built of adobe or wood. A settlement of this kind could easily disappear without trace.

But the Adulis of later centuries, of the fourth to the sixth, the Adulis that served as *the* port for Ethiopia's flourishing Axumite kingdom, could not so disappear. From remarks dropped by Cosmas Indicopleustes (2.103), who paid it a visit in A.D. 525 and saw there a monument erected by Ptolemy III, a handsome marble chair with a Greek inscription, we gain the distinct impression of a full-fledged city. And the only ruins to have come to light in the whole region—ruins, moreover, which would well fit such a city—are those that Salt discovered and Paribeni excavated. However, as we have just pointed out, they are nowhere near the open sea opposite Dissei Island, but halfway down the side of Annesley Bay.

One possible solution to the dilemma is to assume that the site of Adulis was shifted some time after the *Periplus* was written. A reason is not far to seek: the need for water. The rise of the Axumite kingdom increased the amount of traffic coming to the port, and the local population serving it must have grown accordingly. At some point the decision could well have been taken to found a new Adulis on the nearest place where water was available, the banks of a river some twenty miles to the southeast.

We have established that, in the days before the *Periplus,* the

205

harbor of Adulis, the place where ships anchored and unloaded, had been the fine natural basin at Taulud-Massawa. In the days of the *Periplus,* raiders had forced a transfer to Dissei Island. Where was the harbor after the site of Adulis had been shifted, when it was handling the far-flung and active commerce of the Axumites in their flourishing period? Procopius states (*Bell. Pers.* 1.19.22): "The city of Adulis is a distance of twenty stades from the harbor (*limen*)—by that much alone does it miss being on the sea." Cosmas, who, it must be remembered, was there in person, says the same (2.103A): "The city of the Ethiopians called Adulis is near the coast, two miles distant, and is the harbor (*limen*) of the Axumites." A harbor named Gabaza is several times mentioned in connection with Adulis, and commentators have concluded that it was the name given to the *limen* referred to by Procopius and Cosmas.[24]

So, following what seemed to be the clear evidence of two reliable ancient sources, scholars have universally assumed that the harbor of Adulis was on the coast due east of the ruins, presumably just north of the modern village of Malcatto (actually the distance from this point to the ruins is four rather than two miles, but that is not serious). The coast here is, as mentioned earlier, but a very gently shelving beach, no more; the *Periplus* would be fully justified in calling Adulis, as it does other coastal points, *alimenos*.[25] To be sure, the beach here *can* be made into an anchorage; in 1867, when the British were searching for a place to land the expeditionary force that was to march inland and seize the fortress of Magdala, rejecting Massawa because of its lack of water, they chose precisely this beach. However, they had to build a stone jetty three hundred yards long and later add an artificial island at the end to make it serviceable.[26] No doubt the Adulitans could have done the same, but if they did, whatever structures they put up have disappeared without trace. It seems strange that a facility of the magnitude of Adulis's harbor in the fourth to sixth century, a facility that must have boasted warehouses ashore as well as piers running far out into the water, could have vanished so totally. Possibly the structures were of wood, but surely some parts, the foundations for example, would have been of stone. Yet no such remains have ever been reported.

From the eight century A.D. on, as we remarked earlier, the port of the region was Massawa. This was where the earliest Muslim craft put in, where the first Portuguese mssions to Ethiopia landed at the beginning of the sixteenth century, where Charles Jacques Poncet boarded a boat for Arabia in 1700, and where James Bruce disembarked in 1769.[27] It had also been the harbor, as we have seen, before the days of the *Periplus,* abandoned only because of marauding natives. Thus, if we follow all the commentators in placing the harbor of Adulis during its heyday deep in Annesley Bay, its history would have to go as follows: the first known harbor of the region was where we would expect, at Massawa with its deep, well-protected basin; sometime before the second half of the first century A.D., the date of the *Periplus,* it was moved to Dissei Island, since Massawa was too open to raids from the mainland; then it was moved to the beach in Annesley Bay, to remain there all during the thriving centuries of the Axumite kingdom; when that decayed, it was moved back to its original location, and there it stayed for the next twelve centuries.

I would like to suggest a different development, one that will yield a far more consistent historical picture as well as explain why no ruins were ever found along the coast where Adulis's harbor presumably existed. Its presence there rests squarely on the statement by Procopius and Cosmas that Adulis lay two miles inland from its *limen.* I submit that what both mean by this word is not the main harbor, but merely the small-boat harbor, the nearby point on the coast where the small craft which plied between the main harbor and Adulis put in. The main harbor would have been at Massawa. This was the facility where all seagoing vessels anchored; this was the harbor that had its own name of Gabaza.[28] The abandonment referred to in the *Periplus* surely was of short duration. Once the Axumite rulers had established themselves, they must have policed carefully this part of the coast, since all their rich international trade passed through it. And, with the threat of raids removed, there was no reason not to take advantage of the one good harbor of the region, at Massawa. Thus, when the Muslim conquerors took over, they simply continued to use, as was their way, what had been established by their predecessors. In other words, the harbor of Ethiopia, save for the brief moment recorded in the *Periplus,* was from earliest times to today at Massawa. Because of the lack of water, the settlement serving it, sometime after the 1st c. A.D., was shifted to a river site twenty-five miles to the south.

207

Notes

1. Cf. Pliny, *N.H.* 6.172, who refers to Adulis as the *maximum emporium trogodytarum, etiam Aethiopum.*

2. On the Axumite kingdom, see E. Littmann in *RE* Suppl. 7.77-80 (1940), and, on Adulis's importance at this time, G. Hourani, *Arab Seafaring* (Princeton 1951) 42.

3. The *Periplus* devotes a long section (6) to the imports and exports that passed through it. On possible trade with China, see A. Hermann in *Zeitschrift der Gesellschaft für Erdkunde* (1913) 553–55 (but cf. J. Duyvendak, *China's Discovery of Africa* [London 1949] 10–11).

4. On the date of the *Periplus,* see above, chap. 8, n. 4.

5. Cf. L. Casson in *CQ* 30 (1980) 495–96.

6. Coloe = Kohaito, where J. Theodore Bent (*The Sacred City of the Ethiopians* [London 1896] 217–25) discovered ruins.

7. See W. Vincent, *The Commerce and Navigation of the Ancients in the Indian Ocean* ii, *The Periplus of the Erythrean Sea* (London 1807) 117, where he mentions receiving accurate information about the bay only when his book was already in press.

8. Henry Salt, *Voyage to Abyssinia* (1814) 451–53; for the distance inland, see C. Markham in *Journal of the Royal Geographical Society* 38 (1868) 13.

9. Cf. C. Müller's note in his edition of the *Periplus* in *Geographi Graeci Minores* i (Paris 1855) 257–305; Schoff 60; the original entry in *RE* s.v. "Adule" (1894) and the updated one in Suppl. 7 (1940); A. Anfray in *Journal of African History* 9 (1968) 356; L. Kirwan in *Geographical Journal* 138 (1972) 166–69.

10. *Zeitschrift für Assyriologie* 20 (1907) 171–82.

11. "Ricerche nel luogo dell' antica Adulis," *Monumenti Antichi* 18 (1907) 438–572. Recently excavation has been renewed; se H. Sergew, *Ancient and Medieval Ethiopian History to 1270* (Addis Ababa 1972) 74–75 (photograph of ivory tusk found in 1961).

12. Cf. Paribeni's summary (above, n. 11) 565–72. There are no Ptolemaic remains; cf. Kirwan (above, n. 9) 171–72. The large corded amphorae of Egyptian type which Paribeni found (549–50) are to be dated closer to the 3rd–4th c. A.D. than earlier.

13. A. Anzani, "Numismatica Axumita," *Rivista italiana di numismatica e scienze affini* 33 (1926) 5–96. The earliest is of an unknown ruler Endybis (51), the

latest of Hataz II (92, 94). For up-to-date bibliography on the coinage of the kings of Axum, see S. Munro-Hay in *Azania* 14 (1979) 29.

14. Paribeni (above, n. 11) 570–71; Littmann, *RE* Suppl. 7.2. Cf. A. Jones and E. Monroe, *A History of Ethiopia* (Oxford 1935) 45–46.

15. Müller (above, n. 9) 260, offers the desperate suggestion that in the course of time the island disappeared, becoming yoked to the mainland. R. Mauny in *Journal de la Société des Africanistes* 38 (1968) 23, says, "Adulis se trouve près du port actuel de Massawa, au village actuel de Zula," which makes nonsense of the geography.

16. F. Myatt, *The March to Magdala: The Abyssinian War of 1868* (London 1970) 70.

17. Cf. Kirwan (above, n. 9) 166.

18. Vincent (above, n. 7) 93. James Bruce, who was there in 1769, describes the harbor as follows (*Travels to Discover the Source of the Nile* [Edinburgh 1804²] iv 201–2): "Masuah . . . is a small island . . . having an excellent harbor, and water deep enough for ships of any size to the very edge of the island. Here they may ride in the utmost security, from whatever point, or with whatever degree of strength, the wind blows." For details of the harbor, see *Sailing Directions for the Red Sea and Gulf of Eden,* Defense Mapping Agency, Hydrographic Center, Pub. 61 (1965⁵, rev. ed. 1976) 164.

19. *Sailing Directions* (above, n. 18) 166. Most commentators agree that Oreinê = Dissei Island (or Valentia Island, as it was called earlier): Salt (above, n. 8) 451; Müller (above, n. 9) 259; Mauny (above, n. 15) 23, who, mistranslating the Greek of the *Periplus,* puts it "environ 200 stades de l'entrée de la baie."

20. Most commentators agree that the islets are to be connected with islets in the Dahlac group: Vincent (above, n. 7) 105; Müller (above, n. 9) 260; Schoff (above, n. 9) 66; Littmann, *RE* Suppl. 7.1.

21. C. Conti Rossini, *Storia d'Etiopia,* "Africa Italiana," Collezione di monografie a cura del Ministero delle Colonie iii (Milan 1928) 273.

22. Cf. Myatt (above, n. 16) 70; the British in 1867–68 could not use Massawa as a base for their expeditionary force because of the lack of water.

23. When the Portuguese arrived at the beginning of the 16th c., Arkiko was the chief Christian center of the area; see S. Pankhurst, *Ethiopia; A Cultural History* (Woodford Green, Essex 1955) 312–13.

24. An illustration in the Vatican manuscript of Cosmas includes the words *telônion Gabazas;* E. Winstedt, *The Christian Topography of Cosmas Indico-*

pleustes (Cambridge 1909) 337–38. "The Martyrdom of Arethas," *Acta Sanctorum* lvi *October* x (Paris 1869) 747 recounts how Caleb, the king of Axum, when preparing to launch an attack on Himyar in South Arabia in 525, "in a certain harbor (*hormos*) called Gabaza, within the district of the city of Adulis, the costal city (ὑπὸ τὴν ἐνορίαν ὄντι Ἀδουλὶς τῆς πόλεως, τῆς παραθαλασσίας), ordered [60 vessels] to be drawn up on the shore." The editors of this passage take Gabaza (p. 752) to be near the ruins of Adulis, as does Winstedt. Cf. Conti Rossini (above, n. 21) 170, 174.

25. The trading post (*emporion*) of Ptolemais of the Hunts (3) and of Mouza (24).

26. Myatt (above, n. 16) 70–71.

27. Conti Rossini (above, n. 21) 273; C. Rey, *The Romance of the Portuguese in Abyssinia* (New York 1969 [1929]) 38; C. Poncet, *Cairo-Abyssinia and Back,* Hakluyt Society, 2d ser. 100 (London 1949) 154–56; James Bruce (above, n. 18) 201.

28. The sole text to locate Gabaza uses a curious locution, "within the district of Adulis" (see above, n. 24), which argues in favor of putting it further from Adulis than the nearest strip of shore.

10.
Sakas Versus Andhras in the
Periplus Maris Erythraei

The *Periplus Maris Erythraei* is a unique document, the only one of its kind to have survived from the wreckage of the writings of the ancient Greek and Roman world. It is a handbook, drawn up in unvarnished businessman's language, for the use of Greek-speaking shippers, skippers, or agents who, working out of the Red Sea ports of Roman Egypt, sailed south to trade along the coast of Africa or east to trade with the coasts of India.[1] We do not know the date—the guesses at present in favor range from the middle of the first century A.D. to the end—but the outside limits are fairly clear: it cannot be earlier than the opening decades of the first century A.D. or later than the middle of the second.[2]

Most of the text is given over to talk of routes, of moorings, of sailing hazards, above all of the items that could be bought or sold at the various ports of call. In the process, the author every now and then drops names of local potentates or tantalizingly terse bits of information about current or recent events. There are a number of these nuggets embedded in his treatment of the northwest coast of India, an area which, his account makes clear, was of prime commercial importance.[3] The problem is to fit them into a context. For the history of northwest India in the first two centuries A.D. is distressingly obscure, and particularly the chronology. To complicate things further, what the author of the

211

Periplus says has been carelessly, even incorrectly, reported. The purpose of this paper is to present his exact words, clearly and accurately, and then to explore what historical inferences or conclusions may be drawn from them. We shall discover that these are the very opposite of what have been drawn hitherto.

I

The first major port of northwest India that traders from Roman Egypt touched at was Barbarikon, which lay on the coast at the mouth of the Indus; exactly where is not known. It and the lower Indus were ruled, as the author dryly informs us (38), by "Parthian [*sc.* princelings], who are constantly chasing each other out." India proper, in his geographical conception, started just beyond this point. For he continues (41):[4]

> Immediately beyond the Bay of Barake [Kutch] is the Gulf of Barygaza [Cambay] and the coast of the region of Ariake,[5] which is the beginning of the kingdom of Manbanos and, at the same time, of the whole of India. Of this kingdom, the part inland, bordering on Scythia [Sind], is called Aberia [Ābhīra], the coastal part Syrastrene [Surāṣṭra]. . . . The metropolis of the country is Minnagara.

There follows a detailed description of the port of Barygaza (Bharukaccha, modern Broach) on the Gulf of Cambay: the navigational difficulties encountered in getting up the bay to it, the goods to be bought and sold there. He then turns to what he calls Dachinabades, the Deccan, specifically the barren highland. Of the trading centers located here, he reports (51) that

> two are the most outstanding, Paithana [Pratiṣṭhāna, modern Paithan], a twenty-day journey southwards from Barygaza, and, about ten days eastwards from it [i.e., Paithana], another very large city, Tagara [Tēr]. From these there is brought to Barygaza, by conveyance in wagons over very great roadless stretches, from Paithana a very great amount of onyx-colored glassware, from Tagara much cheap cotton goods, all kinds of linen goods, fine cottons, and from the [*sc.* east] coast certain other merchandise which finds a market locally.[6]

He now returns to the part of the coast that reaches from the Gulf of Cambay to Bombay, the northern Konkan (52):

Fig. 11. Northwest India in the First Century A.D.

The local ports, lying in a row, are Akabarou [unidentified], Souppara [Śūrpāraka, Sopāra], and Kalliena City [Kalyāna]; the last, in the time of the elder Saraganos, was an official trading center offering legal protection. [*Sc.* It is so no longer], for, after Sandanes occupied it, there has been much hindrance [*sc.* to trade]. For the Greek ships that by chance come into these places are brought under guard to Barygaza.[7]

What are the Indian names that lie behind the *Periplus'* Manbanos, Saraganos, Sandanes? What were the political or military storms that raised the waves which affected trade in the manner it

213

describes? Practically all writers on India's history during the early centuries of the Christian era have made a stab at answering these questions. For the passages offer unique information, evidence of a kind that is not to be gathered from the other sources we have, a miscellany of statements from writings of a much later age, inscriptions, and, most important, coins.[8]

These sources, fragmentary though they are, make one point clear: there were two bitterly hostile powers in the area at the time, the Sakas and the Andhras. The Andhras, long before the time we are dealing with, had created a sizable empire in the Deccan; pushing steadily upward, by the beginning of the first century A.D. they had moved their northwestern border to beyond Nāsik in the western ghats. The Sakas—the *Sakai* of the Greek writers—were invaders from the north; pushing steadily downward, by the same century they had taken over the area the *Periplus* calls Ariake and become the Andhras' unwelcome neighbors. There followed a seesaw struggle between the two peoples, the course of which is fairly clear, though the chronology is much disputed. A powerful Saka ruler, Nahapāna, whose name is attested on coins and his titles (satrap, later great satrap) and deeds in inscriptions, succeeded in wresting from Andhran hands control of Nāsik, Junnar, and Karle; these were important towns, since they commanded the passes which gave the ports of the northern Konkan access to the hinterland. Subsequently—but how long subsequently is debated—the Andhras under Gautamīputra Sātakarṇi won back what Nahapāna had taken away, only to lose it again under Gautamīputra's son to the Saka ruler Rudradāman. With Rudradāman we finally arrive at a reasonably securely fixed chronological point: the consensus is that he was on the throne between at least A.D. 130 and 150.[9]

All historians of the period are in agreement that one phase or another of this conflict was going on when the author of the *Periplus* made his visit or visits to India and that consequently it provides the key to understanding his observations. Practically all are convinced that the forwarding of Greek shipping to Barygaza which he remarks upon stemmed from a deliberate campaign on the part of the Sakas to extort trade from the Andhras, to divert it to an area totally under their control.[10] All agree that the "elder Saraganos," in whose time Kalliena had been a thriving place where merchants enjoyed legal protection, was an Andhra monarch, Saraganos being a Greek's attempt at reproducing Sātakarṇi, a name born by a number of early Andhra kings.[11] Most are certain that Manbanos, whom the *Periplus* names as king of the realm that included Barygaza, was none other than the conquering Saka ruler Nahapāna.[12] There is only one important point about which opinions differ: many think that, after Saraganos' day, the Andhras continued in possession of Kalliena and the other two ports of the northern Konkan; thus the Sandanes who "occupied" Kalliena would be Andhran, and it has been suggested that he be identified with Sundara Sātakarṇi, a dim and short-reigned Andhran king mentioned in later literature. A minority holds that the Sakas' victorious push along the coast reached as far as Bombay, putting all those ports in their grasp; thus Sandanes would be a Saka, and it has been suggested that he was a subordinate of Manbanos.[13]

In 1947 J. Palmer, in a short but influential paper, touched on yet another aspect of the Saka-Andhra struggle that he perceived in the *Periplus'* words. Palmer was one of those who were convinced that the ports of the northern Konkan had throughout remained under Andhra rule. He argued that these suffered loss not only of seaborne trade but of land-borne as well. For, he pointed out, the normal trade routes from the Andhra centers of Paithana and Tagara passed through the western ghats and ended at these ports; so, when Nahapāna took over Nāsik and the other towns at the head of the passes, inevitably all traffic was blocked. The Andhras' only recourse, Palmer concluded, was to find new routes—hence the *Periplus'* mention of goods traveling long distances through roadless areas to get from Paithana and Tagara to Barygaza. And even this was possible only when there was no "active and violent warfare," when the Sakas presumably would be disposed to handle enemy merchandise.[14]

No one has added anything new to the picture since Palmer wrote. Most have been content to echo his view. Yet a scrutiny of precisely what the *Periplus* says will reveal that the conclusions which he and so many others before him have drawn from it are topsy-turvy. The situation, we shall see, was just the other way round: it was the Andhras who were attempting to prey on traffic bound for Saka ports.

II

Let us consider first the *Periplus'* statement about the forwarding of Greek ships from Akabarou, Souppara, and Kalliena to Barygaza. To begin with, note that the author limits it to Greek vessels alone—in other words, to vessels carrying cargoes from Egypt or preparing to take them to Egypt, in either case goods that were worth hauling so long a distance. Although in other contexts he will talk of Arab and Indian craft, he does not do so here.[15] For all we know, these, trading in less valuable merchandise, tramping up and down on local business, may have continued to use the ports in question freely.

Next, and more significant, his remark is limited to Greek ships which have come to these ports *by chance*. Not a single writer of the many who have cited this passage as evidence has considered the implications of that phrase.[16] The Greek ships that willy-nilly were moved on from Kalliena, say, to Barygaza were those that had arrived accidentally; in other words, Kalliena was not their port of destination. Then what was it? It could not be any to the south, for the next important cluster of ports is on the Malabar coast, and these require different routing and supply a different type of cargo.[17] There is only one possible answer: the destination must have been Barygaza itself, which is just to the north and which, the *Periplus* makes clear, was far and away the major trade center for the region.[18] The ships the author is talking about are those that had overshot the entrance to the Gulf of Cambay and ended up south of it—which is not at all hard to do, since the whole area is lacking in distinctive landmarks and, because of terribly dangerous currents, skippers would tend to stay well offshore.[19] So all those who have cited this passage as evidence that the Sakas were mounting a blockade, or diverting traffic from the Andhras, or in general trying to aggrandize their commercial stake[20] are drawing conclusions that have no basis whatsoever in the text. The forwarding of Greek ships to Barygaza was just the rectifying of a mistake, the making sure that vessels which had strayed got to their proper destination.

Why did not the ships unload or load at Kalliena or Souppara? As Palmer pointed out, the ports of the northern Konkan were the natural outlets for goods from the Deccan, from highland centers like Paithana and Tagara. Caravans traveled westward to

Nāsik, Junnar, and Karle and then into the passes that lead through the western ghats down to the coast. But in this period those three towns were in Saka hands. Thus no trade was moving from the Deccan to, e.g., Kalliena; as the *Periplus* tersely puts it: "after Sandanes occupied it, there has been much hindrance."[21] Consequently there was no reason for ships—or, at any rate, ships from Egypt dealing in items of international commerce—to put in there, and it was useless for those that had blundered there to unload. So they moved on to Barygaza.

But the move, the *Periplus* distinctly states, was done *met' phylaches* "under guard." The guard, it has been assumed by everyone who has cited this passage, was there to keep the Greek ships from getting away, and since they were being conducted to Barygaza, a Saka port, the natural conclusion was that the Sakas were diverting commerce intended for their Andhra rivals. Yet, as we 'have just seen, the Sakas who supplied the guard were not highjacking helpless merchantmen but, on the contrary, were helping them, were ensuring that they got to their intended destination. Why, then, "under guard"?

We must remember that a guard need not always be, like an arresting officer, for the purpose of preventing escape. It can equally be, like the warships that herd a convoy, for the purpose of preventing attack, to make sure that no harm comes to the flock being guarded. That surely is what we are dealing with here.

Under guard against whom? Again there is but one possible answer: against the Andhras. In other words, what the *Periplus* reveals is not the Sakas' diverting of trade from the Andhras, as everybody has thought, but precisely the opposite, Andhra attempts to divert goods from the Sakas. Presumably they sent out raiders from nearby Bombay Island. What prizes they seized they could escort to the port of Semylla, which has been identified with Chaul, just south of Bombay.[22]

Lastly, the *Periplus'* words settle once and for all the one point about which there had been a difference of opinion: which of the rivals at the time controlled the ports of the northern Konkan, Akabarou, Souppara, and Kalliena. The Greek ships that are forwarded to Barygaza under guard are those which "come *into* these places [*sc.* any of the three ports]"—actually enter them; the text is unmistakable on this point.[23] If after entering the ports, they are from there escorted to Barygaza, a Saka possession, it follows that these ports too must have been Saka possessions. And this makes sense, considering the nature of ancient warcraft. Those writers who think the ports were in Andhra hands must imagine that the Sakas maintained patrols up and down the coast to intercept all Greek shipping headed elsewhere than towards Barygaza.[24] This is possible with today's warships; it was possible in Napoleonic times when England's sailing navy blockaded the continent—but it was almost impossible in ancient times: the light and fragile galleys, which were the only known form of warship, were intended for quick decisive clashes, not extended duty at sea. Oversized racing shells, as they have aptly been called, they had room to carry only a bare minimum of provisions; thus they had to stay close to shore so that they could put in nightly to enable the crews to secure food—usually by purchase at a local market—eat and sleep.[25] The warships that escorted Greek merchantmen to Barygaza had to be Saka units based at the ports. A Greek ship would enter, say, Kalliena, discover it was in the wrong place, be told there was no sense in unloading, and the local naval commander—perhaps even Sandanes himself during the years he was the town's chief official[26]— would assign one or more of his units to usher it to Barygaza.

The *Periplus* does mention certain Andhra goods available at Barygaza, glassware from Paithana and cottons and other fabrics from Tagara that had arrived by way of a long and laborious journey "in wagons over very great roadless stretches." Palmer interpreted this traffic as a desperate Andhra expedient, and, to explain why the Sakas cooperated and handled the goods, he had to assume that at the moment Sakas and Andhras were not in a state of "active and violent warfare"—a lame justification for an ad hoc explanation. Palmer's main point was that the Sakas refused to let Greek traders accept Andhra exports at any time, whether hostilities were "active and violent" or not; why should they accept such exports themselves?

If we do not try to read between the lines but take the *Periplus'* words at face value—and, in the absence of information from other sources, this is the only justifiable procedure—we learn that at Barygaza the Sakas were dealing in Andhra goods. And, if at Barygaza, then at all trading centers—which accords well with the Sakas' general concern for promoting trade as reflected elsewhere in the *Periplus,* their escorting of Greek shipping to

218

Barygaza, their supplying of pilot services at the Gulf of Cambay, their enticing of products from all quarters.[27] Then why at Kalliena was there "much hindrance," as the *Periplus* puts it? There is one very reasonable answer—it must have been because of the Andhras, because they stopped goods from leaving their territory to go to Kalliena once "Sandanes occupied it," i.e., once it fell under Saka control. In other words, the Andhras must have instituted an embargo, and this accords well with what we have demonstrated above, that the Andhras were aggressively seeking to interfere with their enemy's commerce.

But what of the merchandise that, we are told, came from Paithana and Tagara into Barygaza? After all, if there was an embargo, it should have been enforced everywhere. The clue to the explanation is provided by the *Periplus'* remark that this merchandise arrived by way of "very great roadless stretches." There was a well-defined route from Paithana to Barygaza, as J. Fleet long ago pointed out. It ran over the highland to Nāsik and then, from the northwest corner of the Nāsik district, traversed the western ghats via Paint to arrive at the coast between Daman and Bulsar, a journey that involved forty miles of difficult descent. Fleet took the mountain segment to be the part referred to by the words "over very great roadless stretches."[28] But such a description hardly fits what is the sole recognized pass through a mountain barrier; if anything, it would imply that the traffic did not go that way but rather avoided it, went where there was no recognized line of travel. Yet why do that? For the same reason that traders have done so through the ages, to avoid the law. In other words, the goods from Paithana and Tagara must have been smuggled. The "very great roadless stretches" most likely refers not to the mountain region after Nāsik but the highland area before it; in traversing this, the caravans avoided the known roads in order to avoid Andhra agents who were enforcing the embargo. Theoretically this clandestine traffic could have gone over back country to the Saka-held towns of Junnar or Karle and used the passes there to get down to Kalliena, a much shorter and less rigorous journey.[29] But, as we have seen there was no sense in doing that: the embargo had been effective enough so that "there was much hindrance" to trade there, and the Greek ships that might eagerly have loaded aboard the glassware and fabrics had been sent on to Barygaza.

219

III

To summarize: the consensus up to now has been that the *Periplus* reflects the impact upon trade of the hostilities between Sakas and Andhras, that the Sakas preyed upon Andhra commerce and the Andhras responded as best they could by using a slow and laborious land route for their overseas exports. This view was based on a careless or mistaken reading of the relevant passages in the *Periplus*. These reflect, to be sure, the impact upon trade of the hostilities, but a careful reading reveals that it was the Andhras who waged war on Saka commerce and not the other way round. They sought to intercept it on the sea and embargo it on the land. On sea, the Sakas responded by conveying Greek shipping safely to Barygaza, on land by welcoming whatever goods were smuggled in over the Deccan highlands.

In the light of this we must revise our conception of the two rivals at this period. In the picture portrayed hitherto, the Sakas appeared as aggressors[30] and the Andhras as on the defensive.[31] The new picture reveals the Sakas, if not on the defensive, at least content with the status quo and the Andhras as pressing attack. Eventually, as we know, the Andhra king Gautamīputra defeated the Sakas, driving them out of Nāsik and Junnar and other places in the area that they had seized. Perhaps the *Periplus* reflects actions that were preliminary to this military thrust.

Notes

1. The following abbreviations have been used:

CHI = K. A. Sastri, ed., *A Comprehensive History of India* ii, *The Mauryas and Satavahanas, 325 B.C.–A.D. 300* (Bombay 1957)

Frisk = H. Frisk, *Le Périple de la Mer Érythrée*, Göteborgs Högskolas Årsskrift 33 (Göteborg 1927)

JA = *Journal Asiatique*

JRAS = *Journal of the Royal Asiatic Society of Great Britian and Ireland*

Kaniska Papers = A. Basham, ed., *Papers on the Date of Kaniṣka* (Leiden 1968)

NC = *Numismatic Chronicle*

Palmer = J. Palmer, "*Periplus Maris Erythraei:* The Indian Evidence as to the Date," *CQ* 41 (1947) 137–40

Raschke   = M. Raschke, "New Studies in Roman Commerce with the East," *ANRW* ii.9.2 (Berlin 1978) 604–1361

Smith   = V. Smith, *The Early History of India* (Oxford 1924[4])

2. On the date of the *Periplus,* see above, chap. 8, n. 4.

3. Cf. *Periplus* 6 (trade with Adulis [Massawa]), 14 (with the ports on the south shore of the Gulf of Aden and on Africa's horn), 54 (with India's Malabar coast).

4. The sole reliable text of the *Periplus* is Frisk's, which totally supersedes C. Müller's (*Geographi Graeci Minores* i [Paris 1855] 257–305). For improvements on Frisk's text, see A. Roos' suggestions in his review in *Gnomon* 8 (1932) 502–505 (those in W. Schmid's review in *Philologische Wochenschrift* [June 1928] 788–94 are unconvincing); G. Giangrande's in *Mnemosyne* 28 (1975) 293–95 and *JHS* 96 (1976) 154–57; and my own in *CQ* 30 (1980) 495–97 and 32 (1982) 181–83; *JHS* 102 (1982) 204–206.

5. The source of the name is unclear. S. Lévi (*JA* 228 [1936] 73) suggested a derivation from a legendary figure Āryaka, who may "représente . . . le pays Ārya, enfin libéré de ses maîtres étrangers." S. Chattopadhyaya, *The Sakas in India* (Santiniketan 1955) 37 suggested Āryaka "the land of the Āryas or the Āryāvarta."

6. Glassware: ὀνυχίνη λιθία, a form of glass rather than agate, as Schoff translates; see A. Kisa, *Das Glas im Altertume* (Leipzig 1908) 543–51. East coast: cf. J. Fleet, *JRAS* (1901) 547–48.

7. On the rendering of the last two sentences, cf. Frisk 86.

8. For the available evidence, see, e.g., Smith 229–32.

9. Extent of the Andhra expansion: Smith 218–19. Andhra-Saka struggle: Smith 220–23 (a brief survey); Chattopadhyaya (above, n. 5) 36–48 (more detailed account).

10. Schoff 198–99: "[The passage] describes clearly enough an Andhra port . . . harried and dominated . . . by the powerful navy of its northern enemy"; Fleet, *JRAS* (1912) 790: "Nahapāna blockaded Kalyāṇ, expressly in order to maintain the commercial supremacy of Broach"; Smith 226: "[Kalliena's] trade was . . . restricted to narrow limits by Sandanes, who may have been a Saka official"; Lévi, *JA* 228 (1936) 75: "Sandanes . . . avait fermé Kalliena (Kalyan) aux bateaux helléniques" (and cf. 92); Palmer 138: "a ruler of Barygaza or his emissary . . . diverted the goods to his own port. . . . He . . . wanted them himself, or at any rate would not let them go direct to the Andhras"; U. Ghoshal, *CHI* (1957) ii 349: "The same care for their valuable commercial interests led the Śaka rulers . . . to obstruct the trade of the port of

221

Kalyāna belonging to their Śātavāhana rivals"; G. Venket in G. Yazdani, ed., *The Early History of the Deccan* (Oxford 1960) 125: "The Sātavāhana ports of Sopārā and Kalyān were closed to all commerce by the action of Nahapāna's successors" (and cf. 104); D. MacDowall, *NC* (1964) 279: "The interruption by Nahapāna of Andhra-Greek trade through Kalliena"; P. Eggermont, *Kaniska Papers* 95: "Sandanes, who is blockading Kalliena"; B. Mukherjee, *The Economic Factors in Kushāna History* (Calcutta 1970) 40: "A phase of the Kshatrapa-Sātavāhana struggle. The enemies of the Sātavāhanas blockaded a port obviously to deprive them of financial gain from commercial transactions between their subjects and the foreign merchants."

11. See the references in the previous note. Also A. Boyer, *JA* n.s. 10 (1897) 138–39; C. Wilson, *Journal of the Asiatic Society of Bengal* 73 (1904) 272–73; D. Sircar in R. Majumdar, ed., *The History and Culture of the Indian People* ii, *The Age of Imperial Unity* (Bombay 1951) 178–79.

12. For a careful presentation of the identification, see Boyer (above, n. 11) 137–138 (and 139–41 for considering him of Saka extraction). Boyer's view has been adopted by most of the authorities cited in n. 10 above (Fleet 785, Smith 221, Lévi 72, Palmer 137, Venket 103, MacDowall 279) as well as many others: J. Banerjea, *CHI* ii 275, and 279; K. Gopalachari, *CHI* ii 309; A. Maricq, *Kaniska Papers* 199; S. Chattopadhyaya, *Early History of North India* (Calcutta 1968²) 83, 128–29. Some reject the identification chiefly on the grounds that the *Periplus* was written before the reign of the Nahapāna of the coins and inscriptions. Thus Schoff (199) believes that there was an earlier ruler of the same name, as does F. Thomas, *New Indian Antiquary* 7 (1944) 83, while Sircar ([above, n. 11] 178–79) and Raschke (631–32) make no attempt at an identification.

13. Banerjea (*CHI* ii 279), Gopalachari (*CHI* ii 308), and all cited in n. 10 above take the ports to be Andhran except Smith (226) and Lévi (92), who consider them Saka possessions, as do Boyer (above, n. 11, 148) and Sircar (above, n. 11, 178–79). Sandanes = Sundara Sātakarṇi: Wilson (above, n. 11) 272, Schoff 198, Venket (above, n. 10) 104. Sandanes = Saka: Smith 226, whose formulation (see above, n. 10) is more accurate than identifying him more precisely as a subordinate of Manbanos (Sircar 179; Raschke 665), or insisting that the two were contemporary (Palmer 139), since the *Periplus* refers to Manbanos as king at the time of writing but to Sandanes' occupation as having happened some unspecified time in the past. Sandanes is mentioned but once in the *Periplus,* in the passage I have translated, a mention that hardly justifies Thomas' view (above, n. 12, 94–95) that "Sandanes . . . in the Periplus is a commanding figure."

14. Palmer 138–39. Cf. Ghoshal, *CHI* ii 349: "The vast trade from . . . Pratishṭhāna and Tagara . . . , instead of finding its natural outlet in Kalyāṇa harbour, was diverted across a long and difficult mountainous country to Barygaza"; Venket (above, n. 10) 125: "All trade found its way across difficult country to . . . Barygaza"; MacDowall (above, n. 10) 278: "Palmer

rightly drew attention to the warfare between the Andhras and western sa-
traps, which explains . . . the difficult route by which goods were brought
down from Barygaza to Paithana and Tagara." MacDowall is careless; the
Periplus refers only to goods going in the reverse direction.

15. E.g., 16, 30 (Arab craft to Rhapta and Socotra); 14, 30, 36 (Indian craft to
    Somali ports, Socotra, and the Persian Gulf). Eggermont, in an ostenta-
    tiously terse summary (above, n. 10) of *Periplus* 52 states: "All ships have to
    go to Broach"; this is not at all what the passage says.

16. Schoff deserves much of the blame, for he grievously misled any who relied
    on his translation by rendering (43) the last sentence of *Periplus* 52: "Greek
    ships landing there may chance to be taken to Barygaza," which is an egre-
    gious mistake. The text reads: τὰ ἐκ τύχης εἰς τούτους τοὺς τόπους
    ἐσβάλλοντα πλοῖα Ἑλληνικά, literally "the by chance into these places en-
    tering Greek ships." Even the translation of the learned Henry Yule goes
    astray: "for if Greek vessels, even by accident, enter its ports, a guard is put
    on board, etc." (H. Yule and A. Burnell, *Hobson-Jobson* [London 1903²]
    149). It has finally been rendered correctly in the most recent English transla-
    tion, G. Huntingford's *The Periplus of the Erythraean Sea*, Hakluyt Society,
    2nd ser., no. 151 (London 1980).

17. For the routing, see *Periplus* 57. For the cargoes, see the convenient sum-
    maries in Schoff 287. The objects of trade par excellence from southern India
    were pepper and malabathrum; for northern India the author includes only
    long pepper and that at the end of his listing (*Periplus* 49), while malaba-
    thrum is not even mentioned.

18. It was the collecting point for products from all over, from the Deccan to the
    southeast (*Periplus* 51), from Ujjain and its environs to the northeast (48),
    even for spikenard from the Kabul valley and Kashmir (48) and silk by the
    land route from China (64). Barygaza is mentioned over twice as many times
    as any other port.

19. Cf. *Periplus* 40. The only indication ships coming from the open sea had that
    they were nearing land was "the approach of huge black snakes."

20. See above, n. 10

21. ἐκωλύθη ἐπὶ πολύ, a deliberately vague expression. The common interpreta-
    tion as a blockade instituted by the Sakas in general (Schoff, Fleet, Ghoshal,
    Venket, MacDowall, Mukherjee [cited above, n. 10]) or by Sandanes in par-
    ticular (Smith, Lévi, Eggermont [cited above, n. 10]) gives the phrase a preci-
    sion, and the verb a meaning, which neither has. Raschke (983, n. 1355) is
    convinced that the forwarding to Barygaza was "the routine enforcement of
    the use of a 'port of trade' by foreign merchants." This overlooks completely
    the explicit causal connection in the *Periplus'* language: the forwarding to
    Barygaza came not only after the hindrance to trade but because of it; see
    above, n. 7.

22. Cf. J. McCrindle, *The Commerce and Navigation of the Erythraean Sea; Being a Translation of the Periplus Maris Erythraei* (Calcutta 1879) 128.

23. The verb is *eisballo* used with the preposition *eis* (see above, n. 16); on this, cf. H. Stephanus, *Thesaurus Graecae Linguae*, s.v.

24. Cf. Ghoshal, *CHI* ii 349: "Foreign ships touching at Kalyāṇa were in danger of being seized and taken to Barygaza"; Palmer 138: "When Greek ships approached Kalliena . . . a ruler of Barygaza or his emissary stopped them." Palmer's presentation is inexplicably confused. He talks (140) of "the Saka blockade of Kalliena"; Kalliena, thus, is an Andhra port. Yet he also talks (138) of how "Sandanes held it" and how "Sandanes is stopping imports to the Andhran dominions." If Kalliena is Andhran, then the Sandanes who held it must be Andhran, and, if so, what is he doing stopping imports to his own country? See Huntingford (above, n. 16) 155 for the same confusion.

25. Cf. L. Casson, *The Ancient Mariners* (New York 1959) 102; A. Gomme, "A Forgotten Factor of Greek Naval Strategy," *JHS* 53 (1933) 16–24, esp. 17–19, 23. Gomme is wrong in thinking there was a distinction between Greek and Roman galleys; they both had the same limitations.

26. Sandanes may have been a contemporary of Manbanos but more likely was not. The *Periplus* (41) uses the present tense in talking of Manbanos, but the aorist in talking of Sandanes' possession of Kalliena and the consequent hindrance of trade (cf. above, n. 21). The aorist, however, can be used in a way best translated by the English present perfect, as in my rendition "there has been hindrance"; cf. A. Robertson, *A Grammar of the Greek New Testament in the Light of Historical Research* (New York 1919[3]) 843–45.

27. Pilot services, *Periplus* 44; products from all quarters, above, n. 18.

28. *JRAS* (1901) 548: "And only there, in the Western Ghauts . . . commenced the real difficulties of the journey—the 'vast places that had no proper roads at all.' " For the route, cf. also *JRAS* (1912) 790.

29. Cf. Fleet, *JRAS* (1912) 790. Writers exaggerate the amount of trade involved. What the *Periplus* lists as coming from Paithana and Tagara hardly justifies such descriptions as "vast trade" (Ghoshal [cited above, n. 14]) or "commodities flowed to Broach through Ozene, Paethan and Tagara" (Chattopadhyaya [above, n. 5] 38).

30. Cf. above, n. 10.

31. Cf. Schoff cited above, n. 10; Venket (above, n. 10) 125: "The economic life of the [Andhra] kingdom was becoming completely disorganized. The prospects were bleak"; Eggermont (above, n. 10): "The power of Ujjain has passed. The same is true of the power of the Āndhra kings."

11.
Cinnamon and Cassia in the Ancient World

W here did the Greeks and Romans get their supplies of cinnamon and cassia? The question, explored at great length during the last century, has not received extended treatment since, although today we have a much better understanding of the botany of the regions involved and the trade of the ancients with them. Nor have any of those who have written on the subject, either then or now, compared what we know of the way ancient dealers handled cinnamon and cassia with our modern way, to see what light this may throw on the problem.[1]

Modern Cinnamon and Cassia

Cinnamon and cassia come from the bark of certain trees of the laurel family (Lauraceae). Cinnamon is—at least in British terminology, which is less confusing than American—the bark of *Cinnamomum zeylanicum* Nees, a tree native to Ceylon but also found in southern India. Cassia is the bark of *Cinnamomum cassia* Blume and certain other related trees native to India, southern China, and mainland Southeast Asia. What distinguishes the two by and large is quality: the first is generally finer than the second.[2]

In their uncultivated state the trees, handsome evergreens, can grow to a height of forty or fifty feet. Under cultivation they are kept low, in the form, more or less, of coppiced bushes. The young trees are ruthlessly cut back to within a few inches from the ground in order to make them form multiple shoots. When these are about three to four feet long and three-quarters of an inch thick, they are the right size for cutting for their bark. A healthy plant will produce three to four such shoots each year. Once the shoots are lopped off, the bark is stripped immediately, since at that stage it peels off easily. The bark from Ceylon trees or others that produce fine grades is then scraped on the outside, leaving it some shade of brown in color. Cassia bark, notably that from China, is frequently left unscraped; its color consequently is that of the tree, some shade of grey. The last step is to let the bark dry, at which time it curls to form the tube-like pieces we are familiar with.[3] Certain types of Chinese cassia are not peeled but shipped as whole branches,[4] a practice that, as we shall see, can be traced back to ancient times.

Ancient Cinnamon and Cassia

The earliest mention of cinnamon and cassia occurs in the Book of Exodus: in 30.23 Moses is instructed to take "principal spices, of pure myrrh five hundred shekels, and of sweet cinnamon [ḳinnemōn beśem] half so much," and in 30.24 to take "of cassia [ḳiddāh] five hundred shekels." The word ḳinnemōn (ḳinnāmōn in Prov. 7.17 and Cant. 4.14), aut sim., from Semitic—specifically Phoenician, according to Herodotus (3.111)—entered Greek as kinnamōmon, a form whose ending possibly arose by association with the spice amōmon. The word in Exodus for cassia, ḳiddāh, appears in Greek as kittō (see below). Another word is ḳeṣi'āh (Ps. 45.9), whence the Greek kasia.[5]

Both Greek terms are treated at some length in Herodotus 3.107–11, a discussion of Arabia as the land par excellence of aromatics. Herodotus is principally concerned with detailing the awesome obstacles blocking access to the two spices and the wondrous ways in which these are circumvented. It is Theophrastus who provides the earliest straightforward description (H.P. 9.5), based, as he is careful to record, on hearsay. And there are full treatments in Dioscorides and Galen. Incidental remarks dropped by Galen, as will appear shortly, are particularly revealing.

All three deal with cinnamon and cassia as two separate products. Their distinction, however, was not based on botanical criteria, as ours is, since the ancients had no idea that different trees were involved. When Galen, for example, states (14.70) that one finds "branches [*akremones*] of cinnamon right alongside shoots [*kladoi*] of cassia," it is clear that, in his view, the two types occur on the same tree. What distinguished one from the other, as today, was quality. Galen (14.63) makes the remark that "the finest cassia is only slightly inferior to the poorest cinnamon"; he is in effect saying that cassia was by definition inferior.[6] Theophrastus' description provides a clue to what the criteria were: cassia, he points out (*H.P.* 9.5.3), has shoots that are not only thicker but fibrous—and, indeed, today as well, the thicker and coarser the bark, the less its commercial value. At times the ancient experts found it hard to draw the line. "I have often seen," declares Galen (14.56), "some branches of . . . cassia precisely similar to cinnamon both in appearance and thinness of bark and, what is more, also in the surest distinguishing characteristics of cinnamon, taste and smell."

The Greeks and Romans went further, as we do, and distinguished various grades of quality within each. This, too, appears in Theophrastus: he was told, he says (*H.P.* 9.5.1), that there are five grades of cinnamon according to the part of the tree that supplied the bark; only the bark, he reminds the reader, is of use, not the wood. The best grade comes from the top of the tree, since this has the most bark, the poorest from the area nearest the root, since this has the least bark, and the middle grades from in between, the grade becoming poorer as one descends. Had Theophrastus actually seen a tree instead of getting his information at second hand, he would have realized that the truth was the reverse: the bark is thicker toward the base than the top, and, anyway, thinner bark is more valuable than thicker. However, within his misinformation we can discern one solid fact: the poorest quality does indeed come from the part of the tree nearest the root, i.e., the lower trunk, since its bark is inevitably thicker and coarser than elsewhere.[7]

The division into five grades must have been standard trade practice for, many centuries later, it reappears in Dioscorides, but without Theophrastus' misleading criterion. Dioscorides' criteria are color, texture, thickness, and such characteristics. Here

227

are his descriptions of the various grades; they are more or less repeated by Galen.[8]

Cinnamon

Best Grade (Dioscorides 1.14.1): The cinnamon called *Mosylon* (obviously named after the port of Mosyl(l)on on the north coast of Somalia just west of Cape Guardafui[9]), so called because of its similarity to Mosylitic cassia; "dark and ash grey on a wine-colored background, thin as to its shoots and smooth, and with many twigs" (τῇ χρόᾳ μέλαν, τεφρίζον ἐν τῷ οἰνώδει, λεπτὸν δὲ τοῖςξ ῥαβδίοις καὶ λεῖον, ὄζοις συνεχέσι κεχρημένον). Cf. Galen 14.257: "The *Mosyllon*, as it is called by the natives, ash grey [*tephrōdes*] in color, with thin shoots and many twigs." However, Galen states elsewhere (14.65) that "the best cinnamon . . . is a mix of milk color [*gala*] and grey [*phaion*] with a touch of dark blue [*kyanon*]."

2nd Grade (Dioscorides 1.14.2): The cinnamon grown in the mountains, markedly light yellow (*hypokirron*), thick and short. Cf. Galen 14.257: "Cinnamon grown in the mountains . . . is yellow [*kirron*], not thin nor long."

3rd Grade (Dioscorides 1.14.2): "Dark, smooth, fibrous, without many knots" (μέλαν καὶ λεῖον, ἰνῶδες δὲ καὶ οὐ πολυγόνατον). Cf. Galen 14.257: Dark, fibrous.

4th Grade (Dioscorides 1.14.2): Light (*leukon*), spongy (*chaunon*), brittle, with a large root. Cf. Galen 14.257: Light, not hard, brittle, with a small (*sic*) root.

5th Grade (Dioscorides 1.14.2): Light yellow (*hypokirron*), bark similar to red cassia, hard to the touch, not very fibrous, thick root. Cf. Galen 14.257: similar to yellow (*kirra*) cassia, smooth.

Pseudocinnamomon (Dioscorides 1.14.3): Similar (*sc.* to true cinnamon) but weaker in strength and smell; also called *zingiberi* ("ginger"). Cf. Galen 14.257: Similar but much weaker in taste and smell.

Xylocinnamomon (Dioscorides 1.14.3): Woody, with long tough shoots and much weaker fragrance. Cf. Galen 14.257: Woody, with tough shoots and different fragrance.

Cassia

Best Grade (Dioscorides 1.13.1): The cassia called *gizir*, dark (*melaina*) and purplish (*emporphyros*), thick, rose-like in smell. Cf.

by a two-syllable native name, the first syllable g and i, the
second z and i"), "very close to cinnamon in all respects."

2nd Grade (Dioscorides 1.13.1): The cassia called *achy*,[10] the same
as what dealers of Alexandria call Daphnitic (almost certainly
named after Daphnos Harbor, a locale on the north coast of
Somalia just west of Cape Guardafui[11]), pale yellow (*enkirros*),
coral-like (*korallizousa*), narrow, smooth, with long, thick quills
(*syringes*). Cf. Galen 14.72: The cassia called *motō* according to
some, that called *arēbō* and Daphnitic according to others.

3rd Grade (Dioscorides 1.13.1): Mosylitic *batos* ([?] other MS
readings are *baktos* and *blastos*).

Cheaper Grades: Dioscorides lists (1.13.2) *asyphē* (*asyphēmōn* in
some manuscripts), dark, unpleasant, with bark that is thin or
splintery (*phloiorragēs*); *kittō* (almost certainly the Hebrew
ḳiddāh; see above); *darka* (*dakar* in some manuscripts, and cf.
the *douaka*[12] of *Periplus* 8). Galen (14.73) lists a type named
syringis as the cheapest of all; its "outer bark, which they also
call *syrinx*, is tough."

Pseudocassia (Dioscorides 1.13.2): This is amazingly similar to
true cassia but given away by its taste; also, the bark clings to
the wood. There is, as well, a better type with a "broad, soft,
light quill" (πλατεῖα σύριγξ, ἁπαλή, κούφη). Cf. Galen 14.258:
Very similar to true cassia, bark clings to the wood, called *zin-
giber* by the natives (cf. under *Pseudocinnamomon* above).

Most of these types of cassia appear in the *Periplus* among the
products listed as available for purchase at the ports of northern
Somalia west and south of Cape Guardafui: "harder cassia" and
douaka at Malao and Moundos (8–9); great amounts of cassia,
enough to require use of larger ships, at Mosyllon (10); cassia,
gizeir, asyphē, motō, magla ([?] possibly not a form of cassia) at
the Trading Post of Spices (12); cassia and *motō* at Opone (13).

It is hopeless to try to correlate each of the ancient descriptions
with a specific grade of cinnamon or cassia known today. The
descriptions are too general, the known grades too varied. Only
one characteristic, color, is precise enough to be of help. Some of
Theophrastus' informants told him (*H.P.* 9.5.2) that there were
two basic forms of cinnamon, dark (*melan*) and light (*leukon*).
These terms could well be applied to unscraped and scraped
bark, since the first is always darker than the other and in some
cases can be almost black, while the second can be as light as the
color of cream.[13] Again, a clear distinction can be made between

the grade characterized as grey or greyish (Cinnamon, Best Grade) and those as yellow or yellowish (Cinnamon, 2nd and 5th Grades; Cassia, 2nd Grade). To the first the obvious parallels are certain types of Chinese cassia, which are definitely grey in color,[14] to the second certain forms of the cinnamon we are familiar with, forms we find described in the literature as yellowish brown or straw-colored.[15]

The red cassia that Dioscorides alludes to (see under Cinnamon, 5th Grade; cf. Scribonius Largus 36: *casiae rufae*) can be compared with types of Chinese cassia that are distinctly reddish.[16] *Pseudocinnamomon, pseudocassia,* and *xylocinnamomon* are puzzling. The ancient descriptions treat the first two as inferior grades rather than adulterated products. The third may be what the Chinese call "wood cinnamon," the unscraped bark of larger trees.[17]

One interesting fact emerges from all the above; the ancients' preference in cinnamon and cassia was, in a way, the very reverse of ours. To us, Chinese grey cassia is a decidedly inferior grade; to Dioscorides and Galen, some forms of it were the finest available. Conformably, Pliny reports (*N.H.* 12.92) that in his day *nigrum,* i.e., some type of what we would call cassia, was preferred. The most prized cinnamon today is light-colored cinnamon, such as comes from Ceylon; to Dioscorides and Galen this was at best second grade. And we shall see below that there were supplies in the imperial storeroom, certainly the finest the market could offer, which were not pieces of peeled bark but whole branches, a form that currently has found favor only among the Chinese.[18]

Ancient Uses of Cinnamon and Cassia

Cinnamon and cassia were expensive, as we would expect of exotic imports. Pliny provides some prices (12.91, 93, 97, 98): a pound of the very cheapest cost five denarii (which would probably buy fifty pounds of wheat[19]), while the best cassia ran three hundred denarii the pound and the best cinnamon at times of shortage could reach fifteen hundred.

Both were in demand by doctors for medical prescriptions, in which they appear either alone, or more commonly, compounded with other ingredients (Dioscorides 1.13.3, 14.4). They were an important element in the *theriaca* (Galen 14.64–65), the prescriptions that began as antidotes against poisonous bites but soon developed into popular cure-alls.[20] As it happens, cinnamon and cassia do possess genuine pharmaceutical properties: as carminatives, antiseptics, and astringents, they still maintain a place in the pharmacopoeia.[21]

But it was not the doctors who caused the trade to flourish so and sent the prices so high, but rather the manufacturers of fragrant unguents, of perfumes. They employed cinnamon and cassia for a number of their concoctions, including some of the most prized, the so-called Magaleion, for example, or the Royal.[22] Cinnamon and cassia perfumes enjoyed particular favor for use on the body—when dead as well as living: at funerals one scented the corpse with cinnamon or cassia or myrrh and threw raw cinnamon or cassia on the pyre.[23] One added cinnamon or cassia to olive oil to improve the smell. As a condiment they served, along with other aromatics, to enhance the taste of wine—but never of cooking. That use, which today has far outstripped all others, is first attested in the ninth century A.D., when the records of the monastery of St. Gallen reveal that the monks seasoned their fish dishes with cinnamon.[24]

How the Ancients Shipped Cinnamon and Cassia

Today cinnamon and cassia are most often shipped in the form of pieces of dried bark. Indeed, one of the keys to success as a cultivator is to recognize the precise moment for stripping the bark. When a shoot appears to be ready for this, a notch is made in it to see if the wood below has reached the requisite state of moistness. If it has, the shoot is lopped off and the bark promptly removed, for any delay will make the job that much harder and affect the quality. The bark—at least the finer grades—is then scraped, dried, and readied for shipment.[25]

Dioscorides' and Galen's descriptions, together with certain remarks they drop, make it clear that this was by no means the standard procedure in ancient times. The dealers who supplied the imperial court—those, in other words, who handled the very best grades—furnished whole branches, sometimes root and all, sometimes even the whole tree, albeit of small size. Galen tells (14.64), for example, how he made up a *theriakon* for Marcus

Aurelius using cinnamon from a "box shipped from the land of the barbarians, four and a half cubits long, in which was a whole cinnamon tree of the first quality." Elsewhere (14.66–67) he talks of boxes stored away under previous emperors which

> contain multi-root types [*polyrrhizoi*] or multi-branch [*polykladoi*], or however one wants to name the different types of cinnamon. It [*sc.* the tree] does not reach up into greater length in the form of a trunk [*premnon*] splitting into numerous branches [*kladoi*]; its form, rather, is like the two types of hellebore. . . .[26] Each is a growth from a single stool [*pythmēn*], like a little bush [*thamniskos*], with six shoots in some cases, seven in others, sometimes a little more and sometimes a little less, not all equal in length, but the biggest of them is not less than half a Roman foot [*sc.* longer than the others].[27]

In another passage (14.56) he talks of having "often seen tall and flourishing cassia that reached the size of a bush [*thamnos*]." We will deal later with the question of where cinnamon and cassia came from and the implications of Galen's descriptions; suffice it to say here that none of the regions that are candidates were ever visited by Galen—or by Dioscorides, for that matter. Neither man could possibly have seen cinnamon or cassia in their native soil. Perhaps there were specimens growing in some botanical garden, in Alexandria, say, where Galen spent a number of years.[28] It is much more likely, however, that the exporting of branches, or even of whole small trees, such as the one that arrived in the four-and-a-half cubit box, was common practice. Dioscorides' descriptions, for example, indicate that some shipments at least took the form of parts of the tree, for on occasion he characterizes a type as "having many twigs" (1.14.1, cited above) or mentions the presence of the root (1.14.2). Merchandising the product in this form never died out: as we noted at the outset, the Chinese still sell certain types of cassia in whole branches.[29]

The Greeks and Romans also received their cinnamon and cassia in the form that we are most familiar with, pieces of peeled bark. The proof is their use of the word *syrinx* "pipe" (e.g., Dioscorides 1.13.1, Galen 14.73), the Greek equivalent of our "quill." And, as mentioned above, the terms "dark" and "light" that describe certain grades would indicate that the bark was shipped both scraped and unscraped, and the scraped would surely have been peelings.

232

The cinnamon and cassia of antiquity must have been considerably less strong than today. For one, they were allowed to age for incredibly long periods of time. Galen once prepared a prescription for Severus with cinnamon he took from boxes marked as having been acquired in the reign of Trajan (14.65), and there were others dating from all the emperors in between. He himself felt that thirty years was about the limit, that after such a lapse cinnamon definitely became weaker (14.63–64). For another, when cinnamon and cassia arrived in the form of twigs or branches, the bark could not possibly be peeled off; some of the wood must have adhered to it and, entering into the concoction of prescriptions and unguents, inevitably reduced the potency.

The Problem of the Source

We come now to the crucial question: where did the Greeks and Romans get their cinnamon and cassia?

The earliest ancient writers had no doubts about the matter: from Arabia, declare Herodotus (3.107), Theophrastus (*H.P.* 9.4.2), and Agatharchides (frgs. 97, 101). Strabo (16.778, 782–83) cites authorities who list Arabia as a key source, and Dioscorides (1.13.1) starts his discussion of cassia by stating that it grows in Arabia. Writers of prose and verse repeat this until well-nigh the end of Roman times.

But Strabo (15.695, 16.774) also mentions another important area, the region south of Egypt that he considered the southernmost inhabited part of the globe, what we today call Ethiopia and Somalia. Indeed, he refers to it as the "Cinnamon Country" (1.63; 2.72, 95, 114, 119, 132). Pliny—who was aware that there was no cinnamon or cassia in Arabia (*N.H.* 12.82)—puts the source here (*N.H.* 12.86), and so do Ptolemy (4.7.34) and a number of others.[30]

A third candidate, clearly the least favored, was India. Strabo, the earliest to mention it, cites certain authorities who claimed that "most cassia comes from India" (16.782) and that "southern India produces cinnamon" (15.695). Apuleius (*Flor.* 6.2) includes *cinnami merces* among the marvels of India, while Philostratus (*V.A.* 3.4) tells of cinnamon growing in the mountains north of the plain of the Ganges.

From our point of view these last are the ones who are reporting the truth of the matter. Some forms of cinnamon and cassia are native to India, and the tree that for the past three hundred years has supplied the world with the best grade of cinnamon is native to Ceylon.[31] Certain varieties that produce cassia—in our sense—are native to mainland Southeast Asia and southern China, and their bark could well have been exported to India to be forwarded from there to the West.

Arabia can be eliminated without further ado. Even though Herodotus and Theophrastus reported that it was the source, and generations of later writers followed them, by Pliny's day, as we have just seen, some people knew better. There is not a trace of cinnamon or cassia there, nor could there be: the plants require a degree of moisture not to be found in that parched peninsula.[32] What led to the misunderstanding? An answer that is frequently offered, and it is eminently reasonable, is that Arabia was the point where buyers from the West secured their supplies, and they took what was merely a point of transshipment to be the point of origin.[33] Vessels carrying exports from India to the West regularly called at a number of ports on the south coast of Arabia, ports from which Arabia's abundant yield of frankincense and myrrh was shipped out.[34] When they arrived with cargoes of cinnamon and cassia, it is reasonable to assume that these would be sold off to the local dealers in aromatics, who would warehouse them along with their stocks of frankincense and myrrh. Buyers from the West would assume that what they purchased there all came from the interior—and the sellers would do nothing to disabuse them. Quite the contrary: to the tall tales already current of how hard it was to come upon frankincense and myrrh, they added equally tall ones about cinnamon and cassia; the winged serpents that guarded the frankincense trees (Herodotus 3.107) were joined by the winged bat-like creatures that guarded the cassia trees (3.110).

East Africa, however, is harder to explain. Cinnamon and cassia are not found there any more than in Arabia. Yet Strabo and others referred to it as the "Cinnamon Country." Even more telling is the testimony of the author of the *Periplus Maris Erythraei*. He was not a geographer like Strabo or an encyclopedist like Pliny but a merchant or ship captain who, on the basis of personal experience, provides an unvarnished account of the products to be bought and sold in the ports from the Red Sea south to

234

Zanzibar and east to India. He lists (8–10) cassia as one of the chief exports of Malao, Moundos, and Mosyllon on the northern coast of Somalia and then, when he comes (12–13) to the Trading Post of Spices and Opone (the first is just west of Cape Guardafui and the second just south of it), adds the information that cassia grows there. Centuries later Cosmas Indicopleustes, another businessman writing from autopsy, states (2.139) that cassia comes from the hinterland of northern Somalia.

Two schools of thought have arisen. One holds that eastern Africa required its reputation as the source of cinnamon and cassia the way Arabia did: we know that Indian products were regularly shipped to African ports as well as Arabian; the shipments must have included cinnamon and cassia, and the traders here as well as there managed to keep secret where they got their supplies.[35] But another school holds that this is too hard to believe. How could such a secret possibly be kept? Pliny, writing in his study might be fooled but hardly the author of the *Periplus* who was there on the spot, who may have traded in the products himself.

Those who wrote on the problem during the last century, when much of Africa was still *terra incognita,* had a ready answer: once the area was thoroughly explored, cinnamon, they asserted, would surely be found growing there.[36] But in 1883 Carl Schumann, at home in botany as well as in Greek, Latin, and Arabic, demolished this possibility in an exhaustive study. He demonstrated that Ethiopia and Somalia lack all the members of the laurel family; in the light of this, there was scant likelihood that two particular members, cinnamon and cassia, would ever be found there. Both require continuous moisture; they cannot stand periods of dryness, and such periods are part of the climate of Ethiopia and Somalia.[37] Time has proven Schumann right: neither cinnamon nor cassia nor any of the laurels appear in the fairly comprehensive studies of the flora of the area that have appeared in recent years.[38]

In this century other ways out of the dilemma have been offered. In 1919 B. Laufer wrote: "It is perfectly conceivable that in ancient times there was a fragrant bark supplied by a certain tree of Ethiopia or Arabia or both, which is either extinct or unknown to us."[39] Twenty years later R. Hennig, unaware of Laufer's work, offered somewhat the same solution: the cinna-

235

mon of the ancients, he declared "unser Zimt keinesfalls gewesen sein kann."[40] And most recently G. Huntingford has suggested that East Africa did indeed have cinnamon at one time but lost it all through some devastating blight.[41]

But if ancient cinnamon and cassia were not what is known by those names today, what were they? What is this African or Arabian tree that either is extinct or has escaped notice? If it is hard to believe that traders in cinnamon and cassia in the ports of Somalia were able to keep the source of their product a secret from the author of the *Periplus,* it is even harder to believe that Ethiopia and Somalia boasted a tree that at one time supplied a fragrant bark in sufficient quantity to take care of the needs of the whole Roman Empire and then disappeared without leaving a trace in the botanical record.

And what grounds are there for thinking that the cassia and cinnamon of the ancients were different from what goes under those names today? Ancient cassia and cinnamon were a form of bark; about that there is no question whatsoever. And, to judge from the use of the word *syrinx* in connection with it (see above), the pieces came in the pipe-like form characteristic of our cassia and cinnamon. What other trees could have been the source? There are very few whose bark serves as an aromatic. Those that produce cassia and cinnamon are far and away the most important—and the only ones found in the parts of the globe within the orbit of ancient civilization.[42]

As it happens, there is no discernible break in the trade in cassia and cinnamon after the end of the ancient world: both remained commercially available all through the Dark and Middle Ages.[43] During these centuries, too, the source was unknown, but there was some improvement in the information available. Arabs as well as Europeans were now interested in geography, and in describing their homeland never list cassia or cinnamon among its products; they knew better. Ibn Khordādzbeh, who wrote between A.D. 844 and 848, includes cinnamon among the items from a place he calls Sila, which was somewhere in the Far East, probably China.[44] Idrisi, writing in the twelfth century, offers China and Malay, and, by the middle of the fourteenth century, Ibn Batuta provides the first certain mention of Ceylon cinnamon, indicating, however, that its exploitation was of recent origin.[45] The very word for cinnamon in Arabic provides a clue: it is *dār ṣīnī,* a borrowing from Persian that means literally "wood of China."[46]

The picture that emerges is consistent. What the ancients called cinnamon or cassia was the same as what we do, the bark of certain trees of the laurel family native to the Far East. Greeks and Romans thought the two came from Africa for the same reason they thought the two came from Arabia: dealers in African ports were just as adept as those in Arabian at keeping quiet about where they got their supplies. Very likely the author of the *Periplus* did his buying—or observed the buying—in the sort of spice bazaars that have been traditional in that part of the world, open air markets where the sellers squat behind their wares, bags or heaps of spices, both local and imported.[47] We can imagine him stopping in front of a heap of cassia, asking—very possibly through an interpreter—"Where does it come from?" and getting in reply a vague sweep of the hand toward the hinterland.

The nearest any ancient author got to naming the true source was India—which, though it had the trees, actually was not a supplier. The evidence is provided by the author of the *Periplus:* in his report on India's exports, there is no mention whatsoever of either cinnamon or cassia. To be sure, he stopped short of Cape Comorin at the southern tip of India and, though he describes the east coast, it is from hearsay and his information is sparse and sketchy.[48] But he personally visited all the west coast, including Malabar, where there are rich stands of a certain type of cinnamon tree, while not too far away is Ceylon, native land of the cinnamon tree par excellence. The Malabar coast, we can only conclude, did not yet exploit its resources, perhaps because they produced a decidedly inferior grade.[49] About Ceylon we can be more definite: its trees were not exploited until the fourteenth century or the very end of the thirteenth.[50]

Thus, to the question posed at the outset of this essay—where did the Greeks and Romans get their supplies of cinnamon and cassia?—we must repeat the answer given over a century ago: from mainland Southeast Asia or southern China.[51] It was an answer based partly on the evidence of the Persian and Arabic words for cinnamon, which, as indicated above, mean literally "wood of China," partly on the mention of China by the early Arab writers, partly on a process of elimination: if India and

Ceylon did not exploit their trees until the thirteenth century and later, the ancients must have been supplied from elsewhere, and the only possible candidates are China and Southeast Asia, home of the trees that produce what we call cassia. Ships from those regions did not sail all the way to the West.[52] They delivered to ports on the east coast of India, whence their cargoes were trans-shipped to Arabian and African ports. For some reason, the Indian informants of the author of the *Periplus* neglected to pass this information on to him.

There is one further point—an important one—to be made about Chinese cassia. The ancients consistently talk of cinnamon and cassia plants as bushes (cf. Theophrastus, *H.P.* 9.5.1: *thamnous*), and Galen even gives a detailed description (see the passage cited above on p. 232). Yet cinnamon and cassia in their native state are trees; it is only under cultivation that they are made to take the form of bushes—bushes which, it so happens, fit Galen's description perfectly.[53] In other words, the cultivating of the trees—as against merely lopping off branches from those growing wild—is a practice that was introduced in antiquity and not just a few centuries ago, as is commonly believed.[54] The credit for its discovery goes to the Chinese.[55]

India may not have exported to the Greeks and Romans any bark from its cinnamon trees, but it did export the leaves from them—although the Greeks and Romans were totally unaware that these leaves had any connection with cinnamon. Malabathron was one of the aromatics that the west received in quantity from India in ancient times (Dioscorides 1.12, *Periplus* 56, 63). Like cinnamon and cassia, it was used in medicines (Dioscorides 1.12) and unguents (Pliny, *N.H.* 12.129). The name is a Hellenization of the Sanskrit *tamāla-pattra*,[56] the leaf of certain cinnamon trees native to India, notably the *Cinnamomum tamala* Nees and the *Cinnamomum obtusifolium* Nees, both of which grow in the Himalayas all across the northern border of India but most commonly in the eastern portion.[57] Though the bark as well as the leaf can be used, and is so today, the author of the *Periplus* makes it clear (65) that what entered the export market was only the leaves, and that these came from one particular area in north-eastern India where it borders on Tibet.[58] From there the leaves were brought by river to the Ganges, whence some was exported directly to the west, but large amounts also went, probably by

238

boat, to south India, to depart from there for the West (*Periplus* 56). The ancients never connected leaf cinnamon with bark cinnamon, and for good reason. For one, they had no idea the two were related; many, indeed, on the basis of the aroma, held that malabathron came from the spikenard plant (Dioscorides 1.12.1). For another, as our discussion has revealed, the two products arose in and were marketed in widely separated places. Malabathron came from the Indo-Tibetan border, and buyers from the west picked it up at the mouth of the Ganges or on the Malabar coast. Cinnamon and cassia came by ship from China and Southeast Asia, and buyers from the west picked them up in Arabian and African ports.[59]

Conclusion

What the Greeks and Romans called cinnamon and cassia is the same as what we do. They imported all grades, even the finest, in the form of twigs, branches, and small trees, as well as bark peelings. We prefer scraped cinnamon bark; they preferred unscraped cassia. Their source was mainland Southeast Asia or southern China. Here, by the second century A.D. or perhaps even earlier, men were cultivating the plants in the fashion used today. Supplies came by boat to the east coast of India, whence they were transshipped to ports on the southern coast of Arabia and especially around the horn of Africa.

Notes

1. The following abbreviations have been used:

   Schumann   = C. Schumann, *Kritische Untersuchungen über die Zimtländer,* Ergänzungsheft no. 73 zu "Petermanns (geographische) Mitteilungen" (Gotha 1883)

   Warmington = E. Warmington, *The Commerce between the Roman Empire and India* (Cambridge 1928)

   Olck's article "Casia" in *RE* 3 (1899) 1637–50 is a comprehensive review with exhaustive citation of the Greek and Latin sources, but he bypasses the problem of where the ancients derived their supplies.

2. H. Redgrove, *Spices and Condiments* (London 1933) 91, 106–107.

3. Redgrove (above, n. 2) 95–100; H. Ridley, *Spices* (London 1912) 205–206, 218–19, 227–31; D. Plucknett, "Cassia" in G. Ritchie, ed., *New Agricultural*

Crops, American Association for the Advancement of Science, Selected Symposium 38 (Boulder, Col. 1979) 149–66 at 153–61 (I owe this reference to Dr. Elmo Davis, Director of Agricultural Science and Technology of McCormick and Company, Inc.); K. Pillai, *The Cinnamon,* Department of Agriculture, Agricultural Information Service, Farm Bulletin no. 3 (Kerala 1965) 21–29. He states (28) that the scraping of the exterior is carried out before peeling. On the color, see especially J. Parry, *Spices: Their Morphology, Histology and Chemistry* (New York 1962) 38, 40.

4. F. Flückiger and D. Hanbury, *Pharmacographia, A History of the Principal Drugs of Vegetable Origin Met with in Great Britain and British India* (London 1879[2]) 533: "Cassia twigs are not as yet exported to Europe, but they constitute a very important article of the trade of the interior of China. . . . In the Paris Exhibition of 1878 we had the opportunity of examining some bundles. . . . The branches were as much as 2 feet in length and of the thickness of a finger."

5. I. Löw, *Die Flora der Juden* ii (Vienna 1924) 108, 113–14; E. Masson, *Recherches sur les plus anciens emprunts sémitiques en grec* (Paris 1967) 48–50. I am indebted to my colleague Robert Stieglitz for invaluable help with the Semitic sources. *Kinnamōmon* first appears in Herodotus 3.107, *kasia* in Sappho, frg. 44 (Lobel-Page).

6. This is implicit in the ancient pharmaceutical rule of thumb that, if cinnamon is lacking, 2 parts of cassia will do as well (Dioscorides 1.13.3; Galen 14.69).

7. Ridley (above, n. 3) 221. He points out that the best quality bark comes from the middle of a shoot, next best from around the tip, poorest from around the base.

8. There were as well subdivisions within grades. Galen, for example, refers (14.63) to the 6 different grades of fine cinnamon in the imperial storerooms.

9. Cf. *Periplus* 10–12; Pliny, *N.H.* 6.174.

10. The word *achy* may be connected with the Hebrew *'aḥu,* meaning, *inter alia,* "reed." The word is itself a borrowing from Egyptian; see T. Lambdin in the *Journal of the American Oriental Society* 73 (1953) 146.

11. Strabo 16.774; cf. *Periplus* 11 (*daphnōn mikros* and *daphnōn megas*).

12. Schumann 18, followed by Olck (above, n. 1) 1646, suggested that *douaka* is connected with the Sanskrit word for "bark" *tvac* (pronounced "twac"). The Prakrit form, which would be contemporary with the *Periplus,* was *taca.*

13. I have myself purchased pieces of unscraped Chinese cassia that can well be described as black. Pillai (above, n. 3) describes (28) newly scraped shoots as "creamy in color."

240

14. F. Flückiger, *Pharmakognosie des Pflanzenreiches* (Berlin 1891³) 608: "seit 1870 gelangt z. B. ein ganz vorzüglicher Zimt als China cinnamon auf den Londoner Markt. Die Herkunft dieses grauen chinesischen Zimts ist nicht bekannt. . . . Dieser graue Zimt ist nicht geschält, von bräunlicher bis hell-grauer Oberfläche, entschieden grau sind namentlich die stärkern Röhren." Cf. Parry (above, n. 3) 40: unscraped China cassia is grey or greyish.

15. Parry (above, n. 3) 38 ("yellowish-brown"), Ridley (above, n. 3) 220 ("light straw color").

16. *Chinese Medicinal Herbs*, comp. Li Shih-chen, trans. F. Porter Smith and G. A. Stuart (San Francisco 1973) 108–109: "[Tan-kuei] . . . is . . . used for a red kind of true cinnamon bark, which comes from a variety of tree found most largely in the province of Kuichou." Cf. Redgrove (above, n. 2) 107: Cassia (in the modern sense) "is reddish-brown in colour, darker and redder than cinnamon."

17. Schoff (83), followed by Warmington (187), suggested that the "false" forms were imported cassia which had been adulterated by admixture with bark from Somalian laurel trees. As mentioned above, the sources do not treat them as adulterated products. Furthermore, as will be shown below, there are no laurel trees in Somalia. The trees in the passage Schoff had in mind (*Periplus* 11) were very likely mangroves, which are common in Somalia and can easily be confused with laurel; see N. Chittick in *Azania* 11 (1976) 124–25. On Chinese "wood-cinnamon," cf. Porter Smith and Stuart (above, n. 16) 108: "Mu-kuei 'wood cinnamon' and Jou-kuei 'fleshy cinnamon' is the unscraped bark of the larger cinnamon tree. . . . The difference between the *mu-kuei* and the *jou-kuei* is that the former is taken from the larger and older branches, and is therefore more woody and less pungent." See also below, n. 29.

18. See the passage from Flückiger and Hanbury cited above, n. 4.

19. Cf. G. Rickman, *The Corn Supply of Ancient Rome* (Oxford 1980) 240.

20. G. Watson, *Theriac and Mithridatium: A Study in Therapeutics,* Publication of the Wellcome Historical Medical Library, n.s. ix (London 1966) 50–51.

21. Redgrove (above, n. 2) 103–104; N. Allport, *The Chemistry and Pharmacy of Vegetable Drugs* (London 1943) 161: "Apart from its value as a carminative, cinnamon possesses some virtue as an intestinal astringent for the treatment of diarrhoea."

22. The Megaleion (spelled Megalleion in Athenaeus 15.690f., where it is said to have been named after Megallos, its inventor) consisted of cassia, cinnamon, and myrrh in a vehicle of resin and oil of balanos (Theophrastus, *Od.* 30; cf. Pliny, *N.H.* 13.13). See Pliny, *N.H.* 13.18 for the ingredients of the *Regale*. To judge from Martial 4.13.3, a common perfume was a mix of cinnamon and nard.

23. Body perfume: Martial 3.53.4, 6.55.1 (of men); 3.55.2 (of a woman). Aromatics at funerals: Apuleius, *Apol.* 32; Martial 10.97.2; Persius 6.34–36. Perfuming the corpse: Martial 11.54.3. At Sulla's funeral, the procession included big images of Sulla and a lictor made of frankincense and cinnamon (Plutarch, *Sulla* 38); these perhaps consisted of a frame of cinnamon branches covered with frankincense gum.

24. Olive oil: Persius 2.64; Vergil, *Geor.* 2.466. Wine: Theophrastus, *Od.* 32, Geoponica 7.13.1, 4 and 8.22.2, 3; Columella 12.20.5; Pliny, *N.H.* 14.107. St. Gallen: Flückiger (above, n. 14) 597, citing Dümmler, "St. Gallische Denkmäler aus der Karolingischen Zeit," *Mitteilungen der antiquarischen Gesellschaft, Zürich* 12 (1859) 139.

25. Ridley (above, n. 3) 218–19; Pillai (above, n. 3) 26–29.

26. The two types of hellebore are generally taken to be the black Christmas rose, a member of the family of Ranunculaceae, and the white Veratrum, a member of the family of Liliaceae. The two are conveniently pictured in G. Majno, *The Healing Hand* (Cambridge, Mass. 1975) 190–91. The Christmas rose, consisting of multiple stems growing up from the stock, is an apt comparison; it replicates on a small scale the look of a cultivated cinnamon bush. Veratrum, with a single stem, is not. However, Theophrastus indicates (*H.P.* 9.10.1) that there was a form of white hellebore which differed from the black only in color.

27. Olck (above, n. 1) 1645 takes the last phrase to mean that the longest shoot was but half a Roman foot in length. This makes no sense.

28. Galen was in Alexandria probably from 152 to 157 A.D.; cf. G. Sarton, *Galen of Pergamon* (Lawrence, Kansas 1954) 18.

29. We may add the crowns of cinnamon—necessarily of woven branches—that Vespasian dedicated and the massive root on view in the temple to the Divus Augustus on the Palatine in Rome (Pliny, *N.H.* 12.94); see also n. 23 above. Since even fine cinnamon intended for emperors arrived in the form of whole twigs, branches, or small trees, the suggestion (Flückiger and Hanbury [above, n. 4] 529) that the ancient terms "false cinnamon" and "wood cinnamon" refer to branches and twigs as against bark peelings has no validity. And since the Greek and Roman references to both cinnamon and cassia mention branches, twigs, and bark peelings but never flowers, there is no validity to Schoff's talk (82) of "the wood split lengthwise, as distinguished from the flower-tips and tender bark" and certainly not to Warmington's idea (186) that by "Cinnamon proper" the Romans meant "the tender shoots and flower-tips and very delicate bark reserved, as Galen shows, for emperors," whereas they meant by "Casia . . . the wood split lengthwise and the bark and root rolled up into small pipes."

30. Cf. Olck (above, n. 1) 1641, where he has collected all the references to the place of origin of cinnamon and cassia.

31. G. Watt, *A Dictionary of the Economic Products of India* ii (Calcutta 1889) 319–26.

32. Schumann 33–38, esp. 37–38.

33. Cf. Schumann 40. There is a full discussion in Warmington 185–94.

34. See above, chap. 8, n. 26.

35. J. D'Alwis, "Cinnamon," *Journal of the Royal Asiatic Society, Ceylon Branch* 3 (1856–61) 372–80 at 376; Schumann 40; Schoff 83, 217–18 (reporting a statement by R. Drake-Brockman); Warmington 191–92. Pliny spins a yarn (*N.H.* 12.87–88) about the Trogodytes—inhabitants of the Ethiopic shore of the Red Sea—transporting cinnamon of Ethiopia over vast oceans to Ocilia in craft which "no rudder steers, nor any oars draw or drive, nor any sails"; the round trip takes at least five years and many of the merchants involved die before it is over. Ocilia, as it happens, is not at the other end of the world but just across the Strait of Bab el Mandeb. The passage has inevitably started the juices of speculation flowing. Warmington explains it as a seller's tall tale to hide the fact that cinnamon came from India. Schoff thinks it reflects India or the Far East as source. J. Filliozat, "Les échanges de l'Inde et de l'empire romain," *Revue historique* 201 (1949) 1–29, suggests (6–8) that Pliny's Ethiopia really is Ceylon (repeated in *Les relations extérieures de l'Inde* [1], Publications de l'Institut français d'Indologie, 2 [Pondicherry 1956] 7–8). J. Miller, *The Spice Trade of the Roman Empire* (Oxford 1969) 153–72, takes the story seriously, explaining it as reflecting shipments by Indonesians in outrigger canoes to Madagascar and Zanzibar and back, a bit of fantasy that has managed to trip the unwary (cf. Majno [above, n. 26] 211, 219; J. Balsdon, *Romans and Aliens* [London 1979] 269, n. 4).

36. W. Cooley, "On the Regio Cinnamomifera of the Ancients," *Journal of the Royal Geographical Society* 19 (1849) 166–91, esp. 191; E. Bunbury, *A History of Ancient Geography* i (London 1879) 609.

37. Schumann 28–38, esp. 38.

38. See P. E. Glover, *A Provisional Check-List of British and Italian Somaliland Trees, Shrubs and Herbs* (London 1947) xviii–xxvi. These pages list all the plants, arranged in "Ecological Successional order"; no laurels appear. Cf. Schoff in *Journal of the American Oriental Society* 40 (1920) 262–63.

39. B. Laufer, *Sino-Iranica*, Field Museum of Natural History, Publication 201, Anthroplogical Series xv, no. 3 (Chicago 1919) 543, followed by M. Raschke in *ANRW* ii.9.2 (Berlin 1978) 655.

40. *Klio* 32 (1939) 330.

41. In the commentary to his new translation of the *Periplus* (*The Periplus of the Erythraean Sea,* Hakluyt Society, 2nd. ser., no. 151 [London 1980]) 134.

42. Redgrove (above, n. 2), after dealing with cinnamon in his chapter ix and cassia in x, devotes xi to "Miscellaneous Bark Spices." He includes: Oliver's bark from Australia, Massoia from Papua, sassafras from eastern United States and Canada and northern Mexico, clove bark from Brazil and the Guianas, and white cinnamon from southern Florida, Jamaica, Cuba, the Bahamas, and the West Indies.

43. W. Heyd, *Histoire du commerce du Levant au Moyen-Âge* ii (Leipzig 1923) 595–96.

44. Schumann 42–46, who reaches the dubious conclusion that Sila is Japan; cf. Laufer (above, n. 39) 542.

45. Schumann 46 (Idrisi), 48 (Ibn Batuta); cf. Heyd (above, n. 43) 597–98.

46. Laufer (above, n. 39) 541.

47. For a vivid description of these bazaars in the years before World War II, see P. Rovesti, "Medicamenti, aromi e droghe nei mercati indigeni dell' Eritrea" and "Indagini sui prodotti erboristici dei mercati abissini in Etiopia" in *Rivista Italiana delle Essenze, dei Profumi e delle Piante officinali* 15 (1933) 19–29 (Eritrea), 179–91 (Ethiopia).

48. Cf. Schumann 19; Bunbury (above, n. 36) ii 472–75.

49. Cf. Heyd (above, n. 43) 598–99.

50. Cooley (above, n. 36) 180–81; D'Alwis (above, n. 35) 375; Schumann 21 and 48; Flückiger and Hanbury (above, n. 4) 520–21; Heyd (above, n. 43) 597–98; Redgrove (above, n. 2) 93–94. The argument is based on negative evidence: neither Cosmas Indicopleustes nor any subsequent writer who mentions Ceylon, European or Arabian, speaks of cinnamon until possibly Giovanni di Monte Corvino (ca. 1292–93) or certainly Ibn Batuta (ca. 1340), whose account reveals that the Sinhalese themselves took scant interest in the trade.

51. Schumann 52–53: "Das Zimtland katexochen des Altertums und des Mittelalters war zweifelsohne China; es besass das fast ausschliessliche Monopol bis zur Auffindung des Gewürzes in Ceylon." Cf. Flückiger and Hanbury (above, n. 4) 520–21, Warmington 187 and 193 (who is more guarded). Schumann was convinced not only that China was the chief source but that it had been so since the days of Middle Kingdom Egypt (6–11). His evidence

was the presumed similarity between the Chinese and Egyptian words for cinnamon, *keï-schi* and *khisīt* in his transliteration. The theory was approved by Olck (above, n. 1, 1639), W. Muss-Arnolt (*TAPA* 23 [1892] 115), Löw ([above, n. 5] 113), and is still alive: see Miller (above, n. 35) 154. Egyptologists today transliterate the word differently and translate it much less precisely; see R. Faulkner, *A Concise Dictionary of Middle Egyptian* (Oxford 1962) 282, s.v., *ḳdtt*, which he renders "a conifer (?)." Half a century ago James Breasted admitted that the word which he formerly translated "cinnamon" (*tyspsy*) was not to be rendered so specifically (see Schoff in *Journal of the American Oriental Society* 40 [1920] 263); Faulkner 294, s.v. *tišps*, translates it "a tree and its spice (?)." In Chinese *kuei* or *kwei* is a general term for cinnamon or cassia (cf. Laufer [above, n. 39] 543), and *kwei-chi* is used of the twigs of the plant or (Porter Smith and Stuart [above, n. 16] 109) the tips of the branches; the latter, it has been suggested (Olck 1640; Löw 113), lies behind the Hebrew and Greek words for cassia.

52. Chinese ships did not enter seagoing trade until as late as the fifth century A.D.; cf. J. Mills, "Notes on Early Chinese Voyages," *Journal of the Royal Asiatic Society* (1950) 3–25 at 6. The merchantmen that plied between Southeast Asia and the east coast of India are mentioned in the *Periplus* (60) in such a way as to make it clear that they were never seen in ports further westward. On the etymology of the name given to these vessels, see A. Christie in *Bulletin of the London University School of Oriental and African Studies* 19 (1957) 345–53, whose explanation identifies them as of Southeast Asia.

53. Cf. the descriptions given in Redgrove (above, n. 2) 95–97 (cinnamon) and Plucknett (above, n. 3) 161 (cassia).

54. Cultivation of cinnamon was introduced in Ceylon by the Dutch ca. 1770; see Flückiger and Hanbury (above, n. 4) 522.

55. Flückiger and Hanbury (above, n. 4) 530 express uncertainty about Chinese cultivation ("We have no information whether the tree which affords the cassia bark of Southern China is culitvated, or whether it is exclusively found wild"). Ridley (above, n. 3) 230 thought it had been carried on since "time immemorial." We know now that it goes back at least to Theophrastus' day.

56. This was first suggested by Garcia da Orta in 1563; see B. Laufer, "Malabathron," *Journal Asiatique* (July–August 1918) 5–49 at 10. The Sanskrit form was transliterated into Greek as *tamalabathra*, which was then divided erroneously into *ta malabathra;* see E. Schwyzer in *Neue Jahrbücher für das klassische Altertum* 49–50 (1922) 460.

57. H. Yule and A. Burnell, *Hobson–Jobson* (London 1903³) 543; Watt (above, n. 31) 319–20. Laufer (see previous note) argued (14–20) that the Sanskrit word did not refer to the *Cinnamomum tamala* Nees, as is commonly held, on the

grounds that the leaves of that tree are today called *tejpāt,* not *tamāla-pattra,* and that the Sanskrit sources never connect *tamāla-pattra* with cassia. Yet Watt cites (319) among the modern names for the tree both *tamálá* (Bombay) and *tamálpatra* (Gujarat). Laufer's own suggestion (38), that malabathron was patchouli, is even more specualtive, for there is not an iota of evidence that patchouli leaves were ever called *tamāla-pattra* in Sanskrit.

58. Schoff (279), followed by Warmington (188–89), place the locus of the trade in malabathron with great precision. G. Coedès, *Textes d'auteurs grecs et latins relatifs à l'Extrême-Orient* (Paris 1910) xviii, is properly cautious: "dans les pays montagneux qui bordent la Chine au sud-ouest, quelque part entre l'Assam et le Se-tchouen."

59. Thus there is no reason to express wonderment, as, e.g., Warmington does (186–87), over the failure of the ancients to realize that malabathron and cinnamon were related.

12.
China and the West

E ven in ancient times East was East and West was West—but the twain did keep meeting, at the edges. It was the lightest of contact, but enough to raise a hotly disputed point: what did each take from the other?

Actually the question involves the whole span of history, for the West went one way and China another, not only in prehistoric times and antiquity but also during the Middle Ages—indeed, right through the days of the industrial revolution, which came to China long after it had swept over Europe. In antiquity the West developed such political forms as democracy and republicanism, which China did not learn until yesterday, while China developed such administrative forms as a civil service, which the West did not learn until yesterday. Western thinkers turned mathematics into a handmaid of astronomy and physics: the Chinese never did. Through all its history China has clung to a system of writing whose likes most of the West gave up three thousand years ago. If the two great centers had arisen and grown in vacuums, sealed off from each other, their separate paths would be understandable. But they did not.

Let us limit ourselves to the first two historical periods, prehistory and antiquity. Each poses a different problem. What prehistorians puzzle over is this: did civilization, after arising in the Near East, spread from there to China as well as to Europe? Or

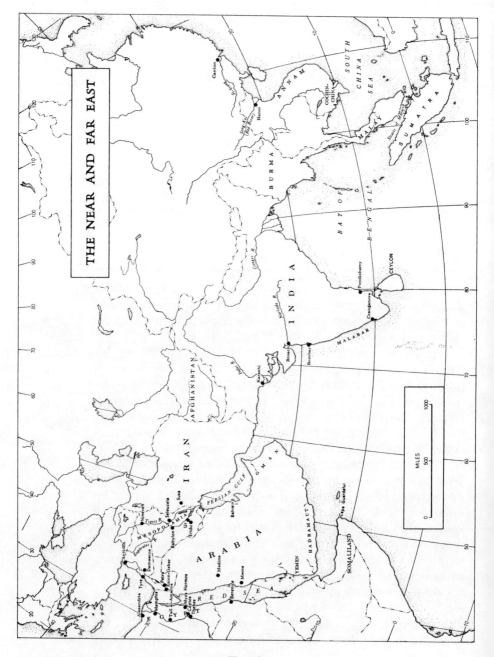

Fig. 12

did the Chinese civilization arise independently? What historians of antiquity puzzle over is this: we know that there was contact between the Greco-Roman world and China, at long distance to be sure, but contact nonetheless and over a considerable stretch of time; it is possible that there was hardly any technological interchange? Specifically, can it be true that the West showed little interest in numerous devices of manifest practical value that the Chinese, precocious inventors, were using?

The Chinese emerged from the Stone Age late, long after the people of Mesopotamia and Egypt. This was grist for the mill of historians of the "diffusionist" school—historians who are persuaded that invention is so precious and rare an act that it occurs only once, at a given time amid a given people, and then "diffuses" to the rest of the world—who until recently were riding high. Why presume that the Chinese independently discovered agriculture, stock-raising, metallurgy, and the other first steps in civilization? Is it not easier to imagine that the knowledge of these fundamental arts traveled from Mesopotamia east across the steppes, where nomads were in constant movement? The scholars who busied themselves with the subject, as it happens, were Westerners, and so their theorizing may well have been colored by geographical allegiance as well as commitment to diffusionism. During the past decades China's new regime has been vigorously promoting research into the country's ancient past, and Chinese archaeologists have been excavating, studying the finds, and drawing their own conclusion. It will come as no surprise to learn that, as they see it, their neolithic ancestors largely made their own way with scant assistance from outside.

China's first settled society arose in a relatively small basin of the Yellow River, the area where it makes its great angle to flow northeast to the Yellow Sea and where it is joined by important tributaries. This was an oasis amid discouraging terrain on all four sides: north lay a windswept plateau; west, semiarid highlands; south, a mountain range; east, swampy lowlands. The rivers of the basin offered such good fishing that it was not until relatively late—some scholars say 5000 B.C., but others put it much after that—that men felt the need to supplement what they could catch by growing food.

Up until the very middle of this century, what excavation had been carried out seemed to show a definite break between the hunter-fisher's paleolithic way of life and the settled neolithic way. For the diffusion-minded Westerner this was proof positive of his case: the changeover was abrupt and tardy because it took place only when agriculture and domestication of beasts, so long known in the Near East, finally arrived in China. The intensive archaeological activity of the last decades has altered the picture considerably. Although it has confirmed that the paleolithic way of life continued for an unusually long time, it has also revealed that neolithic villages whose members raised cereals and grazed sheep go very far back. There is no break; rather, the two ways of life for a long time overlapped. Is it still possible that China's agriculture is indebted to the West?[1]

"It is asking too much of coincidence to assume that such a fundamental revolution as had already occurred in the Fertile Crescent of the Near East should have happened independently a second time in China," declares William Watson, author of a shelfful of works on ancient China. But Kwang-chih Chang thinks differently: "It is all well and good to assume that the idea [of food production] diffused from one region to another, but this assumption is as difficult to prove as it is to disprove. . . . For the present it is best, I think, to concentrate our efforts on learning more about the Neolithic culture in China itself before making any farfetched conclusions"; such is the view he expressed in a book published in 1968. And Chêng Tê-K'un, in an article that appeared in 1973, states flatly, "It was in the Central Plain that typical Chinese agriculture was developed," with not the slightest allusion to possible influence from the Near East in farming or animal husbandry. This is how matters stand at the moment. Let us leave it at that and turn to the next debated aspect of Chinese civilization.[2]

The Bronze Age makes a dramatic entrance in China, for it appears on the stage of history hand in hand with the first central-ized government (the so-called Shang Dynasty), differentiated so-cial classes, specialization of labor, slaves, writing, the chariot—in short, the trappings of a fully developed civilization.

Before 1950 its debut had seemed even more dramatic. Up to then the sole Bronze Age site that had been excavated was An-yang, lying on the northeastern edge of the heartland of neolithic China. Chinese historical accounts list An-yang as the last capital of the Shang Dynasty, dating to the fourteenth century B.C. As

250

the excavation at An-yang proceeded, archaeologists were astounded by what their spades laid bare: a city with a planned quadrilateral shape crisscrossed by streets which were lined with houses, a cemetery with tombs in the form of elaborate chambers where kings had been laid to rest with their chariots amid the bodies of people slaughtered for the occasion, superbly crafted bronzework and jade and jewelry. The archaeologists had never expected such an advanced community, such riches. The Shang rulers and their retainers clearly were wealthy and powerful, men who rode to the hunt and into battle on horse-drawn chariots, who commanded the services of fluent scribes and skilled craftsmen as well as hosts of slaves.

How does one explain this sudden leap in material civilization? Again it was easy for diffusionist-minded Western scholars, particularly since the Shang Dynasty seemed to date from about 1500 B.C., and they knew that, just about then, bronze-accoutered chariot-riding Aryans had moved into and overrun India. Either a portion of them had continued on and made their way into China, or if not that, their martial arts and equipment had.

However, the digging that has been carried out since 1950 makes it clear that An-yang had predecessors. According to Chinese records, the Shang court shifted the seat of its capital six times, and at least two other sites have been discovered. Both are earlier, but they reveal a high level of development consonant with that at An-yang. Furthermore, they also reveal that Shang beginnings predate 1500 B.C., posibly by as much as two or three centuries, and that Shang sites lie over earlier, more primitive sites and derive most of their basic characteristics from these. In short, China's progress could not possibly have been connected with the Aryan push into India.[3]

But the new archaeological discoveries do not completely eliminate the problem, merely narrow it. Three elements appear in the Shang capitals which have no antecedents in the previous neolithic period: writing, the horse and chariot, and bronze metallurgy.

Let us take writing first. Here we find the by now customary division between Western and Eastern thinking. Some of the Chinese authorities insist that the art of writing is totally indigenous and can be traced right down from symbols found on early neolithic pottery; others feel that true writing does not appear before the Bronze Age and prefer to leave the question of its

251

origin open. But the Westerners are well-nigh unanimous: since writing had been in use in Mesopotamia a millennium and a half before its appearance in China, the idea at least must surely have come from there. Even Joseph Needham, author of the monumental multivolume *Science and Civilization in China* and a passionate advocate of China and its contributions to the world, agrees that writing in China was the result of diffusion from the West.

Next, the horse and chariot. "The resemblance of the Shang chariot to chariots made in the Near East towards the end of the second millennium B.C. is too great to be dismissed as a coincidence"; so William Watson, the authority on ancient China whom we cited earlier. "The inference is irresistible: charioteers [from the steppes] must have overrun China also . . . and then proceeded to assimilate a large part of the culture of their subjects"; so William McNeill, in his magisterial *The Rise of the West.* But he adds in a footnote, "I have called the inference irresistible, but many Chinese experts do in fact resist it with considerable emotional energy." Kwang-chih Chang, whom we quoted earlier, sets forth with precision the relevant facts so far uncovered. Horse bones have definitely been found on sites inhabited by certain neolithic peoples. We may be pretty sure they did not use their horses for riding, since this particular art made its debut in human history much later, after the beginning of the first millennium B.C. We are certain they did not use them for food. That leaves only the pulling of carts or chariots—but of these, there is absolutely no trace until we come to the Shang period. Moreover, the horse bones that have been found are very very rare. "A great number of excavations and comparative studies of horse and chariot remains in China and in Mesopotamia must be made before we can be certain about the origin of the horse chariot in the Shang dynasty," Chang concludes. For the present, that seems the appropriate last word on this puzzle.[4]

Finally, the question of metallurgy. For long it seemed that the art of working both bronze and iron had been developed in the West. The earliest known objects of bronze, dating about 3000 B.C., had been found in Mesopotamia; those of iron, dating about 1200 B.C., in Asia Minor. But spectacular new discoveries have changed all this. Recent excavations at Ban Chiang in the northeastern part of Thailand have brought to light finely fashioned bronze spear points which seem to have been made about 3500 B.C. and iron objects which seem to have been made about 1600 B.C. Clearly, if we are to see diffusion at work, the direction of travel was from east to west. And, if to the West, why not to China as well? After all, it is that much nearer. Perhaps not only the technology of bronze but also the tin that went into it, the metal whose source in ancient times is so obscure, came to both China and the West from Southeast Asia. There is plenty of it there; Malaysia is today the world's greatest producer of tin.[5]

One of the curious aspects of Chinese bronze metallurgy is that it started relatively late and then forged ahead with phenomenal speed. The early Chinese bronzes date from the sixteenth century B.C., perhaps a bit sooner but not much. However, by 1300, Chinese smiths were turning out exquisite cast-bronze ritual vessels which are far superior to contemporary work found elsewhere. The diffusionists for long bolstered their case for outside influence by pointing out the absence of any primitive stage in Chinese bronze casting; the earliest pieces discovered were just as fine as the later. Were we to conceive of it as coming into the world fully grown, like Athena from Zeus' head? It was easier to imagine that the Chinese had borrowed a developed technology.

But new finds have produced examples of bronze casting done in rougher, simpler fashion, which indicates that the art did indeed have an infancy. And the Chinese experts have worked out a plausible explanation for China's late start and precocious advance in it. Bronze is worked by casting in molds—and so are forms of ceramics. What the Chinese craftsman did was to adapt a technique he had long perfected in working with clay to the new material; the superb results were a measure of the skill he had acquired. Chêng Tê-K'un, the authority we had occasion to mention earlier, in a recent article offers an appealing reason for the rapid advance of such skill not only in bronze but in clay: the thirst of the Shang rulers. They were heavy drinkers, he reports, and adds darkly, "Many historians have seen this as the main cause of the downfall of the dynasty." Previously, pottery had been rather porous; for holding wine the Shang potters were inspired to produce a finer, impervious ware and did so thriving a business in it that, as excavation has revealed, they were able to afford workshops in many respects as elegant as any palace chamber. Since the majority of the bronze vessels found are also for wine, Tê-k'un deduces that

253

Shang tippling brought boom times to the smiths as well as the potters.[6]

Thus one conclusion is now obvious—at least to Chinese scholars: their ancestors did not learn the technology of bronze from the West. Having settled this problem, if only negatively, we run right into another: why is it that the Chinese continued to make bronze weapons—arrowheads, halberds, daggers—for centuries after iron had come into use for agricultural instruments? A warrior of, say, the fourth century B.C. was still wielding a bronze halberd long after peasants had begun turning fields with an iron hoe. And this brings us to Chinese iron metallurgy, whose history presents even more puzzles than bronze.

The Shang Dynasty, which lasted until about 1000 B.C., knew only bronze. The Chou Dynasty, which dates from about 1000 B.C. until 221, saw the introduction of iron about 500 B.C., but, as we have just noted, for the longest while only for instruments of peace. Finally, in the third century B.C. iron weapons became common. They served the armies of the Ch'in Dynasty, which unified the land, and of the famed Han Dynasty, whose reign, from 206 B.C. to A.D. 220, parallels the rise and heyday of the Romans in the West. The Chinese, thus, were the last among the great culture areas of the Old World to turn to the use of iron.

Did they turn to it because they finally became aware of its existence in other lands? Specifically, did the knowledge of reducing iron from ore and working it, both known, as we have just seen, in Southeast Asia from 1600 B.C., diffuse from there to China—for that matter, to the West as well? To the West, possibly, since the objects found there are of wrought iron, as they are in Thailand. To China, not possibly, for the Chinese smiths, when they finally did turn to iron, went their own special way: they produced objects of *cast* iron.

There are two basic methods for making iron. To make wrought iron the ore is heated in a furnace, which need be no hotter than that used for copper, whose melting point is 1083 degrees Celsius: this results in a "bloom," a spongy mass of fused stone with pasty globules of iron embedded in it. By repeatedly heating this mass till it is red-hot and hammering it, the smith pounds away the slag and integrates the iron globules into a lump of wrought iron. The further processes of reheating, hammering, and quenching to produce iron of increasing strength as well as

254

the various forms of steel need not concern us. Wrought iron was the sole kind known to the West not only during the whole of ancient times but right up to the fourteenth century A.D.

The second method results in cast iron. The ore is heated at a temperature generally of no less than 1400 degrees Celsius, at which point it will liquefy, the slag is drawn off, and the molten iron can be poured into molds just like bronze. (It can also be allowed to cool and then hammered into wrought iron.) Now there are no words at all in Chinese that refer to the reduction of iron ore in a solid form: they all refer to a liquid form. Clearly, then, from the very beginning Chinese smiths knew only cast iron. It would appear that, just as they had transferred their skills in casting ceramics to bronze sometime before 1500 B.C., so, a thousand years later, they achieved a similar transfer from bronze to iron. The great difficulty in making cast iron is to create and maintain the heat. This necessity mothered a series of important inventions, which, like cast iron itself, do not appear in the West until after the Middle Ages. In the West the smiths were content to supply their furnaces with a natural draft by building them on hillsides. For artificial draft all they used were the leather bellows. But neither of these systems was suitable for the production of cast iron. The Chinese at the very outset must have devised a form of blast furnace, no doubt very small at first. By the fourth century B.C. they had invented the piston bellows, and, in the ensuing centuries, introduced even more efficient designs to produce a continuous blast. The water-power mill appears in China in the first century A.D.—not for grinding grain, as in the West, but for driving the bellows of the blast furnaces.

Iron, as Pliny the Elder, the Roman savant of the first century A.D., puts it, is "the best and worst instrument in human existence. We use it to split the soil, plant trees, cut vine props . . . build houses, dress stone. . . . But we also use it for war, murder, brigandage." Incredible as it may seem, the two great centers of ancient civilization through the whole course of their existence chose to go different ways in producing this all-important material. Chinese smiths did turn out objects of wrought iron and steel, but not by the process used in the West—rather, by transforming cast iron. Western smiths did occasionally turn out chunks of cast iron when the temperature in their furnaces accidentally went high enough, but they saw no value in them and

255

tossed them away; archaeologists have found these discards in the remains about Roman iron works.[7]

This fundamental division in the iron technology of East and West brings us to the second question posed at the outset of this chapter: for long there was steady contact between these two greater centers of civilization—is it possible that the Chinese, as precocious in other phases of technology as they were in iron, invented numerous devices of obvious utility which Westerners cavalierly disregarded?

Of the contact there is no room for doubt. It can be traced, without a break, from the third century B.C. on. At that time Chinese silk, transported by caravan through central Asia, began to filter through to the Mediterranean, where its superiority to the only thing the Greeks had, produced from wild Asia Minor silkworms, was swiftly recognized. By the second half of the second century B.C. the Chinese were active in the trade. Each year they dispatched caravans which followed a route that started from Sian, moved along the inside of the Great Wall to its western end, traversed Chinese Turkistan by looping either north or south of the vast salt swamp in the Tarim basin, snaked through the Pamir mountains to Merv, and from there proceeded across the desert to link up with age-old trade routes across Persia and Mesopotamia to the Mediterranean. During the days of the Roman Empire, not only silk but camphor, cinnamon, jade, and other objects were included, though silk was always far and away the most important. It was exchanged for cash. A few Western objects have been found in the Far East—some Roman glass in Korea and perhaps in China, some gems and a Roman bronze lamp and a Greek bowl in Indochina—but these probably drifted there or were carried by travelers as souvenirs.

Neither the Chinese nor any other people involved in the trade went the whole distance. Somewhere in the Pamirs the Chinese caravanners turned their merchandise over to either to local traders or to Indian middlemen who had come up from the south. The Indians hauled their share back home to forward it to the West by ship, while the others plodded on to Persia, where they met up with Syrians and Greeks who took care of the final leg.

It was only on very rare occasions that East and West met face to face. We know of only two, mentioned in the Chinese records. In A.D. 97 an official Chinese envoy, Kang Ying, was sent on an embassy to the West. He got only as far as Mesopotamia, for there he was told that to go farther involved a voyage on ship that might last two years, that people who did it fortified themselves with food for three years just to be on the safe side, that many lost their lives; it sounds very much like a cock-and-bull story concocted by the local business interests to discourage any attempts on China's part to cut them out of their position as middlemen, but Kang Ying swallowed it. The second occasion was in A.D. 166 when, according to a Chinese account, "the king of Ta-ts'in, An-tun, sent an embassy who, from the frontier of Jih-nan [Annam] offered ivory, rhinoceros horns, and tortoise shell. From that time dates the [direct] intercourse with this country." Ta-ts'in was the Chinese name for the Far West, and An-tun is Antoninus, the family name of the Roman emperor Marcus Aurelius. The account goes on to comment in raised-eyebrow fashion on the very commonplace gifts the embassy brought for the Chinese emperor; there were, for example, no jewels. No doubt it was not an official body at all but a group of shippers trying to get their Chinese silk without the intervention of middlemen. In any event, the direct intercourse could not have lasted very long, since we hear of no further meetings.

Since the contact between East and West was indirect, the information that came back to either side was necessarily second-hand. Some of it was solid. Greek and Near Eastern traders were able to pick up from the middlemen with whom they worked place names and other points of geographical interest, which is why the geographers of the first and second centuries A.D., when the silk trade was at its height, are so much better informed about central Asia and Indonesia than their predecessors. But what filtered through to the man in the street was often fanciful hearsay. The Romans got the impression that the Chinese were all supremely righteous; the Chinese that Westerners were all supremely honest. Apparently some information about iron came through. Pliny the Elder, in the discussion of iron in his encyclopedia, mentions *Sericum ferrum,* "Chinese iron"; of all the types of iron, he writes, "It is Chinese iron that takes the palm. The Chinese export it along with textiles and skins." There is something askew here, since what we would call Chinese iron (that is, cast iron) is hardly the finest type there is. Caravans from the East often brought in iron from India, which Pliny may have

257

thought came from China. It was produced in Hyderabad and was a superb steel, the very same that in Islamic times served the smiths of Damascus for their celebrated blades.[8]

Let us admit that the contact was indirect, that misunderstandings were common, that Westerners and Easterners rarely came face to face—yet the contact was there, and if there were few times when Greek and Chinese communicated directly with each other, there were plenty when their agents or employees did. There was enough contact, one would think, for each side to hear about each other's discoveries, especially for Westerners to hear about the immensely useful devices one saw in Chinese workshops, houses, ports. For some mysterious reason, they paid them no heed whatsoever. Take so simple and practical a thing as the wheelbarrow. The Chinese were trundling around these humble but superbly efficient instruments by the third century A.D. and very likely before, but the Europeans did not adopt them until the Middle Ages. Westerners waited until the ninth century A.D. to use cranks or to mount in gimbals things which have to be kept level like shipboard lamps, until the twelfth to introduce treadles, until the eighteenth to cool themselves with rotating fans, all of which the Chinese had been using since the second century A.D. Not until after the Middle Ages did Westerners equip their forges with power-driven bellows or introduce the blast furnace, both of which, as we have seen, the Chinese had by the first century A.D. Not until after the eighteenth century did they build suspension bridges held up by chains, which the Chinese had been building since the sixth century A.D. Not until the sixteenth did they fly kites, a pastime the Chinese had been enjoying since 400 B.C.[9]

Fans, gimbals, kites, and the like—these are only gadgets and toys. But, as we have seen in connection with the fashioning of iron, the indifference extended to far more than gadgets and toys. Perhaps the most striking case in point is naval technology. The various seamen—Greeks, Arabs, Persians, Indians, Malays, Chinese—who plied the sea lanes between the West and China passed each other on the water and rubbed shoulders in port; one would expect at least some interchange. Yet, with one exception, there was practically none of any significance.

We have already described the land route over which Chinese products came to the Mediterranean world. There was an equally

258

important route by water. The first leg ran from the Red Sea or the
Persian Gulf as far as India, and ever since the first century B.C.,
this had been largely in the hands of Greek skippers, although
Arabs and Indians must have some share. In the Indian ports the
vessels loaded up not only with Indian goods, principally pepper
and other spices, but also Chinese, principally silk. Some of these,
as pointed out earlier, had come to India by way of Indian middlemen who had purchased them from caravanners in central Asia.
The rest were brought in by ship from farther east. Initially, this
eastern leg of the route was totally in the hands of Indian and
Malay seamen, but by the first century A.D. the Greeks who sailed
to India began to cut in and by the second were actively involved,
at least part of the way. At first they cautiously coasted around the
shores of the Bay of Bengal, but eventually they learned to cut
right across from southern India to the Malay Peninsula. On occasion they went farther, into the Tonkin Gulf beyond, for they
clearly knew Sumatra, although they seem to have confused it with
Java. The great geographer Ptolemy, who wrote in the second
century A.D., mentions an island called "Iabadiu," which, he adds,
means "island of barley"; the name surely is a garbling of Java
Dvipa "island of millet," what we call Java, but the description he
gives better fits Sumatra, and, in any event, anyone coming from
the West must pass Sumatra to get to Java. Greek sailors who
penetrated this far met up with the Chinese at a port which Ptolemy calls Cattigara, and where Cattigara is has triggered the usual
scholarly wrangling; the prime contenders are Hanoi, Canton,
Hanchow, and Borneo, with the odds favoring Hanoi. Cattigara
was as far as Westerners ever got. The third and last leg of the
route, between Cattigara and China itself, was shared by Chinese,
Malay, and Indian seamen. One of the most interesting archaeological finds of the postwar period was the discovery of a settlement of Indians near the modern village of Oc-eo at the mouth of
the Mekong River in the southernmost part of Vietnam; it dates
from at least as early as the second century A.D. and lasted at least
as late as the fifth. Excavators have unearthed the remains of a
typical Indian temple, relics of the cults of Siva and Vishnu, gems
with Brahmi inscriptions on them. There were even some objects
from further West, gems engraved with Roman or Roman-
inspired figures and several Roman coins of the second half of the
second century A.D. It must have been Indian traders, such as

259

those who settled here and elsewhere in the region, who passed on to the Greeks the few scraps of information they acquired about China. In a handbook of instructions drawn up in the first century A.D. for Greek skippers and merchants in the Far Eastern trade, all the author can tell of what lies beyond Malaya is that "at the very north, on the outside the sea ends in a certain place, and here lies a huge inland city called Thina, from which originate raw silk, silk yarn, and silk cloth. . . . But it is not easy to go to this Thina; for rarely do people come from there, and not many." Three centuries later a Roman geographer candidly informs his readers that after "Cattigara, the leading port of the *Sinai,* [is] the end of the known and inhabited land in the regions of the south. . . . There are no witnesses to point out the course beyond the port of the *Sinai* unless it be some god who knows." *Sinai* was the name the Greeks gave to the Chinese they encountered in these southern regions; it derives from the Ch'in Dynasty, the first to rule a united country, including the area of the Chinese ports, and from *Sinai* comes our "China." (The northern Chinese, whom the caravanners along the land route dealt with, were called *Seres,* from the Chinese *ssu,* "silk.")

There was, thus, a mélange of Indian, Malay, and Greek ships plying the waters from the southern tip of India all around the Bay of Bengal to Malaya, and Indian, Malay, Chinese, and an occasional Greek ship beyond. In other words, some Greek crews had the chance to see Chinese junks with their own eyes, and many more to hear about them from Indian or Malay sailors, to whom the sight of a junk was a daily occurrence.

With the fall of the Roman Empire, the sea trade with China by no means came to an end. The Greeks made their exit, but their role was taken over by the Persians and also by the Chinese. Whereas up to, say, the third century A.D., junks rarely went west of Malaya, from the fifth century on they sailed regularly all the way to the head of the Persian Gulf, where they discharged cargoes for Babylon.[10]

The contact, then, that might lead to exchange of ideas, new wrinkles, techniques, types of equipment, or what have you, existed for centuries. Yet the seamen involved—Greek, Arab, Indian, Persian, Malay, Chinese—sturdily resisted temptation. The Chinese took nothing from the others, and the others, with one exception, took practically nothing from the Chinese—and therein lies the puzzle, for the Chinese had a great deal to offer.

Chinese seagoing junks, observed Marco Polo, "have . . . one . . . deck . . . and on this deck there are commonly in all the greater number . . . quite sixty little rooms or cabins, and in some, more, and in some, fewer, according as the ships are larger and smaller, where, in each, a merchant can stay comfortably. They have one . . . rudder and four masts. . . . Some ships, namely those which are larger, have besides quite thirteen holds, that is, divisions, on the inside, made with strong planks fitted together . . . if by accident the ship is staved in any place. . . . the water cannot pass from one hold to another, so strongly are they shut in." Staterooms, rudder, rig, watertight compartments—Polo's eye caught precisely the features in which a junk differed for the better from the ships he was familiar with. When a merchant booked passage on a Greek or Roman vessel, he got for his money nothing more than a spot on deck where at night he was entitled to spread bedding and put up a little shelter. The same rough-and-ready accommodations were all that were available on Arab, Persian, or Indian craft, a far cry from a private cabin where travelers could "stay comfortably." The single rudder, about which we will have more to say later, made its appearance on junks by the first or second century A.D., seven or eight hundred years before it turns up anywhere else. Junks had watertight compartments from the second A.D., sixteen hundred years before they are found anywhere else.

Most surprising of all is the total indifference of other seamen to the merits of the Chinese rig. The four masts Polo mentions were rigged with the distinctive type of sail that junks had been carrying since the third century A.D. and still carry today, the Chinese balance lug. The balance lug, to begin with, is one of the class of rigs called fore-and-aft—that is, with the sails set along the axis of the ship, running from fore to aft rather than crosswise—whose great advantage is that they enable a vessel to steer much closer to the wind than the square sails favored by the Greeks and Romans and other maritime nations of the age. Arabs, Persians, and Indians, by the time the Chinese were shar-

261

ing the Indian Ocean with them, had adopted the lateen, itself a fore-and-aft sail but lacking many of the virtues of the Chinese version. The Chinese balance lug is stiffened by a series of parallel battens that reach from one side of the sail to the other, like so many horizontal stripes. From the after end of each batten a line—the sheet—runs down to the deck. By trimming this web of sheets, the sail can be set as well as the scientifically designed canvas of a modern racing yacht. The battens serve yet another all-important purpose, the shortening of sail, the reducing of the surface exposed to the wind when it gets too strong. This advantage would have been of minor interest to the Greeks and Romans, who had an equally efficient system, a web of vertical lines that rolled up the canvas much like a Venetian blind, but should have been of keen interest to the Arabs, Persians, and Indians. The lateen sail drives beautifully in both light and strong winds but is a hazard when the wind gets too strong, for there is no way to shorten it: all a crew can do is lower it and stow it away, and replace it with a smaller storm sail—a proceeding that is slow, cumbersome, and apt to be dangerous. But shortening sail on a junk is simplicity itself: the deckhands simply slack off the halyard (the line that holds the sail up), thereby allowing the sail to drop down, and, as that happens, the area between the lowest two battens folds up like an accordion; if they want to shorten sail further, they keep slacking off on the halyard and letting more battens pile up one upon the other. When the danger has passed, all they have to do to return to full sail is to haul the halyard tight again.[11]

Though seamen of other nations turned up their noses at the junk's rig and other useful features, there was one Chinese contribution they may have adopted: the mariner's compass—if, as some say, the West borrowed it from China. A fiery argument rages over the point. E. G. R. Taylor, the ranking British authority on the history of navigation, asserts, "As to the common story that it [the magnetic compass] had been brought in [to the West] from China by Arab sailors, there is no evidence whatsoever to support it." Needham, in his great history of Chinese technology, which we referred to earlier, stoutly affirms the opposite.

Needham presents lucidly and in detail precisely what China knew not only about the compass but about magnetism in general. The compass is one of the world's seminal inventions, Needham points out, for it is the earliest example of the dial with self-moving needle and, consequently, the direct ancestor of all the myriad types that today stud the spectrum of instruments from the housewife's stove to the atomic scientist's computer. The Greeks and Romans and other ancient peoples knew the sundial—but the sundial has no movable pointer. They had self-moving pointers such as weathervanes, but they never combined these with a dial. A Greek wreck of the early first century B.C., which was discovered off Anticythera, an islet just south of the Peloponnese, yielded up a spectacular example of ancient technological sophistication, a device for showing the position of heavenly bodies at any given moment. It had a series of dials which swiveled to indicate desired positions by means of most delicate and elaborate gearing, but the apparatus was not self-moving; it had to be activated by hand. Until a lucky archaeological strike changes the picture, the compass' claim to the lofty distinction Needham assigns it is unassailable.

The first to note the attractive powers of a magnet was Thales, a Greek philosopher and scientist of the sixth century B.C., though we know about his achievement only through mention of it by Aristotle, who lived two centuries later. The earliest Chinese reference dates to the third century B.C. Clearly, then, the West was first off the mark.

But China very quickly caught up and shot ahead. What triggered this speed was not technological precocity but the flourishing art of geomancy. The geomancer, the "earth-diviner," was an all-important figure in China from about 400 B.C. on. He was called upon to predict, by the special supernatural means at his disposal, what was the divinely recommended spot for placing a city, a tomb, a building, or what have you. In practicing his art, he would take cognizance of the general nature of a terrain, of the various topographical features—of streams, woods, and so on—and, of course, in the process, establishing directions was of the essence. In a work written in A.D. 83, the author tells of a certain type of spoon, a "south-controlling spoon" or a "south-pointing spoon," which when "thrown upon the ground . . . comes to rest pointing at the south" (of course, the other end pointed north, but Chinese always favored orienting toward the south). If Chinese scholars are right in arguing that the spoon was one carved of lodestone, then China was aware of the magnet's uncanny gift for indicating direction as early as the first century A.D., a thousand years before the West. The geomancers of the age used an elaborate diviner's board for their work, and we know what it looked like both from descriptions and some actual fragments that have been found. It consisted of a square plate marked with twenty-four compass points and certain other directions, upon which was mounted a pivotal disk marked with the twenty-four points. In the center of the disk was engraved the Big Dipper, and as the disk was turned, the handle of the Dipper served as a pointer. However, to explain the "south-pointing spoon," Chinese scholars imagine that there was yet another kind of geomancer's board in which the disk was replaced by a spoon-shaped pointer carved from lodestone or magnetized steel; when the spoon was placed on the lower square plate, it duly turned till it came to rest facing south. The explanation is bolstered by a scene of A.D. 114 which, carved in relief and depicting various forms of magic and gadgetry, includes an object that appears to answer this description.

There is a statement in another work dating from the Han period (ca. 206 B.C.–A.D. 220) which seems to show that these "spoons" were used for more practical purposes as well as geomantic hocus-pocus. It mentions that, in a certain area, when people "go out to collect jade, they carry a south-pointer with them so as not to lose their way." We have not the slightest idea what this "south-pointer" looked like, but it certainly sounds as if it were some magnetic device to show direction.

The first unmistakable description of a compass dates from A.D. 1044. A Chinese handbook on military technology completed in that year explains that

> when troops encountered gloomy weather or dark nights, and the directions of space could not be distinguished, they . . . made use of . . . the south-pointing fish to identify the directions. . . . A thin leaf of iron is cut into the shape of a fish two inches long and half an inch broad, having a pointed head and tail. This is then [magnetized]. . . . To use it, a small bowl filled with water is set up in a windless place, and the fish is laid as flat as possible upon the water-surface so that it floats, whereupon its head will point south.

This is the form the Chinese compass was to maintain until the sixteenth century—a pointer of lodestone or magnetized iron (later steel) floating in a bowl on the rim of which were inscribed the various directions. In this instance the device was used on land, but little more than half a century later we find it on the sea: in a text written in A.D. 1117 and perhaps referring to events that go back to A.D. 1086 we read that a ship's pilots "at night . . . steer by the stars, and in the daytime by the sun. In dark weather they look at the south-pointing needle." For a long time western scholars, fighting hard to keep credit for the invention in their part of the world, interpreted the passage to refer to non-Chinese craft, but this, it turns out, was based on a mistranslation; in any event, the context makes it perfectly clear that the author is talking about Chinese ships. Moreover, in an account of a diplomatic mission from China to Korea in 1123, the writer reports that

> during the night it is often not possible to stop . . . so the pilot has to steer by the stars and the Great Bear. If the night is overcast then he uses the south-pointing floating needle to determine south and north.

There are extant a number of specimens of the sort of compass described in these passages, dating from a slightly later period (Ming Dynasty, 1368–1644). They are in the shape of a small bowl (six inches in diameter is a common size) made out of bronze or wood with a very wide rim around which are indicated the twenty-four points of direction (the Chinese favored, in addition to south over north, twenty-four points as against the West's sixteen or thirty-two).[12]

So much for China. Now the West. In Europe there is no series of steps such as took place in China, from an embryonic form used for magical purposes through some sort of gadget for orienting oneself on a dark night to a needle floating in a bowl which served as a rough and ready direction-finder either on land or sea. The first preserved mention of a compass is at the same time our first indication that the West was aware of the magnet's capacity for indicating direction. An English monk, Alexander Neckam, writing in 1190 reports that

> sailors . . . when in cloudy weather they can no longer profit by the light of the sun, or when the world is wrapped up in the darkness of the shades of night . . . touch the magnet with a needle. This then whirls round in a circle until, when its motion ceases, its point looks direct to the north.

Neckam, to be sure, does not say that the needle floated in a bowl of water. That it did is evident from the very next reference to a compass, in a poem by a French monk, Guyot de Provins, written in 1205. He had been on the Third Crusade (1189–92), so very likely he reports what he saw in the course of his journeying to and from the Holy Land. There is an art sailors have, he explains,

> which cannot deceive, through the special property of the magnet. An ugly brownish stone, to which iron willingly attaches itself . . . when a needle has touched it . . . they put it in water. . . . Then it turns its point right to the [pole] star.

Next come two references from Arab sources. One, dating 1232, refers to voyaging on the Indian Ocean and mentions a mysterious iron fish which, when rotated in a bowl of water, settles to point south. The other tells of the use of a floating compass needle during a voyage in the eastern Mediterranean in 1242 and adds the remark that in the Indian Ocean sailors use iron fish, not needles.

So it seems beyond dispute that the earliest form of compass was a pointer floating in a bowl of water which marked north-south, and that this was in use among the Chinese around A.D. 1100 or a little earlier, in any event almost a hundred years before anywhere else. It made its way westward at least as far as the Indian Ocean, for what is described in the Arab references, a fish-shaped pointer indicating south, is unmistakably Chinese. But did it travel from there to the Mediterranean? Or did the Mediterranean somehow come up with its own version, as claimed by E. G. R. Taylor—who points to the significant fact that the Arab word for the compass is neither an adaptation nor translation of the Chinese but a borrowing from Italian.[13]

Moreover, there is another matter to consider. Exactly what do we mean by the word "compass"? If we mean the primitive device that enabled a sailor to orient himself in a general way during an emergency, then yes, the Chinese were the inventors and the West possible borrowers, for the Chinese were the first to reach this goal. But if we mean what every ship has carried for the past five hundred years, the device set up in front of the helmsman by which he steers at all times, the device in whose terms a ship's navigator lays all courses, then the situation is just the reverse: the compass was a Western invention which the Chinese borrowed almost two centuries later.

In 1269 a brilliant medieval technological thinker, Pierre de Maricourt, wrote a treatise on possible uses for a magnetized pointer. All involved a "dry" pointer—that is, a pointer not floating in water but set horizontally on a vertical pivot. One of his designs included a dial marked off into 360 degrees, with not only a pivoted pointer but a needlelike wire sitting atop it which would enable the user to sight compass bearings very much in the manner we do today. To be sure, this was just something on paper; from a remark he drops it is perfectly evident that on shipboard skippers were still managing to get along with a needle floating in water.

However, a Catalan savant, Ramon Lull, writing some twenty years later, talks of a ship's navigator establishing his position by using the needle together with charts and mathematical tables. This seems far more than one could do with a compass whose function was merely to show where north or south lay. Again, we must recognize that such navigators must have been very rare, that most skippers went on steering by the sun and the stars, breaking out the needle and bowl only for an occasional peek.

Then, around 1300, the basic step toward the modern compass was taken. Tradition credits it to a certain Flavio Gioja of Amalfi, which at that time was a great port, precisely the sort of place to generate maritime inventiveness. Who Gioja was—or if there really was a Gioja—we have no idea. Obviously, he did not invent the compass from scratch. What he must have done was to take a pivoted dry pointer, such as Pierre de Maricourt had conceived of for his theoretical constructions, and attach it to a card on which compass bearings were marked—probably sixteen of them, since this is the number on early wind roses figured on charts—so that, when it swiveled, the whole card swiveled with it. He may also have been the one who got the idea to package the pointer-cum-card neatly in a box. The Italian word for compass is *bussola* which means literally "box," and there is even a reference in an Italian work dated 1315 to a portable compass mounted in a box covered by glass. The last essential step was to add the lubber line—that is, a line indicated on the box which, when the box was set up in front of the helm, coincided with the fore-and-aft axis of the vessel. Thus the steersman, when he

267

looked at the compass and saw that the lubber line was aligned with, say, northwest, knew that his ship was heading in that direction. This last step must have been taken by the fifteenth century.

In its finished form the compass swiftly became essential equipment on all Western vessels, for it revolutionized the art of navigating and piloting a ship. Skippers no longer set courses by the stars or sun but by points of the compass, and their helmsmen steered with their eyes on the compass as well as on the stars, sun, direction of the waves and wind, or the like. Dutch and Portuguese ships brought the new device into Oriental waters, where the Japanese picked it up, and then the Chinese from them. This is incontrovertible, for, in a Chinese work of 1570, we read that

> the needle floating on water and giving the north and south directions, is ordinarily called the Wet Compass. In the Chia-Ch'ing reign-period [1522–1566] there were attacks of Japanese pirates, so from that time onwards Japanese methods began to be used. Thus the needle was placed in the compass box, and a paper was stuck onto it carrying all the directions. . . . This is called the Dry Compass.

At the present moment, that is where the matter stands. The Chinese invented the first compass, a primitive form of direction-finder for emergencies. Westerners, probably the Italians, invented the modern compass, a device used at all times by helmsmen to keep a ship steadily on course. How and where the West got its version of the magnetized needle, which it converted into the modern compass, is still very much a mystery.[14]

When Dutch and Portuguese vessels entered oriental waters, the Chinese, as we have just seen, were quick to borrow their style of compass, but they turned a blind eye to their style of rig—yet it was precisely this, square sails superimposed one over the other on lofty masts to produce towering pyramids of canvas, that gave the West control of the oceans both economically and militarily until the coming of steam. The Japanese, who had borrowed the compass even before the Chinese, paid scant attention to both the Chinese and the western rig, preferring for the most part to lumber along under their traditional single huge square mainsail, a rig scarcely better than what the ancient Egyptians used forty-five hundred years earlier. And they never bothered to introduce watertight compartments, nor did the West until as late as the end of the eighteenth century.

By at least the second century A.D., junks had given up the long steering oars on each quarter, which all craft had been carrying since time immemorial, in favor of the ancestor of the modern rudder, the flat blade hung vertically at the stern; this had no effect on the ships of other nations, which clung to the old system. Not until 1200 does the stern rudder appear in Europe—but then, for mysterious reasons, seamen, who for so long had turned their backs on the device, rushed to adopt it, so that within a few hundred years it supplanted steering oars on seagoing vessels all over the globe.[15]

The route that brought Chinese silk to the ports of the Mediterranean was long and arduous, whether by land or sea. Yet men continued to traverse it for over eight hundred years, until the day, around A.D. 550, when two Persian monks arrived from China with a few precious silkworms that they had smuggled out hidden in bamboo canes and therefore started the West on making its own silk. During all this time the thin but steady stream of merchants, porters, drivers, seamen, and so on that flowed back and forth never thought to bring back, along with the bales of silk, some of the many good things China had to offer. China, to adapt Emerson's words, had made not only one but several better mousetraps, yet people, far from beating a path to her door, did not even bother to knock when there. We have talked of the wheelbarrow, crank, kite, "south-pointing needle," Chinese lugsail, stern rudder; there were others, including that discovery so crucial for cultural history, the art of printing with type (done in China at least a millennium before Gutenberg). Eventually all were gratefully adopted, but only after a lapse of centuries, in some instances over a millennium. Why the delay? The answer surely involves deep-seated differences in attitudes, casts of mind, values, and the like, and we lack the information to lay these bare.

Notes

1. For the diffusionist view, see, e.g., S. Cammann, "The Interchange of East and West" in *Asia in Perspective* (Philomathean Society, University of

Pennsylvania, Philadelphia 1959) 3–28. Chinese draw their own conclusions, cf. W. Watson, *China* (New York 1961) 15. First settled society in a small basin, Kwang-chih Chang, *The Archaeology of Ancient China* (New Haven 1968[2]) 85. Argiculture arose ca. 5000 B.C., Chêng Tê-k'un, "The Beginning of Chinese Civilization," *Antiquity* 47 (1973) 197–209 at 204. Others put it later, cf. Needham i 83; Watson 36. Neolithic in China goes far back, Tê-k'un 203–204.

2. "It is asking," Watson (above, n. 1) 36. "It is all well and good," Chang (above, n. 1) 84. "It was in the Central Plain," Tê-k'un (above, n. 1) 206.

3. Entry of the Bronze Age, Watson (above, n. 1) 57. An-yang, Chêng Tê-k'un, "New Light on Shang China," *Antiquity* 49 (1975) 25–32; Chang 234. Aryan influence on China, Watson 57; W. McNeill, *The Rise of the West* (Chicago 1963) 106, 108. An-yang's predecessors, Tê-k'un (1975) 25; Chang 238–39.

4. Chinese writing indigenous, Tê-k'un (above, n. 2) 28; cf. Chang (above, n. 1) 238, who prefers to leave the question open. Idea from the West, M. Pope, *The Story of Archaeological Decipherment* (London 1975) 182. Needham on writing, i 248. "The resemblance," Watson (above n. 1) 94. "The inference," McNeill, (above, n. 2) 219. Chang on horses, (above, n. 1) 237. Debut of horses for riding, J. Anderson, *Ancient Greek Horsemanship* (Berkeley 1961) 10–14. "A great number," Chang 238.

5. Discoveries at Ban Chiang, *Transactions of the Connecticut Academy of Arts and Sciences* 46 (1976) 99, 131; *Expedition* (summer 1976) 11–37. Recently doubts have been raised concerning the early dates assigned; some would prefer to put them much lower.

6. China borrowed bronze casting techniques from West, Watson (above, n. 1) 80; absence of primitive stage, 57. Rougher, simpler bronzes, Chang (above, n. 1) 238. From clay to bronze, Tê-k'un (above, n. 2) 29–30; cf. Chang 239, 248. "Many historians," Tê-k'un 29.

7. Iron utensils for agriculture, Watson 142, 144; J. Needham, *The Development of Iron and Steel Technology in China* (London 1958) 3–4. Iron weapons in the 3rd c. B.C., Watson 144; Needham, *Dev. of Iron* 6. Chinese last to turn to iron, Needham i 99. Casting is prime Chinese method, Chang 314–16. Wrought iron technique, C. Singer, *A History of Technology* i (Oxford 1954) 593. Cast iron in West in 14th c., Needham, *Dev. of Iron* 9. Cast iron technique, Chang 314–15; no Chinese words for reduction of iron ore, 315. West uses natural draft, Singer ii (1956) 73. Chinese blast furnaces, Needham, *Dev. of Iron* 18; piston and water-driven bellows, ibid. "The best and worst," Pliny, *N.H.* 34.138. Western smiths discard cast iron, Singer ii 56.

8. Silk trade, L. Casson, *Travel in the Ancient World* (London 1974) 123–25. Western objects in China, M. Wheeler, *Rome Beyond the Imperial Frontiers*

(London 1954) 175; *Fasti Archaeologici* 10 (1955) no. 2925, 22 (1967) no. 410. Kang Ying, F. Hirth, *China and the Roman Orient* (Shanghai 1885) 39; cock-and-bull story, 164–66; "the king of Ta-ts'in," 42; group of shippers, 176. Solid information about place names, E. Warmington, *The Commerce between the Roman Empire and India* (Cambridge 1928) 125. Chinese righteous and Westerners honest, M. Cary and E. Warmington, *The Ancient Explorers* (New York 1929) 83. "It is Chinese iron," Pliny, *N.H.* 34.145. Probably Indian iron, Schoff 171–72.

9. The wheelbarrow, Singer (above, n. 6) ii 770. Gimbals, Needham iv.2.229–31, 233–34; crank, 111–19. Treadles, L. White, *Medieval Technology and Social Change* (London 1962) 117. Rotating fans, Needham iv.2.150–51, 224, 586; suspension bridges, iv.3.198–99, 207–208; kites, iv.2.573, 577, 580.

10. Sailors and routes east of India, Warmington (above, n. 8) 126, 129; Java and Sumatra, 128–29. Cattigara, Warmington 125–26; W. Hyde, *Ancient Greek Mariners* (New York 1947) 229–30. Seamen on last leg to China, J. Miller, *The Spice Trade of the Roman Empire* (Oxford 1969) 184–87. Oc-eo, Wheeler (above, n. 8) 172–74. "At the very north," *Periplus* 64. "Cattigara, the leading port," Marcian, *Periplus of the Outer Sea*, trans. W. Schoff (Philadelphia 1927) 27. Etymology of *Sinai*, Needham i 168–69; of *Seres*, ibid. Rise of the Persians in trade, Hasan Hādī, *A History of Persian Navigation* (London 1928) 64–65. Chinese in the Persian Gulf, Warmington (above, n. 9) 358.

11. "Have but one deck," Marco Polo, bk. 3, chap. i (Yule ii, 249–51), translated as in Needham iv.3.467. Greeks and Romans travel on deck, Casson (above, n. 8) 154. Single rudder, Needham iv.3.650, 652; watertight compartments, 420–22, 695. Chinese balance lug, L. Casson, *Illustrated History of Ships and Boats* (New York 1964) 176–77; Needham iv.3.601. Shortening sail on a lateener, Casson, *Ill. Hist.* 163.

12. "As to the common," E. Taylor, *The Haven-finding Art* (London 1956) 96. The compass a seminal invention, Needham iv.1.239. Orrery found in a Greek wreck, D. de Sola Price, *Gears from the Greeks* (New York 1975). Thales, Needham iv.1.231; earliest Chinese references to magnetic attraction, 232; geomancy, 240–42. "south-controlling spoon," 261–62; "thrown upon the ground," 262; diviner's board, 262–65; disk and spoon 266–67; "go out to collect," 269; "when troops encountered," 252; "at night . . . steer," 279; "During the night," 280; Ming Dynasty specimens, 286–88.

13. Neckam, B. Kreutz, "Mediterranean Contributions to the Medieval Mariners Compass," *Technology and Culture* 14 (1973) 367–83 at 368–69; Needham iv. i.246. Guyot de Provins, Kreutz 369; Needham iv.1.246–47. Arab sources, Kreutz 369–70; Needham iv.1.247. Arabic term for compass from Italian, Taylor (above, n. 12) 96.

271

14. What do we mean by compass, Kreutz (above, n. 13) 372–73. Pierre de Maricourt, Kreutz 371; Needham iv.l.246. Ramon Lull, Kreutz 371. Gioja, Needham iv.1.249, 289. Pointer on card in box, Kreutz 372. Dutch and Portuguese ships bring compass, Needham iv.1.290; "the needle floating," 289.

15. Japanese rig, Casson (above, n. 11) 179. Watertight compartments in West in late 18th c., Needham iv.3.695; stern rudder in 2nd c. A.D., 650. Stern rudder in Europe, G. Laird Clowes, *Sailing Ships* i (London 1932) 34–35.

Index

Acknowledgment of Sources

The several studies in this volume appeared in slightly different form in the publications noted below; permission to reprint is gratefully acknowledged. The study on cinnamon and cassia in the ancient world is published here for the first time.

Expedition (summer 1979) 25–32: "Traders and Trading in Classical Athens" (Chapter 1).
Transactions of the American Philological Association 106 (1976) 29–59: "The Athenian Upper Class and New Comedy" (Chapter 2).
Transactions of the American Philological Association 85 (1954) 168–87: "The Grain Trade of the Hellenistic World" (Chapter 3).
Memoirs of the American Academy in Rome 36 (1980) 21–33: "The Role of the State in Rome's Grain Trade" (Chapter 4).
The Bulletin of the American Society of Papyrologists 15 = Studies Presented to Napthali Lewis (1978) 43–51: "Unemployment, the Building Trade, and Suetonius, *Vesp.* 18" (Chapter 5).
J. Thorndike, ed., *Mysteries of the Past* (New York: American Heritage 1977) 140–54: "Energy and Technology in the Ancient World" (Chapter 6).

J. Thorndike, ed., *Discovery of Lost Worlds* (New York: American Heritage 1979) 108-25: "The Scrap Paper of Egypt" (Chapter 7).

Transactions of the American Philological Association 110 (1980) 21–36: "Rome's Trade with the East: The Sea Voyage to Africa and India" (Chapter 8).

Coins, Culture, and History in the Ancient World: Numismatic and Other Studies in Honor of Bluma L. Trell (Detroit: Wayne State University Press 1981) 113–22: "The Location of Adulis (*Periplus Maris Erythraei* 4)" (Chapter 9).

Journal of the Social and Economic History of the Orient 26, part 2 (1983) 164–77: "Sakas versus Andhras in the *Periplus Maris Erythraei*" (Chapter 10).

Mysteries of the Past 188–206: "China and the West" (Chapter 12).

Lionel Casson is currently professor of classics at New York University. During his distinguished career he has been awarded two Guggenheim fellowships and a senior fellowship of the National Endowment for the Humanities. He received an NEH grant to serve as director of an NEH Summer Seminar at the American Academy in Rome in 1978. At the Academy he has also directed the Summer Session in Classical Studies and served as Andrew W. Mellon Professor of Classical Studies (1981-82). Among his many publications are *Excavations at Nessana* ii, *Literary Papyri* (1950); *The Ancient Mariners* (1959); *Ships and Seamanship in the Ancient World* (1971); *Travel in the Ancient World* (1974); and *Daily Life in Ancient Rome* and *Daily Life in Ancient Egypt* (1975).

The manuscript was edited for publication by Carol Altman Bromberg. The book was designed by Mary Primeau. The typeface for the text and the display is Mergenthaler VIP Times Roman, based on a design by Stanley Morison in 1932. The book is printed on 55-lb. S. D. Warren's '66 and is bound in Holliston Mills' Kingston Natural Finish cloth over binder's boards.

Manufactured in the United States of America.